CHRISTIAN ORIGINS
AND JUDAISM

Christian Origins
and Judaism

W. D. DAVIES

THE WESTMINSTER PRESS

PHILADELPHIA

Printed in Great Britain

Dedicated

to

The Faculty of Divinity Past and Present

and

T. H. Robinson
H. H. Rowley

Sometime Professors of Semitic Languages
The University of Wales

ABBREVIATIONS

CDC   The Damascus Fragment (Zadokite)
DSD   The Manual of Discipline
DSH   The Habakkuk Commentary
DSIa The Isaiah Scroll
DSS   The Dead Sea Scrolls
DST   The Psalms of Thanksgiving
1QM   The War between the Sons of Light and the Sons of Darkness
1QSa The Two-Column Document

All other abbreviations used are customary and self-explanatory

CONTENTS

PREFACE

As the title suggests, most of the studies in this volume arose from, and all have been influenced by, a concern to understand the interaction of Christianity and Judaism in the first century.

Republished on request, they have previously appeared as follows: I in the *Union Seminary Quarterly Review,* Vol. XV, No. 2, New York, January 1960, pp. 83–98; II in *The Expository Times,* Vol. LIX, T. and T. Clark, Edinburgh, 1948, pp. 233–237; III in *Mélanges Bibliques en l'honneur de'A. Robert* (Travaux de l'Instit. Cath. de Paris, 4), Bloud et Gay, Paris, 1957, pp. 428–456; IV in *The Background of the New Testament and its Eschatology: Studies in Honour of C. H. Dodd,* edited by W. D. Davies and D. Daube, Cambridge University Press, 1956, pp. 124–152; V and X in *Religion in Life,* The Abingdon Press, Nashville, Tenn., Vol. XXVI No. 2, 1957, pp. 246–264 and Vol. XXI, No. 2 1952, pp. 264–274 respectively; VI in *The Harvard Theological Review,* Vol. XLVI, No. 3, Cambridge, Mass., July 1953, pp. 113–139; VII in *The Scrolls and the New Testament,* edited by K. Stendahl, Harper & Brothers, New York, and S.C.M. Press, London, 1957, pp. 157–182; VII in *New Testament Studies,* Vol. 2, No. 1, Cambridge University Press, 1955, pp. 60–72; IX as a monograph by James Clarke and Co., London, 1950. Permission by all the publishers concerned to use these materials is hereby gratefully acknowledged.

What I owe to other scholars appears only in part from the footnotes. My greatest debt, across the years and seas, is to Professors C. H. Dodd and David Daube and Dr. J. S. Whale for conversations and correspondence in criticism.

I should like to thank my publishers, the printers and readers for the care they have taken with the work, and especially Mr. Arthur J. Bellinzoni, jun., who helped with the correction of proofs and prepared all the indices with meticulous thoroughness.

W. D. DAVIES.

New York, 1961.

A QUEST TO BE RESUMED
IN NEW TESTAMENT STUDIES

At the end of the last century, and in the early decades of this, New Testament scholarship was largely absorbed in what we have come to know as the Quest of the Historical Jesus, who stands behind the devotion and dogmas of Christendom. In this quest to discover what actually happened in the life of Jesus, students generally were dominated by literary and textual interests, and, especially in certain centres, such as Chicago, by a concern to understand the matrix within which Christianity arose in all its sociological complexity. The typical products of this period were detailed commentaries, for example, that of McNeile on Matthew, meticulous studies of the Gospel sources, such as the *Oxford Studies in the Synoptic Problem*, and Canon Streeter's work on *The Four Gospels* (1924), and more wide-ranging volumes exploring the world of the first century, both the Judaism of Palestine and the philosophies, mysteries, cultic underworld and Higher Paganism of the Graeco-Roman world. To recall the works of this period is to recognize at once its Herculean achievements and the vitality of that concern to which we have referred. To it we owe the large measure of agreement which has been reached on the nature of the documents of the New Testament, their dates, places of origin, structures, sources and literary characteristics, our deeper understanding of the background of the New Testament, and, in the theological field, our conviction that docetism is dead as a door nail.

But great as were the achievements of those who sought the Jesus of History, they were bought at a price. While on the popular level, and in the piety of the Churches, they were used to present a human Jesus, the Exemplar, and helped to create appreciation for the essentially humane character of the Lord, on the academic level, more often than not, those same achievements produced bewilderment which often led to cynicism. To read in the New Testament, in a British university at least, in the late twenties and early thirties of this century, was to be introduced into a tangled world of literary, textual, historical and other theories, and a maze of details, lexicographical, grammatical and other, which revealed within the New Testament no apparent pattern of any kind. Apart from the Epistles which, despite the tortuousness of much of their thought, were well defined units whose intent could be ascertained with some clarity and certainty, the New Testament documents presented to the student the appearance of a mosaic. But even the term 'mosaic' suggests a diversified unity, and even beauty, which the splintered, student's New Testament of the thirties lacked. Dissection of the New Testament seemed to have ended in murder. Threading carefully from one word or pericope in the sacred text to the next, through reams of heterogeneous notes, was like going through the thick undergrowth of a dark forest. Occasionally a detail of the study might shed a warming and heartening light, just as a sudden ray of sunshine brightens a dark wood, but students could seldom find much meaning or purpose in the details that confronted them. The wood was lost in the trees. The New Testament, regarded as a library of books, spoke with a multiplicity of voices, so that its witness was not only diffuse but confusing—in connection with the foundation document of the Faith, a state of affairs most disturbing.

Nor was the immediate impact of the new discipline which first appeared in Germany at the end of the First World War, and subsequently spread to England, America and elsewhere, reassuring. On the contrary, it only made confusion worse confounded. Form Criticism attempted to go behind the written sources upon which the Gospel writers had drawn and to examine the oral tradition which preceded all such sources; and it revealed that that oral tradition had not only been transmitted to meet the various needs of the Christian Community but had been fashioned and inevitably modified by those needs. Source criticism had been a plague, but Form Criticism, at first at least, proved to be a nightmare. In the hands of its most extreme practitioners, for example, Karl Ludwig Schmidt, the Gospel tradition about Jesus disintegrated into isolated units having no organic connection. The various stories put together by Mark, for example, were often compared to a 'string of beads without a string', i.e., its various pericopae had no inner connection. Details of topography and chronology which occur in the Gospels were claimed to be almost entirely without credence, and any hope that the Gospels might give us a coherent account of the life of Jesus was abandoned. By and large, it was the faith of the community, not facts about Jesus, which emerged in the Gospels, and the various forms which the Gospel tradition assumed were governed by the preaching, teaching, catechetical, baptismal, cultic, and liturgical needs of the Faith. Further, those Form-Critics who urged that the Gospels were concerned with the Theology of the Church and not with history, so that they could not be taken seriously as sources for knowledge of Jesus, found to hand a contemporary understanding of Christianity which declared that such knowledge even if it could be attained with certainty was irrelevant and largely unnecessary. Docetism had died in the early years of the century, and now the Quest of the Historical Jesus also seemed to be preparing for an inevitable and an unlamented death.

II

But the reaction to the state of affairs that I have described was not long in coming. And oddly enough Form Criticism, despite its disintegrating impact on the Quest for the Historical Jesus, provided the point of departure for this reaction.

The point at which the rot of dissection in New Testament studies was stopped was the discovery of the significance of the preaching of the early Christians. Dibelius and others have claimed that it was this preaching which most influenced and moulded the oral tradition which lay behind the written Gospels. But the change from the analytic to the synthetic approach to the New Testament is rightly and especially associated with the work of my revered teacher, Professor C. H. Dodd. In his well-known inaugural lecture he pleaded for a new emphasis in New Testament studies on the unifying and integrating factors in the New Testament documents, and in 1936 he published the small but weighty volume, *The Apostolic Preaching and its Developments*. In this, with typical freshness and clarity, he uncovered behind the various strata of the New Testament documents a common unifying core, the preaching, or to use the now familiar term, the Kerygma, of the primitive community. This core turned out to be a series of events—the life, death and Resurrection of Jesus of Nazareth, in which the glory of God was declared to have been revealed, i.e., the decisive act of God for man's salvation. It is not necessary to give in detail here the separate items of the Kerygma. What must be insisted upon is that the disclosure of a common core within the variety of the New Testament, which lent to the whole of it an unmistakable unity, was liberating and invigorating; it is no exaggeration to claim that it delivered students of my generation from a sense of befuddled futility in New Testament studies. The late thirties were a thrilling time: new vitality and energy were abroad. The tyrannous heterogeneity of the data seemed successfully challenged at last.

But was our deliverance premature? Was the new liberation deceptive? Critics of the new synthetic approach were not wanting. The emphasis which Professor Dodd, and others who followed him, placed on the Kerygma, as constituting the unity of the New Testament, did not go unchallenged.

First, the plague of sources is still with us. In isolating the primitive preaching, Dodd had appealed to the early chapters of Acts as preserving it. But is this position really tenable? Those chapters, it was now urged, present, not so much the earliest preaching, as an idealization: the author of Acts describes not what prevailed at the first, but what ought to have prevailed, both then and in his own day. In short, Acts cannot be taken as a reflection of a primitive stage in the early Christian movement.

Secondly, much has been made of the arbitrary selectiveness which enabled Dodd and others to discover the pattern of the Kerygma in the New Testament. The fact that the motifs of the Kerygma recur in various documents does not necessarily imply that they were more significant for early Christians than others which do not appear in the New Testament. Account should be taken of statistical accident in the preservation of these motifs, if their importance is not to be exaggerated.

Thirdly, the suspicion was inevitable that contemporary theological and ecclesiological movements had here influenced students of the New Testament. The emergence of the ecumenical movement, in particular, provided the urge to seek for a ground for the unity of the Churches within the New Testament itself. The disclosure of the Kerygma satisfied this urge by going behind the conflicting theologies of Christendom to a focal point of unity within the New Testament around which Churches, otherwise divided, could now be united. The implication is that the Kerygma is not so much the result of objective, scientific study of the New Testament, as of well-defined theological and ecclesiastical concerns, however unconsciously these may have been at work. The theory of the Kerygma was fathered by ecumenical enthusiasm rather than by exegetical exactitude, and was a superb example of wishful thinking.

On these grounds many have not been moved by the Kerygmatic approach to the New Testament, which we welcomed so enthusiastically. To counter these criticisms, however, is not difficult. Let us take each in turn. First, the date and character of the preaching reported in the early chapters of Acts must always be open to dispute. While many scholars take the view that the speeches in Acts 1–5 are late, and designed to instruct the Church at the close of the first century, if not in the second, others have discovered behind them Aramaic sources containing very early tradition. But the reality of the Kerygma does not stand or fall with the data of Acts. The evidence culled from the Pauline epistles and elsewhere, not to mention the Kerygmatic interest traceable in the Gospels themselves, is very cogent. To question the existence of a common core of early Christian preaching is to ignore much evidence outside Acts altogether. We need not spend long over the second objection. It is doubtful procedure to claim for what does not appear in the New Testament a significance equal to that of the elements of the Kerygma, which appear very frequently in it. What is often mentioned is likely to have been central. An illustration may help. I have been associated in America with two universities, which I name with honour.

During five years spent at the one the word 'alumni' scarcely ever came to my ears: during four years at the other, I was seldom free from its sound. Was this statistical difference in the incidence of the term 'alumni' significant in the life of the two universities? It most certainly was. It would be no great exaggeration perhaps to say that while the one university produced alumni, the other university was maintained by alumni. Statistics are not always misleading. The items which recur in the New Testament in its various strata can rightly be taken to indicate what was of real significance in the life of the communities which produced it. As for the third criticism, it is to be readily admitted that the New Testament student is necessarily the child of his time, and, if he is at all alive, he brings to his task of interpretation the influences and concerns of his age. There can be little doubt that theological and ecclesiological interests which have moved our time have not left the student of the New Testament untouched. But this cuts both ways. The times which may condition our exegesis may also illuminate it. Is it not true, in more spheres than one, that these times of 'the breaking of the nations' have opened our eyes to things which in more velvety days were hidden from us? Not far from my home in Wales there is an old Norman Castle, Castell Dinefwr. In summer when the trees which surround it are in full leaf the castle is hidden: it can be seen only in glimpses. But when winter comes, and the trees have lost their foliage, the castle walls stand forth in the stark clarity of their ancient splendour. The living of our days has been wintry, but may it not have helped us to see with a new awareness the constitutive structures of the New Testament documents? Even if it were admitted that the emphasis on the Kerygma in recent scholarship was the result of conscious or unconscious pressures to discover a New Testament ground for the unity of the Church (a view to which I could not subscribe), this would not necessarily belittle the validity of the Kerygmatic emphasis.

I submit that the unity which the uncovering of the Kerygma gave to the New Testament, opened the way for the understanding of the early Christian movement at a deeper level than was possible when it was mainly regarded as a collection of documents each of which had its own peculiar emphasis. Early Christianity did not merely spread by the diffusion of a vague, contagious friendliness, centred in Jesus, but unreflecting: it was dominated by the burning enthusiasm of a great conviction, the nature of which is revealed to us in the Kerygma, namely, that in Jesus of Nazareth the purpose of God revealed in the Old Testament is fulfilled and the New Age inaugurated. If we had lacked evidence for the Kerygma, we should have had to invent it in order to explain the missionary intensity, the theological vitality, and deep fellowship which the New Testament reveals. This is not to claim that the Kerygma can be itemized and classified with strict rigidity; there is variety within the Kerygmatic unity; but it does mean that it is unthinkable that we should repudiate the Kerygmatic emphasis in the work of Professor C. H. Dodd and others, however much modification may be required in details.

III

The Kerygmatic emphasis, however, has brought its own dangers. These arise partly from the very cogency with which the Kerygma was presented and partly from the ease with which it could be exploited by those theologies usually referred to as theologies of the Word or of Crisis. These inevitably coloured much recent New Testament exegesis, and especially the 'Biblical Theology', which began to be popular at the same time as did the term 'Kerygma'. It is not easy to pin-point the danger to which we have referred. Perhaps it can best be expressed in terms of isolation. The discovery of the Kerygma within the complexities of the New Testament was liberating. But the Kerygma now came to be isolated. Its items seemed to become a series of bare bones, and the Kerygma itself a kind of skeleton almost devoid of all flesh, which could be impressively rattled on occasion as the essence of the New Testament. The danger arose of treating the Kerygma as if it existed in a vacuum, and cutting it off or isolating it particularly from two things. First, there was its threatened separation from the milieu within which it emerged. While I hasten to note that those to whom we owed the disclosure of the Kerygma never fell victims to this danger, it is scarcely an exaggeration to say that, in Europe at least, as emphasis on the Kerygmatic core of the New Testament intensified, interest in its factuality, by which I mean its rootedness in the world of the first century, waned. There was traceable in some quarters an impatience with the kind of labours that had occupied the scholars of the earlier years of this century. It became fairly common to criticize so-called Liberal-scholarship in favour of a more positive Kerygmatic approach to the Christian documents, which could presumably dispense with such labours. But, in the second place, and equally serious, the Kerygma came to be isolated from the tradition, contained especially in the Synoptic Gospels, about the historical Jesus. The Kerygma was sometimes used perilously like a theological 'Open Sesame' to the Faith of the New Testament. Albeit on a far more moving and profound level, reference to 'The Event' which constituted the Gospel became familiar to us, but 'The Event' was treated as a self-enclosed entity proclaimed by the Church, while the historical data about the life of Jesus were claimed to have become blurred in memory, so that they were, finally, undiscoverable in detail.

Thus the emphasis on the Kerygma often had a strange two-fold dénouement. On the one hand there arose a marked lack of interest in the life of Jesus. The claim that the preaching of the Church constituted the core of the New Testament, although that preaching was centred in Jesus of Nazareth as Lord, tended to shift emphasis away from Jesus Himself to the faith of the community. Lives of Jesus became scarce, and such as did appear were treated as negligible, because it had become a commonplace in many theological classrooms that Form Criticism in its various emphases had made the writing of a life of Jesus a scientific impossibility. Either from an unconscious urge to make a virtue out of necessity (because, in any case, the Jesus of History could not be known), or from genuine theological conviction, the Kerygma of the Church came to be regarded as alone significant and determinative for Christian Faith. This led to the further claim that the Church itself was from the first uninterested in the Jesus of History as such. With this decline in the seriousness with which the historicity of the detailed Gospel tradition was treated, it is not surprising that the door was open for what, with all due deference, we must be allowed to characterize as an extremely subjective, typological and patternistic interpretation of the Gospel Tradition, associated particularly with Dr. A. M. Farrer.

On the other hand, there was another development. Because, it would seem to us, the Kerygma increasingly came to be interpreted as an Event hanging in mid-air, as it were, a phenomenon in a vacuum, the necessity to give it meaning became urgent. It is dangerously easy to be facile at this point, and I am fully aware that I may here be guilty of theological naïveté, but I venture to suggest that as long as the Jesus of History was a significant factor in the interpretation of the Faith of the New Testament, the works and words of Jesus themselves provided a content for the Kerygma which was religiously and ethically enriching. But once the Kerygma was materially divorced from these, it could not but become to some extent an empty shell, or, as I have before expressed it, a skeleton with no flesh. And it is of the nature of skeletons that they call for explanation. This is, in part, the reason for the urgency with which Bultmann has called for demythologizing. When the Kerygma had become mainly a bare divine action from beyond, that touched earth only at the point of the Cross, its mythological character became markedly prominent at the expense of its historical substance, and so Bultmann came to explain the mythology not so much in terms of its historical content as of his own philosophic presuppositions. Exegesis, no less than nature, abhors a vacuum. The neglect of the historical Jesus left the house of the Kerygma empty for the entry of things other than the works and words of Jesus.

I would not presume to dismiss the challenge raised by Dr. Bultmann: into its philosophical and theological ramifications I am not equipped to enter. I have merely set it within the framework of recent New Testament studies. I have mentioned demythologizing here because it is part and parcel of that situation which has produced a most striking phenomenon in much recent New Testament scholarship: namely, the paradox that, while great emphasis is laid upon the preaching of the Early Church as the declaration of an event or series of events as of crucial significance, there has been a growing scepticism as to the precise historical content of that event. The Kerygma, it has been claimed, rests on historical events; but the substance of these in history is declared to be either unimportant or unknowable. Thus far, at any rate, the Quest of the Historical Jesus has had this paradoxical dénouement.

What should we say to this? I suggest that there are two approaches to the problem which we should avoid. First, we should resist the temptation of simplifying the problem raised by Form Criticism as to the possibility of disentangling the works and words of Jesus from the interpretations placed upon them by the Church. We may illustrate such simplification from Professor Harald Riesenfeld's well-known lecture at the International Congress on the Gospels, Oxford 1957, with much of which I find myself in agreement. In a brilliant manner he argued that the words of Jesus had been preserved intact in the New Testament along the channels of a largely fixed Christian tradition which treated them as a Holy Word. But if such were so rigidly the case, the divergencies, which the same materials in the various strata of the tradition present, become inexplicable. At this point, we must allow to the Form-Critic the full weight of the fact that the tradition has in fact been modified in the course of its transmission. We cannot by-pass Form Criticism: its insights must be accepted and taken at full value. In the second place, we should avoid an alternative simplification, arising from factors we have already indicated, namely, that which despairs of ever solving the paradox with which we are concerned and rests content with the affirmation that the Kerygma, as the proclamation of the Church, must alone suffice for us, its precise relationship to the historical Jesus being left undefined. To this we must answer that such a position is ultimately self-contradictory and self-destructive. It asks us to rest in a paradox too acute to be accepted. The salient fact must be recognized that the early Christian movement began under the impulse of Jesus of Nazareth. The Kerygma revolves around Him, and we must therefore assume that the Kerygma itself implies that if Jesus, the Christ, be not taken seriously as a 'fact' in history, He is in a real sense a contradiction in terms. This is, we may argue, why the Gospel tradition in the Synoptics, not to speak of John, has been preserved, and, this being the case, it is justifiable to claim that the paradox at which we have arrived must somehow be transcended: the quest of the historical Jesus must go on.

IV

May I indicate briefly two needs which seem to present themselves in this area of New Testament study?

First, we have insisted that Form Criticism has established its case that the tradition about the works and words of Jesus has been moulded in the course of its transmission by the needs of the Church: but this is not to admit that the tradition owes its origin to the Church. The tradition about Jesus has its source in His activity: it is not the creation of the community, however much coloured by its needs. The task therefore, is to separate, if possible, an original deposit of tradition, with its many starting points, from its increasing modification. To do this a primary requisite is that there should be certain criteria available by which the historicity and authenticity of the tradition in its various parts could be tested. The point is this: Roman and Protestant scholarship in the Synoptics has been made difficult and frustrating because of the extreme subjectivity of its approach. Each student has felt free, not only to make his own assumptions, but to create his own criteria. The establishment of the criteria must precede any renewed quest of the historical Jesus, and it is already afoot as can be seen, for example, in the work of Käsemann, Bornkamm, Fuchs, Stauffer, and Robinson.

Only the briefest statement of such possible criteria can be attempted here. But, first, let me repeat the assumption I have already made, namely, that, since the Kerygma points to history, it is reasonable to assume that the tradition about Jesus purports to preserve historical data, and that the intention of the Evangelists was, in large part, historical. This is not to deny that interpretation and consequent modification have coloured that intention, and, indeed, that it may not be finally possible to separate fact from interpretation, but I am saying that it is reasonable to examine the Gospels for their historical contents. This assumption being made, some criteria for this examination may now be mentioned. Three types appear:

(a) *The Literary*: Source criticism of the Synoptics and John is temporarily under a cloud in some quarters, but there can be little doubt that the comparison of the same traditions, as they are preserved in different sources, can lead us to the earlier forms which they assumed and thus to their more 'historical' form. For example, a comparison of the triumphal entry in Mark 11:1–11 with Matt. 21:1–14 and Luke 19:28–38, reveals developments in the tradition which can with some safety be eliminated. Again at Mark 11:11, the evangelist's loyalty to his source, as compared with what we find in Matthew and Luke, has preserved what we must regard as historical, even at the cost of smoothness. Similarly it is possible by the comparison of the Gospels to detect special interests which have moved their several authors, and to allow for these in the assessment of the tradition they preserve. For example, it may be argued that Mark has been careful to eliminate any political emphasis from the ministry of Jesus.

On the Form-Critical side, not only must greater caution be exercised in passing from judgments of form to judgments of historicity, but recognition must be more generously given to what is frequently forgotten. It is this. The mere fact that modifications introduced into the tradition can be detected, implies that what has been modified can also be identified and often treated seriously as history. We may illustrate this from Mark 2:20, which reads: 'The days will come when the bridegroom is taken away from them, and then they will fast on that day.' It has often been urged that these words were added by the primitive Church to justify the practice of fasting, which Jesus, in His day, had not countenanced. But, as Professor Moule has recently insisted, even if this be granted, it only makes more probable the historicity of the first part of the story. What is applicable in Mark 2:18 ff. is applicable wherever event and interpretation are contiguous. As for the parables and words of Jesus, Professor Jeremias has showed us the way to separate the authentic from the interpretative in a volume which is already a classic. It now begins to appear perhaps that Form-Critical methods, applied with literary vigour, and without prejudice to historicity as such, may turn out to be a weapon which, so far from attacking and dismissing historicity, will be its active defender.

(b) *The Historical*: In addition to literary criteria, supplied by source and Form Criticism, strictly historical considerations can be brought to bear on the tradition. Of late it has been frequently asserted that the Gospels are not biographies. But this admission must not be too exclusively interpreted. As a genre of literature, biography, in its mature form, has emerged only in the last three centuries; and it has assumed three forms: (1) That in which the biographical data are fused, the biographer himself being present in the work as omniscient narrator (we think of Morley's *Life of Gladstone* as one example of this). Obviously the Gospels are not biographies in this sense. (2) That in which there is a free creation, in the biographer's own words, the result being something akin to the painter's portrait—an impression, which may, in fact, be more 'true' than the first type of biography mentioned. But, again, the Gospels are not such individualistic, impressionistic creations; the role of the community in the formation of the tradition rules out such extreme personalism. (3) That in which the biographer arranges traditional documentary and other material to produce an integrated work. With this last type the Gospels can broadly be compared, i.e., they manipulate traditional material with seriousness. Nothing is gained by insisting that the Gospels are what they are not, i.e., biographies, but nothing is gained either, indeed much is lost, by ignoring the fact that their intention is fulfilled in the presentation of the story of a life. To this 'story' it is reasonable to apply tests of historical reliability.

Thus, for example, the Gospels contain references to names, places, itineraries, and apparently pointless details, which, were the intent of their authors merely interpretative or theological, are hard to explain. Such details surely point to historical reminiscences, which were regarded as preserving points of significance, and must be exploited as clues to the course of the life of Jesus. At certain points of the narrative the mention of actual eyewitnesses must be significant; other pericopae invite the application of our knowledge of first century conditions to determine whether they can be dated during the ministry of Jesus or must be relegated to a later time. Despite the special problems posed by the writing of 'history' in the first century, and the peculiar character of the Gospels, historical probability must be given its due weight.

(c) *The Theological*: Lastly, any assessment of the historical value of the tradition must make use of theological probability. Thus there are elements in the Synoptics which are self-authenticating, i.e., which it is improbable that the Church, in the light of its theological development, should ever have invented. On the other hand, the absence of other elements is equally significant. While I was preparing this lecture there came into my hands the volume of essays in memory of the late beloved Professor T. W. Manson, who would, I think, have endorsed most, if not all, of what I have tried to say here. In an essay in it entitled 'The Intention of the Evangelists', Professor Charles Moule of Cambridge points out the almost complete absence in Mark of the great Pauline motifs in Christology, pneumatology and sacramentalism—a fact difficult to understand if we are to find in that Gospel the faith of the Church. I cannot offer here a full substantiation of Moule's claim 'that all four Gospels are alike to be interpreted as more than anything else evangelistic and apologetic in purpose, and that the Synoptic Gospels represent primarily the recognition that a vital element in evangelism is the plain story of what happened in the ministry of Jesus'.[1] But it confirms my contention to the hilt that the character of the Gospels does not make the quest of the historical Jesus an impossibility.

But though easy to state, criteria are notoriously difficult to apply; and even the most thorough application of these suggested literary, historical and theological criteria is not likely to provide an 'Open Sesame' to breach the curtain of historical scepticism set up by so much Form-Critical scholarship. Moreover, I am fully aware that their application can prove fruitful only if the assumption be accepted that the Kerygma itself necessarily takes that which 'actually happened' seriously. And this insistence on the necessity of 'history' for the Kerygma itself leads me to the second need in New Testament scholarship at this time; namely, a recovered sense of the importance of the matrix within which the Gospels emerged, i.e., the world of the first century. Impatience with the kind of scholarly activity involved in the meticulous exploration of that world must be challenged. I may be allowed to refer, in illustration, to yet another castle of my boyhood—Castell Carreg Cennen. This stands giddily on a steep cliff, which falls sheer for five hundred feet: to look at it,

[1] *New Testament Essays; Studies in Memory of T. W. Manson.* A. J. B. Higgins, ed., Manchester, 1959, pp. 175 ff.

on this side, is to see a structure almost suspended in mid-air; its base is lost to sight: it erupts without warning, inexplicable and strange, among the soft limestone hills around. But, from the other side, the castle looks quite different. There the ground gradually rises from the river valley till it reaches the outer wall of the castle, which, from this point of view, appears to grow naturally out of the ground, 'to belong' to its world after the manner which Frank Lloyd Wright taught us to appreciate. The castle seen from one side seems a strange eruption, a crag, like those that jut out, without father or mother, so to speak, in the deserts of Arizona; from the other, it seems a natural evolution, a peak rising gradually to its majestic height. So is the figure of Jesus. As bare Kerygma looked at *in vacuo*, He is an erupting Word, unaccountable, original. But looked at across the complexities of first century Judaism He is the culminating Word— part of a continuum. The life of Jesus must appear a strange Keryg- matic 'oddity' unless it be rooted in its native soil, where alone it can be understood in its proper relations.

Fortunately that soil can now be examined with a new thorough- ness because of the discovery of the Dead Sea Scrolls, not to speak of the finds at Chenoboskion. An understanding of the thought-world of Jesus at a new depth is now made possible. It promises to reveal far more clearly how the Judaism into which Jesus was born was heir not only to the Old Testament, but also to the rich heritage of the Graeco-Oriental setting. This means that the whole of the Near Eastern complex has to be exploited in the interests of a more profound understanding of Jesus. As we might expect, the com- plexity of Jesus is matched by the complexity of that world. A true appreciation of that world would not only illumine Jesus and the Gospels, but also serve as a check on certain exegetical developments. Let me illustrate from the work of two scholars, standing at opposite poles, to whom I have already referred. Professor Riesenfeld's treat- ment of the words of Jesus as a more or less fixed tradition, we may be allowed to suggest, would have gained in precision and probability from a clearer awareness of the nature of that tradition in first century Judaism to which he himself refers. It was not a static but a dynamic force; it was constantly creating and absorbing into itself new developments. And this is precisely the process revealed in the

New Testament, the fact, which, indeed, constitutes the very heart of the problem with which we are concerned. Similarly Dr. Bultmann's plea for demythologizing the New Testament, because it implies a tripartite conception of the Universe, which is no longer acceptable to the scientific mind, does not do justice to aspects of mythology in Judaism, and elsewhere, which are more significant than the spatial, and which might, were they better understood, prove of profound value in the interpretation of the Gospel even today. The first plea should not be for the rejection or reinterpretation of mythology, however much that might ultimately be thought to be necessary, but its true appreciation within a highly complex and enriched Judaism. So too in the light of recent studies in the nature of that Judaism, particularly by Professors Daube, E. R. Goodenough and Lieberman, much of the conventional dichotomy between Hellenism and Judaism calls for revision—a fact of far reaching consequences in many spheres, and not least in the quest of the historical Jesus. In short, a prerequisite for the resumption of that quest is a deeper attention to the roots of Jesus, if I may so express it, in His own times. We are driven back again to a renewed emphasis on those detailed background studies, which recent Kerygmatic and theological interests have tended, not always unconsciously, to belittle.

These then are the two needs: the rigid application of as satisfactory criteria as we can establish for the documents in the case, and a new intensified dedication to the study of Christian Origins within Judaism as an integral part of the Ancient Roman-Graeco-Oriental world. To put this in perspective, we are to resume the Quest of the Historical Jesus except that that task is now undertaken in a post Kerygmatic and post Form-Critical era, with all that this implies. Professor J. M. Robinson has called for a new quest, which he distinguishes sharply from that of the early years of the century. For reasons which I cannot develop here, I prefer to advocate resumption of the old quest on a new level, because the recovery of the intention of Jesus and His understanding of existence, such as Robinson desiderates, is inseparable from the recovery of what He did and said.

To some this lecture may have appeared as a knocking at doors that have long been open; to others as a futile exercise in reviving dead horses. This is perhaps inevitable, since I have presented the elements of the New Testament scene as they have passed through the crucible of my own experience, which is necessarily conditioned and limited.[2] In particular, I am not tempted to underestimate the full force of the impact of Form Criticism in this field. I am also aware that any advocacy of a renewed quest of 'the historical Jesus', especially without more careful definition of what is meant by that term than I have been able to present here, prompts theological questions which it would be presumptuous on my part to discuss. I will merely state, in theological justification of the position I have been advocating, that it would seem to me essential that there should be no incongruity between the Jesus of History and the Christ of Faith. The problem of their congruity cannot be silenced or shelved. Should they be incongruous, while a Theology of the Word might be possible, a Theology of the Word made flesh would hardly be so, and it is to such a Theology that the New Testament commits us.

[2] In this essay, which constituted my Inaugural Lecture at Union Theological Seminary, I have avoided any treatment of the rise in Germany of the problem with which it deals, in the work of M. Kähler and J. Schniewind and others. My aim has been to state it as it most directly presented itself in my own work. Very recently an extensive literature on the theme has emerged, typified especially in James M. Robinson, *A New Quest of the Historical Jesus*, 1959.

II

APOCALYPTIC AND PHARISAISM

The special problems connected with the teaching of Jesus arise partly from the juxtaposition within it of two things, eschatological concepts and religio-ethical ideals. And it is with an unsolved problem in the Jewish background of Jesus suggested by this juxtaposition that we shall here be concerned. This problem is best formulated by asking how first-century Judaism dealt with the tension between eschatology and ethics, or, more concretely, what the relationship was between Apocalyptic and Pharisaism.

Let us begin by asking what is meant by the eschatological background of Jesus. Schweitzer gives to this question a definite answer. To him the life of Jesus is controlled by a consistent, eschatological dogmatism, which can 'only be interpreted by the aid of . . . Jewish apocalyptic literature'. Jesus 'is simply the culminating manifestation of Jewish apocalyptic thought'. *But this Apocalyptic thought is to be divorced utterly from the Rabbis*.[1] Similarly Otto regarded Jesus as an *'ober gᵉlila'ah*, a Galilean itinerant preacher of eschatology, an eschatology which contained Hellenistic elements, and also Oriental elements which it shared with the Apocalyptic teaching of the Aramaic and Syriac world. Jesus, the Galilean, belonged to an Oriental-Hellenistic-Jewish Apocalyptic and Gnostic tradition *from which official Judaism had turned away*. Further, Galilee was not Judaized till a century before Christ; its Jewish inhabitants had the character of a Dispersion, and 'were relatively untouched by the direct doctrine and scholastic training of Judaea and Jerusalem'.[2] This sharp separation of Apocalyptic from Pharisaism has been

---

[1] *The Quest of the Historical Jesus*, pp. 365 ff.
[2] *The Kingdom of God and the Son of Man*, pp. 13 ff.

urged by Bousset, who contrasted Apocalyptic, the product of popular circles, with the learning of the Scribes,[3] and by Box,[4] Charles,[5] Herford,[6] Moore,[7] and most Jewish scholars.[8]

To follow Schweitzer and Otto, then, is to sever Jesus from the main stream of Judaism and connect Him with a sectarian Apocalyptic tradition within it. But this the Synoptic tradition of Jesus will not allow us to do, because, in the light of that tradition, this view of Jesus presents three difficulties. First, the insistence of Jesus on religio-ethical ideals becomes a difficulty, because Apocalyptic, while not unconcerned with ethics,[9] is not primarily concerned therewith. It is significant that Schweitzer has to explain away the ethical teaching of Jesus as an *Interimsethik*, and that Otto has to insist that the ethical interest of Jesus is inconsistent with His expectation of the near approach of the End and is a mark of the irrationality of the eschatological type to which He belongs.[10] *But we must recognize that the teaching of Jesus is not merely of crisis significance but is itself revelatory.*[11] Secondly, the eschatological ideas of Jesus are to be paralleled not from the Apocalyptic literature, but from the Old Testament;[12] and Mark 13:32 alone should make us suspicious of the authenticity of those bizarre Apocalyptic elements ascribed by the tradition to Jesus. Thirdly, to regard Jesus as an Apocalyptic visionary is to do violence to the tradition preserved in the Gospels in another way. T. W. Manson has protested against the view that Jesus was a simple, untutored carpenter. His humble origin does not imply that Jesus could not have been a scholar (cf. e.g., Hillel and Akiba); Jesus was called Rabbi, and knew not only classical Hebrew but also the Hebrew of the Schools, a language which He used in learned arguments with His opponents.[13]

[3] See Kittel, *Die Probleme des palästinischen Spätjudentums und das Urchristentum*, pp. 11 f.
[4] In *Abingdon Bible Commentary*, pp. 843 ff.
[5] *The Apocrypha and Pseudepigrapha of the O.T.*, ii, p. vii.
[6] *Talmud and Apocrypha*, pp. 263 ff.
[7] *Judaism*, i. p. 127.
[8] E.g., Schechter.
[9] Wilder, *Eschatology and Ethics in the Teaching of Jesus*, pp. 17 ff.
[10] *Op. cit.*, pp. 59 ff.
[11] See W. Manson, *Jesus the Messiah*, pp. 77 ff.
[12] T. W. Manson, *The Teaching of Jesus*, pp. 260 ff.
[13] *Op. cit.*, pp. 46 f.

It is at this point that we can best protest also against any rigid differentiation of the Judaism of Galilee from the orthodox Judaism of Jerusalem. Knox [14] has emphasized that there was no essential dichotomy even between Palestinian and Hellenistic Judaism, and how much less was there then, probably, between Galilean and Jerusalem Judaism. On the one hand, there was a Graeco-Jewish atmosphere in Jerusalem as well as in Galilee, and Rabbinism no less than Apocalyptic was open to and receptive of Hellenistic and other influences.[15] On the other hand, the Synagogue everywhere gave to Judaism a marked unity, and the educational 'system' served the same end.[16] Through synagogues and schools a constant interchange of ideas took place between Jerusalem, Galilee, and other places. Pupils in large numbers went from the 'secondary' schools of the provinces to the 'colleges' at Jerusalem. Thus, it was probably Galilee that produced Shammai. In addition, it has often been argued that the record of Galilee in the revolt of A.D. 67 to 70 points to a peculiarly Galilean fanaticism.[17] But, in fact, it was in Jerusalem that enthusiasm for the war reached its highest pitch.[18] In any case, not only may Galilean enthusiasm be interpreted differently, as a mark of loyalty to Jerusalem and Judaism, but we know that Jesus rejected all warlike fanaticism. Grant,[19] summarizing Lohmeyer, rightly claims that the Jews of Galilee in their origin and religious outlook had strong affiliations with Jerusalem. The upshot of all this is that, though Jesus doubtless spoke with a Galilean accent, He was not therefore necessarily outside the main stream of orthodox Judaism.

What we have written above makes us question that view of Jesus which confines Him to an Apocalyptic tradition divorced from Pharisaic Judaism. There are elements in Jesus which connect Him both with Apocalyptic and Pharisaism; and this leads us naturally to ask whether between Apocalyptic and Pharisaism there was such a cleavage as so many scholars have suggested. We begin by referring to those scholars who have rejected that cleavage. These are Torrey,

[14] *Some Hellenistic Elements in Primitive Christianity*, p. 2.
[15] See W. D. Davies, *Paul and Rabbinic Judaism*, pp. 5 f.
[16] See N. Drazin, *History of Jewish Education from 515 B.C.E. to 220 C.E.*; N. Morris, *The Jewish School*; Luke 5:17.
[17] Merrill, in *HDB*, ii, p. 102.
[18] Gwatkin, in *Peake's Commentary*, p. 610.
[19] *The Earliest Gospel*, p. 13.

Porter, Bonsirven, Kautzsch; and even Charles dates the cleavage in its deepest form after A.D. 70.[20] Fully to substantiate the claim of these scholars a thorough comparison of the Apocalyptic literature with relevant Rabbinic material alone would suffice, but the following facts are significant.

(1) In its piety and in its attitude to the Torah Apocalyptic was at one with Pharisaism. Both Charles [21] and Ginzberg [22] admit that the attitude of Apocalyptic writers towards the Torah was not different from that taken by the Rabbis. In 1 Enoch 99:2 we read: 'Woe to them that pervert the words of righteousness, and transgress the eternal law' (cf. 5:44/99:14).[23] The Assumption of Moses is the work of a Palestinian Pharisee who glories in the Law (1:16; 10:11 ff.; 12:10 ff.; Charles, op. cit., ii, pp. 407, 411). The Testament of the XII Patriarchs, which weds a deep ethical concern with Apocalyptic interest (T. Judah 24:1; 25:3; T. Levi 8:14; 19:9, 10, 12; T. Dan 5:10), constantly exalts the Torah (T. Reub. 3:8, T. Levi 13:2, T. Judah 18:3, etc.). In 2 Baruch the centrality of the Torah is evident (15:5; 38:2; 59:2; 77:15), and in 4 Ezra the author is concerned with the demands and efficacy of the Torah no less than with visions (e.g., 7:8; Charles, op. cit., ii, p. 555).

It is not merely in their estimation of the Torah that Apocalyptic writers agree with the Rabbis, they also reveal an ability to discuss questions of Halakah. It is Jubilees that is most illuminating at this point. It reveals a preoccupation with the Torah and a marked ability to manipulate its details in true Rabbinic manner. The author deals with the Calendar (2:9; 6:22), with the law governing the Sabbath, on which he is more severe than the Rabbis (2:27, 31; 50:8, 12); he has his own Halakah on tithes (32:9–11), where he again differs from the Rabbinic Law (see T. B. Sukkah, ad loc.), as he does also in dealing with marriage (4:15), and with circumcision (15:14). His version of the Noachian commandments is older than that of the lists found in Rabbinic sources (7:20), and he also preserves an older Halakah than the Talmud in connection with the festival of Sukkah (16:21). Despite his Apocalyptic interest (e.g., 1:29; 23) the author of

[20] See *Paul and Rabbinic Judaism*, pp. 9 f.
[21] *Op cit.*, ii, p. viii.
[22] In *Journal of Biblical Literature*, xli, p. 134, n. 47.
[23] See Kaplan, in *Anglican Theological Review*, xii. pp. 531 ff.

Jubilees thus reveals a concern with the *Halakah* which leads him to demand a stricter obedience than the Rabbis themselves.[24] Similarly, The Dead Sea Scrolls reveal a group of people who, while demanding a stricter adherence to the Torah than the Pharisees themselves (e.g. on divorce[25]), combine with their zeal for the Torah a marked eschatological interest.

(2) There is a community of eschatological doctrine between the Pharisees and the Apocalyptists. If there was a cleavage between them, it is difficult to understand how Pharisaism had absorbed so many Apocalyptic ideas. R. Johanan b. Zakkai (first century A.D.) was so convinced of the speedy appearance of the Messiah that he modified his ordinances regulating a certain religious ceremony in view of this expectation (*T. B. Rosh Ha-Shanah*, 30a), and in *T. B. Berakoth* 29b, it is confirmed that he expected the Messiah in the near future.[26] According to R. Eliezer b. Hyrkanos[27] the days of the Messiah would last forty years, and in his name a small apocalypse has come down to us.[28] R. Jose, the Galilean (A.D. 120–140) estimated the Messianic reign at sixty years (*Midrash Tehillim* 90:17). More significant still are the beliefs of Akiba. 'To him', writes Danby, 'is due the present system of grouping the *Halakoth*, their more exact definition, and still more, their closer approximation to the Written Law,'[29] and yet it was such a man who remained unwavering in his faith in the advent of the Messiah, and who championed the cause of Bar Kokba. Nothing could more point to the reality of eschatological beliefs among the Rabbis and to the falsity of the customary distinction between fanatic Apocalypticism and sober orthodoxy.

More important than the isolated cases where Rabbis show an eschatological interest is the fact that Judaism came to accept in general the main elements in the eschatological schema or schemas of the Apocalyptists. Kohler's article on 'Eschatology' in *The Jewish Encyclopaedia* reveals this. The evidence cited by Kohler is often too late for our purpose, but much of it is relevant. The following items

[24] See Finkelstein, in *Harvard Theological Review*, xvi, (1923).
[25] *C.D.C.*, 7:1 f.
[26] Silver, *History of Messianic Speculation in Israel*, p. 14.
[27] *T. B. Sanhedrin*, 99a.
[28] *Mishnah, Sotah* (the end).
[29] *The Mishnah*, p. xx.

of belief, among others, are common to Rabbis and Apocalyptists:

The travail of the Messianic Times	(*Mishnah, Sotah,* end; *T. B. Sanhedrin,* 96b–97a; *Derek Eretz Zuta,* 10; *Mishnah, Eduyoth* 2:10; *T. B. ʿAbodah Zarah,* 3b).
The Gathering of the Exiles	(*T. B. Megillah,* 17b; *Mishnah, Sanhedrin,* 10:3).
The Days of the Messiah	(See references above).
The New Jerusalem	(*T. B. Baba Bathra,* 75a–b; *T. B. Taʿanith,* 5a).
The Judgment	(*T. B. Kiddushin,* 40b).
Gehenna	(*T. B. Sotah,* 10b).

We should in addition note the importance attached by Pharisaism to belief in the Resurrection, a belief which grew up in Apocalyptic circles (see, e.g., *Mishnah, Sanhedrin* 10:1; *T. B. Sanhedrin,* 90b). Silver [30] has maintained that the chronological system of the Rabbis had led them to believe 'in the first and early half of the second century . . . that they were living at the close of the fifth millennium—the last millennium before the thousand years of peace which were to close this mundane cycle'.[31] And there can be little question that in the time of Jesus and after A.D. 70 many of the greatest leaders of Judaism to a considerable extent shared the eschatological hopes of the Apocalyptists. This is further borne out, indirectly, by the opposition to Messianic calculations in the Talmud. In *T. B. Sanhedrin,* 97b–98a R. Eliezer b. Hyrkanos disputed (despite his own calculations) with R. Joshua, and insisted that redemption could only come by repentance. R. Eliezer's plea, however, had to wait till later centuries before it found much support, and most of those passages opposing the calculation of the End are late.[32]

(3) The view is to be suspected that Apocalyptic stands for a popular interest, while Pharisaism is 'scholastic'. By its very nature Apocalyptic is a gnosis meant for the initiated: it dealt with visions given to the elect: it had an esoteric character however much its ideas were diffused by preachers like the *'ober gᵉlila'ah.* On the other hand, to separate Pharisaism too much from the popular piety is erroneous. Ginzberg [33] urged this strongly. So, too, Kittel has urged the variety of elements in the Talmud and its popular appeal; and

[30] *Op cit.,* p. 16.
[31] See *T. B. Rosh Ha-Shanah,* 31a; *T. B. ʿAbodah Zarah,* 5a, 9a.
[32] Silver, *op. cit.,* pp. 195 ff.
[33] *Op. cit.*

both Kittel [34] and Moore [35] refer to the discussions between Jesus and the Scribes and Pharisees as recorded in the Gospels as evidence for the popular relevance of Pharisaism. The latter by its very nature was intensely relevant to the life of the people: it involved a highly noticeable discipline which compelled it to be in the public eye.[36]

The above considerations at least invalidate any complete differentiation of Apocalyptic from Pharisaism. But we have now to face a difficulty. Why was it that the Apocalyptic literature found no place in the Jewish Canon of Scripture? It has been held that this latter fact points to a deliberate rejection of that literature by Judaism, a rejection prompted by the anti-Apocalyptic bias of the Rabbis.[37] Contributory to this rejection was the popularity of Apocalyptic in Christian circles, and the fixation of the Jewish Canon has been regarded as a direct reaction against the growth of Christian literature.[38] Moore [39] argued that it was the danger to the Synagogue from the circulation of the Gospels and other Christian books that led to the authoritative definition of the Canon of the Hagiographa. He justified his position by referring the phrase 'external books' in *Mishnah, Sanhedrin* 10:1 to heretical, and particularly to early Christian writings. Eissfeldt [40] points to the danger of Apocalyptic-syncretism within and Christianity without as the two factors leading to the fixation of the Jewish Canon; this is also forcibly expressed by Torrey.[41]

This difficulty, the rejection of Apocalyptic from the Jewish Canon, has been met by those who have regarded Apocalyptic as integral to the main current of Judaism with the contention that Judaism after A.D. 70 became far more unified than it was previously, and that literature which might well have played a marked part before A.D. 70 after that date lost its prestige; hence the exclusion of the Apocalyptic literature from the Canon reflects not so much conditions in the time of Jesus as the disillusion with and reaction against

[34] *Op. cit.*, pp. 12 f.
[35] *Op. cit.*, i, p. 132.
[36] See Finkelstein, *The Pharisees.*
[37] Box and Oesterley, *The Religion and Worship of the Synagogue*, p. 41.
[38] Cf. Loewe, in *ERE*, vii, p. 594. See also Ryle, *The Canon of the O.T.*, pp. 168 ff.
[39] See Ginzberg, *op. cit.*, pp. 115 ff.
[40] *Einleitung in das Alte Testament*, p. 624.
[41] *The Apocryphal Literature*, pp. 14 f.

Apocalyptic speculation after A.D. 70. Now it is clear that the Jamnia period was marked by struggles against Christian and Gnostic influences, struggles which, in view of its Hellenistic elements, and popularity among Christians, would doubtless reflect unfavourably on the Apocalyptic literature. Moreover, despite Moore's salutary protest,[42] we must think that the experiences of the first and second centuries did at least make Judaism more reserved and cautious. Thus the argument that the rejection of Apocalyptic from the Canon reflects not the attitude of Judaism to Apocalyptic in the time of Jesus, but after A.D. 70 must be given its due weight. But it is, nevertheless, precarious. We have seen that eschatological speculation continued unchecked after A.D. 70. Danby's words in connection with Messianic, eschatological and other ideas in Judaism are pertinent here. He writes: 'So long as there was no infringement of the plain and established sense of Scripture, and so long as it made for popular edification, the imagination was allowed free play.'[43] It was in the realm of ceremonial observance, not otherwise, that Judaism was most modified by A.D. 70. Moreover, after A.D. 70, although the more 'liberal' *Halakah* of the School of Hillel replaced the more severe and traditional *Halakah* of the School of Shammai, there is evidence that the attitude towards the Canon was more open than before A.D. 70; thus books were included after A.D. 70 which the School of Shammai had previously excluded, i.e., Ecclesiastes, Esther, Song of Songs.[44]

Useful as the view that the Jamnia period saw a change in the attitude of Judaism towards Apocalyptic, which accounts for its exclusion from the Canon, would be for our thesis, that in the time of Jesus they were not to be too sharply distinguished, we have seen reasons for not pressing it, even while recognizing its possible force. But we now suggest that the assumption which led us to discuss this possible change, namely, that the fixation of the Jewish Canon implies a rejection of the Apocalyptic literature, is itself questionable. Zeitlin [45] has revived the belief in the existence of the Great Syna-

---

[42] *Judaism*, iii, pp. 17 ff.
[43] *Op. cit.*, p. xvi, n. 1.
[44] See Ginzberg, *op. cit.*
[45] 'An Historical Study of the Canonization of the Hebrew Scriptures', in *Proceedings of the American Academy for Jewish Research* (1932), pp. 152 f.

gogue, and has claimed that the Canon was fixed at a meeting of the Great Synagogue in A.D. 65. More customary is it to connect the fixing of the Canon with the meeting of the Sanhedrin at which Gamaliel was deprived of the patriarchate of Jamnia, somewhere between A.D. 73 and 80 (see *Mishnah, Yadaim* 3:5). But it is probably erroneous to think of any specific date for the fixing of the Canon, as if the Canon was formed to meet a particularly urgent situation. Apart from the question of the historicity of the Great Synagogue,[46] the passage from *Mishnah, Yadaim* 3:5 by itself would seem to preclude the final delimitation of the Canon in A.D. 65. As for the date more customarily suggested, Christie [47] has pointed out that '*that day*' to which Ben Azzai refers in *Mishnah, Yadaim* 3:5 was a very crowded one; discussions took place on so many subjects that there would be no time for dealing with the Canon, and in any case it was a meeting at which it was most unlikely that a subject which seriously divided the Schools of Shammai and Hillel would have been raised at all. But even if we reject Christie's dismissal of Ben Azzai's evidence, there are numerous passages in the *Gemara*[48] which show that the question of the Canon was still open to discussion in the third century A.D. It would seem that the fixation of the Canon is to be regarded not so much as a reaction to a definite situation in which Apocalyptic and other literature was deemed to be dangerous, as a process whereby certain books gradually made their way to acceptance in the Synagogue; this process extended over centuries, and is not to be associated with any anti-Apocalyptic bias. Significant in this respect are those criteria which emerge as having governed the canonicity of various books. Zeitlin [49] has shown that two factors chiefly determined the acceptance or rejection of any book: first, the view that prophecy had ceased from Israel after Daniel in the Persian period, and that, therefore, all books written after that time could not be considered; this was an early view, not one artificially introduced in A.D. 65 or at Jamnia.[50] The other factor was the congruity of the contents of any book with the Torah. It

---

[46] See Moore, *op. cit.*, iii, pp. 10 ff.
[47] *JTS.*, xxvi, pp. 347 ff.
[48] *Ibid.*, pp. 352 ff.
[49] *Op. cit.*, pp. 141 ff.
[50] Ps. 74:9.

was this that led, for example, to discussions on the canonicity of
Ezekiel.[51] In addition, a certain self-consistency was also demanded
for canonicity,[52] and the originally Hebrew character of any book.[53]
It would appear that canonicity would not be denied to any book,
even an Apocalyptic one, that complied with these criteria; the
inclusion of Daniel in the Canon is significant in this respect. Equally
significant was the failure of books such as Ecclesiasticus, Judith,
Psalms of Solomon, and 1 and 2 Maccabees to achieve canonicity,
a fact which shows that such failure was not confined to Apocalyptic
books. It was not the presence or absence of Apocalyptic speculation
that determined canonicity, but other factors, and the exclusion of
the Apocalyptic literature is no proof that the Rabbis scornfully
dismissed it, but merely that the bulk of that literature could not be
considered for canonicity because it fell short of certain conditions.
We are probably to think of the fixation of the Canon as implying
not so much the deliberate *rejection* of the Apocalyptic literature as
the tacit assumption on the part of the Rabbis that it could not be
canonized.

What we have suggested above is confirmed when we recall that
non-canonicity did not necessarily imply heresy. Moore took the
term חצונים (external) to refer to 'heretical' and especially Christian
literature. It is thus rendered (i.e., by 'heretical') by Jastrow and
Danby. But the latter notes that it really refers to books excluded
from the Canon;[54] and that the translation 'heretical' is almost
certainly erroneous is shown by Ginzberg.[55] This leads us to point
out what was meant by the prohibition to read the 'external books'.
Zeitlin[56] claims that this prohibition was absolute. But a passage in
T. B. Sanhedrin, 100b, makes it clear that the prohibition refers not
to the reading of non-Canonical literature as such, but to reading it
aloud in public, and this included public study and liturgical
recitation.[57] Thus its exclusion from the Canon did not mean that
Apocalyptic literature could not be read; it was its public reading

[51] *T. B. Shabbath*, 13b.
[52] *Ibid.*, 30b.
[53] See Ginzberg, *op. cit.*
[54] *Op. cit.*, p. 387, n. 5.
[55] *Op. cit.*
[56] *Op. cit.*, p. 155.
[57] *The Jewish Encyclopedia*, iii, p. 148.

and deep study that was forbidden. Torrey [58] does not refer to this point of view at all; he asserts almost dogmatically that Judaism did away with the 'external books' after A.D. 70 by destroying them systematically and thoroughly so that the Semitic originals of such books have been lost. We prefer to follow Ginzberg, who writes: 'The disappearance of the Apocalyptic literature from among the Jews shows as little opposition on the part of the Rabbis to it as the disappearance of Judith shows any opposition of the Rabbis against this genuinely Pharisaic writing.'

What is the outcome of all our discussion on the Canon? It is this, that while it may not be possible to establish certainly that even if after A.D. 70 there was an anti-Apocalyptic bias among the Rabbis—there was no such bias before A.D. 70—it is precarious to assume that the exclusion of the Apocalyptic literature from the Canon implied a set hostility to it on their part.

In the light of all the above, we can now draw certain tentative conclusions. To deny the difference of emphasis in Apocalyptic and Pharisaism would be idle, but it is grievously erroneous to enlarge this difference into a cleavage. The truth about the relation between Apocalyptic and Pharisaism probably lies between the two extreme positions taken by Moore and Torrey. To some elements in first-century Judaism, like the Zealots, Apocalyptic was doubtless the breath of life; to others like the Sadducees, it was perhaps bizarre and slightly ridiculous; to the Pharisees it presented a less easily assessable phenomenon. Various Rabbis differed in their reaction to Apocalyptic, much as modern Christians differ in their view of Second Adventism. Just as an English Knight could say that 'We are all Socialists now' without implying that we were all members of a Socialist Party, so, too, we can probably claim that the Pharisees were all 'Apocalyptists' in the sense that Pharisaism had been infiltrated with Apocalyptic ideas. It was the fanaticism with which these ideas were held that differentiated the Apocalyptists from the Pharisees; but even in the fervour of their beliefs we must not too rigidly separate them; the figure of Akiba is sufficient warning against this.

The juxtaposition of eschatology and religio-ethical ideals is now

[58] *Op. cit.*, pp. 14 f.

seen to be native to Judaism. Even as the Synoptic tradition suggested, so, too, historical probability necessitates that Jesus' eschatological interest should not confine Him to a narrow Apocalyptic background, which was especially typical of Galilee; it can co-exist with the strictly [59] Pharisaic stream of first-century Judaism, to which Rabbinic elements in the Synoptic presentation of Jesus pointed us, elements which should also make us chary of connecting Jesus too exclusively with 'the quiet in the land'. In short, the background of Jesus is the rich complex of a Judaism which was liable to a dynamic irruption of the Prophetic tradition, but in which also Apocalyptic and Pharisaic elements were constantly coming to terms and mutually modifying one another. The relevance of this to the contemporary theological situation will be obvious. Fully to appreciate the Jewish background of Jesus is to recognize that the 'Jesus' of Harnack and the 'Christ' of Schweitzer need not be mutually irreconcilable, but can be one and the same Person. It is no accident that the Gospel of 'Christian Rabbinism', Matthew, is the most eschatological of the Gospels. [60]

[59] On the danger of emphasizing that Pharisaism was the *main* stream of first-century Judaism, see Morton Smith in various articles and my forthcoming work on Judaism in that period in *The New Peake Commentary*, edited by M. Black and H. H. Rowley.

[60] See further J. Bloch, *On the Apocalyptic in Judaism*, Philadelphia, 1953; T. W. Manson, 'Some Reflections on Apocalyptic' in *Aux Sources de la Tradition Chrétienne: Mélanges offerts à M. Maurice Goguel*, Paris, 1952, pp. 139 ff.; E. Stauffer, *Die Theologie des Neuen Testaments*, 1948, pp. 3 ff.

MATTHEW 5:17, 18

The special problems connected with the Gospel according to St. Matthew arise largely from its ambivalence, that is, the juxtaposition within it of apparently contradictory traditions about the life and teaching of Jesus. The 'particularism' of 10:5 is offset by the 'universalism' of 8:11 ff. and 28:16–20; then again in 23 the recognition of the validity of the teaching of the Scribes and Pharisees in 23:1–3 is followed in 23:3 ff. by a violent denunciation of them. Similarly in 5:17–20 and 5:21 ff. we are presented with what appear to be mutually exclusive attitudes to the Law of Moses. These various instances of ambivalence are often ascribed to the presence in Matthew of material drawn from different sources which reflect the interests of the various groups from which they emerged. In particular, Matthew has incorporated in his Gospel material from the source generally called M which is especially tendentious. In this essay we shall be concerned with the example of ambivalence last mentioned in 5:17–18. Do the apparently inconsistent attitudes to the Law of Moses, which it ascribes to Jesus, merely reflect the mind and practice of the Church from which Matthew emerged, or of the Churches from which he acquired his traditions, or do they derive from the practice and teaching of Jesus Himself? In short, does 5:17–18 merely reflect contradictory sources or a contradiction which marked the actual Ministry of Jesus, *Gemeindetheologie* or history?

Let us begin by asking what the pericope taken at its face value means; does it imply a contradiction at all? Matthew's intention in placing it at this point in the Sermon on the Mount seems clear, because it is given a well-defined position. Assuming, without discussion, that primarily at least the Sermon is directed to the

Church, we find that, after describing the blessedness offered by God's grace to His own (5:1–12), Matthew designates the Christian community as the salt of the earth (5:13) and the light of the world (5:14). As such it constitutes a peculiar people which is called upon to bring forth good works and thereby glorify God among men (5:16). The remainder of the Sermon, apart from the conclusion in 7:13 f. is a description of these 'good works': they are summed up in what is usually called the Golden Rule, which appears in the climacteric verse in 7:12. Explicitly, in the description of its blessedness in 5:1–11, and implicitly, in the description of the demands made upon it, the Christian community is set over against the Old Israel. The New Israel is to fulfil a function similar to that of the Old in glorifying God in good works. But what is the relation between the 'good works' of Christians and those of the Old Israel? Do they differ in essence from each other or is it that Christians are to abound more and more in the same kind of good works that characterize the Scribe and Pharisee, as 5:20 seems to suggest? Is the righteousness expressed in obedience to the Law radically different from the righteousness demanded of the new eschatological community? Or, expressed more concretely, what is the relation of the Gospel to the Law? And Matthew begins by rejecting the view that the relation between the old and the new righteousness is one of stark opposition. It was not to annul the Law of Moses that Jesus came: mere iconoclasm on the part of Jesus is at once ruled out. At the very least the phrase οὐκ ἦλθον καταλῦσαι implies that the mission of Jesus did not have as its aim the abrogation of the Law. The attitude of Jesus to the Law was not one of outright rejection nor of uncritical conformity but of 'fulfilment' (πληρῶσαι).

What does the term πληρῶσαι mean here?[1]

---

[1] Interpreters of it fall roughly into two groups. There are, first, those who seek to establish the underlying Aramaic which Jesus used and which πληρῶσαι is intended to translate, and thus claim that there is no contradiction between 5:17 and 5:18. The following suggestions are to be reckoned with. (a) That πληρῶσαι is to be understood in the light of *T. B. Shabbath*, 116a-b as a translation, or rather a mistranslation, of the Aramaic, *wlo' l'wspy*; with this improbable view we shall deal at length below. (b) More frequently the term πληρῶσαι has been interpreted as a translation of some form of the Aramaic *qûm*. Branscomb urges that the immediate context in verses 18 and 19 favours this view, as does Rabbinic usage. He cites M. Aboth IV, 11 and suggests as a translation of 5:17: 'I came not to destroy the Law but to establish it.' He expounds this to mean the establishing of the heart of the

Its total setting in the Sermon on the Mount demands that
πληρῶσαι in Matt. 5:17 should refer primarily at least not so much
to any act or acts of obedience in the life of Jesus or to the totality of
that life as one of obedience, as in Matt. 3:15, and elsewhere, as to His
teaching, which is here specifically under consideration, and to His
relation, not to prophecy, but to the Law, i.e., the demand of God as
such (the phrase 'the Law and the prophets' we take here, with most
commentators, as a pleonasm for the Law itself). The fulfilment
referred to in Matt. 5:17 Matthew would understand in the light of
the whole of 5:17-48, and in our judgment the meaning that
Matthew imparts to πληρῶσαι in Matt. 5:17 is that Jesus has fulfilled
the old Law in that He has brought what amounts to new demands.
Whether Matthew is thinking of Jesus as a New and Greater Moses

---

Torah, 'its deeply humanitarian and ethical spirit'. Equally strongly and with more
copious illustrations from the Rabbis, Dalman insisted on the same underlying
Aramaic for πληρῶσαι in 5:17. . . . He translates it by 'to make valid' which
essentially has the same connotation as Branscomb's 'to establish'. It may well be
that the translations of Branscomb and Dalman are legitimate but the following points
deserve notice. The term *hmt q y γ m* in Aboth IV, 11 is differently understood by
Jastrow, who interprets *qûm* there to mean 'to study and to observe the Law'.
Moreover, Branscomb does not note and Dalman passes over too easily the fact that
the term πληρόω is used in the LXX only to translate forms of the verbs *ml'* and *klh*
(it agrees with this that the Syriac versions read *'elo' de malê*, for ἀλλὰ πληρῶσαι in
5:17). This is particularly the case, since, if, as Branscomb and Dalman claim, the
term meant 'to establish', he had to hand such a familiar term as ἵστημι, the one
used by Paul in Rom. 3:31. The renderings of Branscomb and Dalman, therefore,
cannot be regarded as certain; to accept them would be to recognize that there is
possibly no fundamental contradiction between Matt. 5:17 and 5:18.
    But all attempts at finding the Aramaic which underlies πληρῶσαι must be
conjectural, and many scholars, who constitute the second 'group' referred to above,
have sought to interpret πληρῶσαι primarily in the light of Matthean usage. Thus
some have found it possible to translate πληρῶσαι simply as 'fulfil' in the sense of
'obeying the Law'. This is perhaps the meaning of the elusive phrase, πληρῶσαι πᾶσαν
δικαιοσύνην, Matt. 3:15 (cf. Rom., 8:4; Gal., 5:14) where it seems to mean to keep
every ordinance of the Law of God and thus to establish it. And it has been argued that
Matt. 5:17 means that Jesus, as in Matt. 3:15, came to fulfil the Law in His life of
obedience. Apart from the emphasis on the obedience of Jesus elsewhere in the New
Testament, this understanding of 5:17 is rendered more plausible also by the use of
πληρόω elsewhere in Matthew in the phrases ἵνα πληρώθη τὸ ῥηθεν διὰ τοῦ προφήτου
and ἵνα πληρωθῶσιν αἱ γραφαὶ τῶν προφητῶν to characterize specific events in the
ministry of Jesus (see Matt. 2:17; 2:23; 26:54 etc.). Again this understanding of
πληρῶσαι makes it possible, perhaps, to remove the apparent contradiction between
Matt. 5:17 and 5:18. See Harvey Branscomb, *Jesus and the Law of Moses*, New York,
R. R. Smith, 1930; Gustaf Dalman, *Jesus-Jeshua*, English translation, London, 1929;
David Daube, *The New Testament and Rabbinic Judaism*, London, 1956, p. 60;
Marcus Jastrow, *Dictionary of the Talmud*, London, 1930, and commentaries.

or not, need not, for our purpose, concern us: suffice it to say that Matthew here seems to present Jesus in a legislative cloak, because in at least three of the 'Antitheses' in Matt. 5:21–48 Jesus contravenes the provisions of the Jewish Law and proclaims new commandments (see below). We can reinforce this understanding of πληρῶσαι, for Matthew, in Matt. 5:17 by reference to the fact that the whole of the 'Sermon' is summed up in a 'new' commandment in Matt. 7:12 which plays an important part in Matthew's Gospel.[2] There can be little doubt that it is as the inaugurator of a New Torah which included specific commandments which He Himself promulgated while on earth and the promulgation of which He entrusted to His emissaries after His death (Matt. 28:20) that Jesus appears to Matthew as fulfilling the Law.

The term πληρῶσαι in its present setting, then, would seem to refer to the advent of a new 'Law', which transcends, and even, in parts, annuls the Old Law. But in Matt. 5:18, 20 the validity of the Old Law is asserted unequivocally. This is the contradiction which we have to examine. Matthew presents Jesus, if our interpretation of the text is correct, as affirming the Old Law while He annuls it. How is this contradiction to be understood?

II

One way to resolve the contradiction, as was previously hinted, is to explain it in terms of source criticism or, better, *Gemeindetheologie*. Thus Bultmann finds in Matt. 5:18, 19, as indeed in the whole of Matt. 5:17–19 a creation of the Palestinian, Jewish-Christian Church. 'V. 18 kann in seiner prinzipiellen Formulierung und in seinem Widerspruch zu primarer Überlieferung nur Gemeindebildung sein, und V. 19 kann keine Polemik gegen jüdische Gesetzeslehrer sein, sondern nur gegen die Hellenisten gehen . . . Matt. 5:17–19 gibt also die Stellung der konservativen palästinensischen Gemeinde im Gegensatz zu der der hellenistischen wieder. . . .'[3] Two considerations make it possible to doubt this view. First, the occurrence of

---

[2] Eduard Schweizer, *Theologische Literaturzeitung*, No. 8, 1952, pp. 480 f., Matt. 5: 17–20. *Anmerkungen zum Gesetzesverständnis des Matthäus.*

[3] R. Bultmann, *Die Geschichte der synoptischen Tradition* ², Göttingen, 1931, p. 146.

Matt. 5:18 in a slightly different form in Luke 16:17, in a Gospel which can hardly be accused of any Jewish-Christian sympathies, proves that most of the substance of the verse is no creation of Matthew or of his Church. The context in Luke 16:17 suggests that there also, as in Matt. 5:18, the verse is appended as a kind of comment on the relation between the old and the new order (Luke 16:16). T. W. Manson [4] has urged that there it is an ironical comment, which has been misunderstood by Matthew. The assertion of the eternal validity of the Law he finds impossible on the lips of Jesus. Perhaps Luke 16:15 lends some force to Manson's detection of irony here, but this is always a delicate process, and it is safer not to resort to it. Marcion, at least, found it necessary to take Luke 16:17 seriously and substituted for τοῦ νόμου the words τῶν λόγων μου.[5] That the words are conceivable in a serious sense on the lips of Jesus is sufficiently attested by their preservation in Matthew if not in Luke.

Secondly, it cannot be sufficiently emphasized that the passage Matt. 5:17–20 does not necessarily demand a *Sitz im Leben* outside the Ministry of Jesus. It is to be admitted at once that the prohibition μὴ νομίσητε κ.τ.λ. could well reflect the situation in the Church in Matthew's day at a date later than the Ministry of Jesus. Matthew elsewhere makes it clear that there were many in the Church contemporary with him who found ἀνομία attractive; moral laxity, for ἀνομία at least signified this, was a menace both present and future (Matt. 7:23; 13:41; 24:12),[6] so that Matt. 5:17 utters a prohibition relevant to Matthew's day, when it was possible to urge that Jesus was an iconoclast who urged, among other things, the annulling of the Law. The advent of the Messiah was the end of the Law in the sense that He abrogated the Law: for this had He come.[7] But it is a safe principle to exhaust the possibilities of a setting in the life of Jesus for any sayings ascribed to Jesus before ascribing them to a setting in the life of the primitive Church. And it is possible

---

[4] T. W. Manson, *The Sayings of Jesus*, London, 1949, *ad loc.*

[5] E. Nestle, *Novum Testamentum Graece* [21], Stuttgart, Privilg. Wurtt. Bibelanstalt, 1952, *ad loc.*

[6] The exact significance of the term ἀνομία in Matthew is not always easy to determine.

[7] It is possible, but not certain, that ἦλθον in Matt. 5:17 should be given a Messianic import as has been claimed for ἐξῆλθον in Mark 1:38 and for ἀπεστάλην in Matt. 15:24.

to find a setting for all the elements in Matt. 5:17-19 during the Ministry of Jesus.

First, apparent indifference to the demands of the Law often marked the activity of Jesus (Mark 2:1-14, parallels Luke 13:10 f.; 14:1 f.; John 5:9 f.; 9:14 f.; Mark 2:18 f.; 7:1 f.; 10:1 f.; John 2:19; Mark 14:58), so that the charge that He came to annul the Law could easily arise, and in His teaching, as we saw, for example in Matt. 5:21 f., there are direct contraventions of the Law of Moses. Certainly the Jewish leaders could be excused for proffering a charge of antinomianism against Him, and equally certainly the common people, who heard Him gladly, might have reasonably understood Him as breaking down the fences and proclaiming an unrestricted freedom. Foe and friend could find sufficient cause both in the practice and teaching of Jesus to stimulate the suspicion of iconoclasm, so that Matt. 5:17 could have been called forth by conditions during the Ministry itself.

Secondly, the assertion of the validity of the Law 'till heaven and earth pass away' might well reflect discussions on this problem between Jesus and His opponents. The 'doctrine' of the eternal validity of the Law would almost certainly be familiar to Jesus: moreover, it is possible that He was also familiar with speculations as to the role of the Law in the Messianic Age.[8] And Huber [9] may be right that the charge that Jesus was annulling the Law was rooted in opposition to the Messianic claim that this involved: part of this claim might have been regarded as the 'right' to 'annul' the Law.

Thirdly, the reference in Matt. 5:19 to the doing and the teaching of the Law finds a suitable background in those discussions going back at least to Hillel and Shammai as to the priority to be given to the knowing and doing of the Law. The reference to the least of these commandments reflects distinctions made by the Rabbis between heavy and light commandments, distinctions with which Jesus would be familiar, and Mark 12:28 and Matt. 23:23 furnish the setting against which sayings such as Matt. 5:19 are to be under-

---

[8] On this see W. D. Davies, *Torah in the Messianic Age and/or the Age to Come*, Philadelphia, 1952.

[9] Hugo Huber, *Die Bergpredigt*, Göttingen, 1932, p. 70.

stood. There was also considerable contemporary discussion about the degrees of literalness or severity with which the Law was to be observed.[10] Moreover, the recognition of the existence of gradations of rank in 'the Kingdom of heaven' is consonant with what we find elsewhere in the teaching ascribed to Jesus. (Luke 12:47 f.; Mark 10:40.) There is nothing in Matt. 5:17-19, then, which cannot be connected with the circumstances of Jesus' own ministry, and Bultmann and others, who explain away the contradiction which these verses present in terms of later disputes within the Church, are not necessarily to be followed. The disputes reflected in Matt. 5:17-20 are such as could have arisen during the activity of Jesus Himself.[11]

III

But it is possible to by-pass the contradiction which Matt. 5:17-18 offers while fully recognizing this last point. This is evident in Schoeps' rightful plea that the attitude of Jesus to the Law should be understood over against the contemporary discussion within Judaism. These discussions, he insists, centred chiefly on the authority of the oral tradition, and in the time of Jesus the movement which culminated in the codification of the Mishnah was in violent process and Jesus was actually involved in it. It was not the Law as such that was the object of Jesus' criticisms but the traditions which the Rabbis had built as a fence around it and to which an authority even superior to that of the written Law was accorded.

From this point of view, that Jesus did not attack the Law as such, but merely the παράδοσις τῶν πατέρων, which had grown around it, Matt. 5:18 with its assertion of the validity of the Law till heaven and earth should pass offers no contradiction to the customary position of Jesus. Schoeps [12] accordingly interprets πληρῶσαι in Matt. 5:17 in the light of T. B. Shabbath, 116 a–b, (see p. 433 n).

[10] On all this see H. Strack - P. Billerbeck: *Kommentar zum Neuen Testament aus Talmud und Midrasch*, Munich, 1928, *ad loc.*

[11] Compare J. Schniewind, *Das Evangelium nach Matthäus*, Göttingen, 1950, p. 56.

[12] Hans Joachim Schoeps, *Revue d'Histoire et de Philosophie religieuses*, t. XXXIII, 1953, pp. 15 f., *Jésus et la Loi juive*, p. 2. 'La critique que Jésus fait de la Loi, les divergences existant entre sa pensée et son attitude et la tradition juive, tournent entièrement autour de parties de la Loi qui ne constituaient pas encore de son vivant

He takes the phrases quoted there to preserve the words actually
uttered by Jesus. Jesus expressed Himself on the Law in terms of
Deut. 4:2, which reads *l' tspw 'l hdbr 'šr 'nky mṣwh 'tkm wl' tgr'w
mmnw lšmr 't mṣwt* (cf. Deut. 13:1).

Jesus refused to add to the Law *wl' l'wspy*, but Matthew misunderstood *wlō'* for *éllā'*. The actual words that Jesus uttered,
however, were 'I have not come to diminish the Law: I am not
come to add to the Law, i.e., in the way the elders do with their
traditional interpretations.' The intention of these words was to
express Jesus' opposition not to the Law itself but to the scribal
tradition that had grown around it. Thus the meaning of πληρῶσαι,
does not imply any contradiction with Matt. 5:18: an expression
of the validity of the Law in every jot and tittle, was fully consonant
with Jesus' understanding of πληρῶσαι. But Schoeps' view not only
demands a confusion of *wlō'* and *éllā'* by Matthew. If Deut. 4:2 and
13:1 lie behind the Aramaic words which Jesus spoke, it is strange
that Matthew should translate *ysp* by πληρῶσαι rather than by
προστιθέναι or προσθεῖναι which is found in the LXX, which Matthew
often used. It is easier to believe that the quotation in *T. B. Shabbath*,
116 a–b has been assimilated to the M.T., and supplies us, as
Dalman [13] puts it, with a coined phrase from Deut. 4:2. Moreover,
the passage is late and its text corrupt.[14] To go behind the Greek
of Matt. 5:17 to a late, corrupt Talmudic text for the understanding
of Jesus is to employ Procrustean methods.

[13] *Op. cit.*
[14] See B. H. Branscomb, *op. cit.*, p. 229 for details.

une *halacha* définitivement stabilisée.' The passage from *T. B. Shabbath* 116a–b reads
as follows:
'Imma Shalom, R. Eliezer's wife, was R. Gamaliel's sister. Now, a certain philosopher lived in his vicinity, (116b) and he bore a reputation that he did not accept
bribes. They wished to expose him, so she brought him a golden lamp, went before
him, (and) said to him, "I desire that a share be given me in my (deceased) father's
estate." "Divide," ordered he. Said he (R. Gamaliel) to him, "It is decreed for us,
Where there is a son, a daughter does not inherit." (He replied), "Since the day that
you were exiled from your land the Law of Moses has been superseded and another
book given, wherein it is written, 'A son and a daughter inherit equally.' " The next
day, he (R. Gamaliel) brought him a Lybian ass. Said he to them, "Look at the end
of the book, wherein it is written, I came not to destroy the Law of Moses nor to
add to the Law of Moses, and it is written therein 'A daughter does not inherit where
there is a son.' " Said she to him, "Let thy light shine forth like a lamp." Said R.
Gamaliel to him, "An ass came and knocked the lamp over!" '

But, apart from the understanding of πληρῶσαι, can Schoeps justify his contention that at no point does Jesus annul the Law, His criticisms being directed to the oral tradition? He denies that in the Sermon there is any questioning of the authority of the Law. That Sermon is merely an exegesis of the Law revealed in the Old Testament;[15] Jesus in the Sermon propagates no new law: He merely expounds the old. The words ἐγὼ δὲ λέγω ὑμῖν, he claims, supports this view. Schoeps, who unfortunately does not enlarge on this last phrase, nor support his interpretation, may well be right in his understanding of it, *taken in isolation*.[16] But it is difficult to agree with him that there is no contravention of the Law of Moses in the Antitheses. There are items in the Antitheses where the old Law's demands are radically deepened (with these we shall deal later); there are others where the Law itself is cited and particular provisions abrogated (Matt. 5:31, 38). It is only by a *tour de force* that the Antitheses can all be referred to tradition.[17] Lagrange [18] is here to be followed. Nor is it correct to isolate the phrase ἐγὼ δὲ λέγω ὑμῖν, which *in itself* may merely mean that Jesus is here offering His own interpretation of the Old Law, from its total context in the Sermon. Jesus is here speaking as the Christ of the Mount, and the overwhelmingly solemn nature of the setting of the pronouncements must be given full force. Whether Matthew is thinking of a New Moses or of a Messianic Torah, expectations of which would be known, or of the Son of Man, giving His commandments which were ultimately to be proclaimed to the world (28:16–20), it is clear that the phrase ἐγὼ δὲ λέγω ὑμῖν has here a peculiar force.[19] The occurrence of ἀμήν in 5:18 before the first occurrence of λέγω ὑμῖν adds weight to this view: the use of ἀμήν in this way by Jesus is, as far as we know, unique.[20]

---

[15] *Op. cit.*, p. 7.

[16] Morton Smith, *Tannaitic Parallels to the Gospels*, Philadelphia, 1951, p. 27 f.

[17] As Krister Stendahl, *The School of Matthew*, Uppsala, 1954, points out, the discoveries at Qumrân may illumine the background of such verses as Matt. 5:43.

[18] Le P. M.-J. Lagrange, *L'évangile selon Saint Matthieu*, Paris, 1948, *ad loc.* Lagrange writes: 'Car il ne souffrait pas de dire qu'il ne fait pas allusion à la loi de Moïse, mais seulement aux commentaires qu'en donnaient les Pharisiens. C'est bien la Loi ancienne qu'il cite.'

[19] See the discussion in Morton Smith, *op. cit.*, pp. 27 f. Contrast recent treatments by J. Jeremias and E. Percy.

[20] *Op cit.*, pp. 69 f. See also C. K. Barrett, *The Gospel According to St John*, London, 1955, p. 155.

Schoeps' interpretation of the Antitheses corresponds with his treatment of certain other passages where the question whether Jesus abrogated the Law emerges: these are Mark 2:23–3:6; Matt. 12:1–14; Luke 6:1–11 on the observation of the Sabbath; Mark 7:1–23; Matt. 15:1–20 on the Laws of Purity; Mark 10:2–12; Matt. 19:1–9 on Divorce. In the case of the story in Mark 2:23 ff. no direct provision of the Law is involved, and Jesus is concerned with Rabbinic interpretation; in Mark 3:1–6, however, the regulation in Exod. 16:25 is involved and it is significant that Jesus justifies the action of His disciples by appeal to a Biblical tradition: this in itself means that He has no intention to question the written tradition but merely its interpretation. In finding Jesus in both these cases to be primarily concerned with the rabbinical interpretation of the Law Schoeps may be right, but he has also to admit that even here it is clear that for Jesus 'la volonté de Dieu et la Loi ne sont pas exactement équivalentes aux yeux de Jésus: il est plus conformé à la volonté de Dieu de faire le bien (guérison de l'infirme) que d'observer de façon stricte le commandement du Sabbat pourtant préscrit par Dieu lui aussi'.[21]

It is a short step from this last to the radical criticism of the Torah itself, and it is difficult to agree with Schoeps that in Mark 7:1–23 we do not get this. The pericope Mark 7:1–13 is concerned with the washing of hands, a traditional development, so that here Jesus is concerned with Rabbinical or scribal rules, as Schoeps rightly insists. But it is other in the pericope Mark 7:14–23. This, taken at its face value, declares the abrogation of the laws of clean and unclean, laws which, unlike those dealing with the washing of hands, were written. Schoeps gets over the difficulty thus created for his theory in two ways. First, he maintains that in thus attacking ceremonial laws Jesus is merely concerned to emphasize the ethical ones, and, secondly, he follows some other scholars in rejecting the authenticity of Mark 7:15 f. By this means he is able to dispense with what he calls 'la seule (parole) qui témoigne d'une opposition effective à la Tora. . . .'[22] But against the first point we note that the setting of the pericope in Mark, as in Matthew, is significant. The section

---

[21] H. J. Schoeps, *op. cit.*, p. 10.
[22] *Ibid.*, pp. 15 f.

Mark 7:1 f. follows the feeding of the five thousand and the walking on the sea: in short, it follows what we may regard as a kind of climax in the popularity of Jesus towards the close of the Galilean ministry, when the *'am ha-aretz* had been increasingly attracted to him and had compelled into the open the issue of things clean and unclean. This is made even more clear in Matthew [23] where the discussion on the washing of hands, etc. is occasioned not by any specific act on the part of the disciples of Jesus, who in Mark had been seen eating unwashed by Pharisees and certain of the Scribes from Jerusalem (Mark 7:1, 2), but apparently by the preceding narrative in Matt. 14:13 f., Mark's parenthetical explanation of the occasion of the discussion on the hand washing being omitted by Matthew. Moreover, the phrases ἀκούετε καὶ συνίετε (Matt. 15:10) and ἀκούσατέ μου πάντες καὶ σύνετε (Mark 7:14) suggest a most solemn announcement not merely a correction of emphasis in the traditional attitude to things clean and unclean in favour of ethical rather than ceremonial seriousness. Similarly we must question the second point which Schoeps makes. The phrase καθαρίζων πάντα τὰ βρώματα in Mark 7:19 is almost certainly an addition of an editorial kind. It may also well be that Mark 7:18–23 is a targumic section, formulated by the Church, aimed at bringing out the true meaning of the teaching of Jesus, but, as Taylor has recently urged, the crucial saying Mark 7:15 is unquestionably genuine.[24] At the least we can assert that, *by implication*, Jesus in this verse publicly annuls the written Law; that both His practice and His teaching were not made more explicit so that the early Church could still hesitate on the issue of things clean and unclean (Acts 10:14, 15, 28 f.; Gal. 2:11–17; Rom. 14:14; Col. 2:20–22) belongs to a principle of reticence which also emerges elsewhere in His Ministry and to which we shall refer below.

The same uneasiness arises over Schoeps' treatment of Mark 10:1 ff., the discussion on divorce. For Jesus' appeal here is essentially to the aboriginal will of God in creation.[25] Owing to the hardness of men's hearts there has slipped in between man and God's original

---

[23] On this see B. W. Bacon, *Studies in Matthew*, New York, 1930, pp. 224 f.

[24] Vincent Taylor, *The Gospel According to St. Mark*, London, 1953, p. 342.

[25] See on this B. H. Branscomb, *op. cit.*, pp. 149 f.; C. H. Dodd, 'Natural Law in the Bible', *Theology*, Report No. 17, London, May and June 1946, p. 5.

purpose for him a law: but this last is, therefore, not a true expression of the divine will in its nakedness, but merely a concession to human weakness. Nevertheless, it should not here be overlooked that Gen. 1:27 is also part of the Torah, and it is perhaps safer to follow Schoeps at this point when he insists that Jesus is here appealing to one part of the Law (Gen. 1:27; 2:24) over against another (Deut. 24:1 ff.).

It follows from all the above, however, that Schoeps' attempt to relate the conflict of Jesus with the Law exclusively to the fence which had grown up around it, the παράδοσις τῶν πατέρων, must be rejected; and it is not justifiable by this means to remove the contradiction between Matt. 5:18 and the attitude to the Law revealed by Jesus elsewhere.

The same must be asserted of Huber's [26] treatment of the passage. He connects Matt. 5:17 f. particularly with the preceding verses in Matt. 5:13-16. There are addressed the disciples who were, according to Huber, of the 'am ha-aretz. The disciples had taken over the functions designed for the Old Israel, but because the good works to which they were being called did not depend on the observance of the Law, they were not to consider that Jesus had annulled the Law. The Law remained: Jesus only attacked the tradition.[27] It is from this point of view that Huber goes on to interpret καταλῦσαι in Matt. 5:17. It refers to Jesus' rejection of the Rabbinic interpretation of the Law. This in fact undid the Law while it sought to interpret it: the fence designed by the Rabbis to protect the Law itself annulled it. The same side glance at Rabbinic interpretation appears in Matt. 5:19 in Jesus' use of ποιήσῃ and διδάξῃ—the former term refers to the Pharisees, the second to the Scribes: Jesus here by implication warns against Pharisaic practice and Scribal teaching, respectively.

Huber is right in setting the teaching of Jesus over against contemporary discussions within Judaism. But, nevertheless, his understanding of Matt. 5:17 f. exclusively in the light of Matt. 5:13 f. and his assumption that the disciples as 'am ha-aretz were consciously and minutely being contrasted with the Scribes and Pharisees, as such, leads him to what we cannot but regard as forced exegesis of

[26] Op cit., ad loc.
[27] Ibid., p. 66.

Matt. 5:17 f., this despite the fact that these two groups are explicitly mentioned in Matt. 5:20. It is not likely that in Matt. 5:19 the term λύσῃ refers to the activity of Scribes or Pharisees, who manipulated the Law as did Hillel for example, in the introduction of the prosbul, and that ποιήσῃ and διδάξῃ are to be pinned down and sharply differentiated as referring to Pharisees and Scribes. This is at least as uncertain as the other extreme view that Matthew is here governed by anti-Pauline motifs.[28] Furthermore while the words τῶν ἐντολῶν τούτων τῶν ἐλαχίστων [29] are a difficulty [30], since they have no precise antecedents to which they can point, it is difficult to believe that the reference in λύσῃ and διδάξῃ should be to Pharisees and Scribes: John the Baptist, even though the greatest born among men, was not in the Kingdom; it is, therefore, hardly likely that Pharisees and Scribes should have been regarded as even least in the Kingdom. The words in Matt. 5:19 surely have in mind any Christian who regarded the moral law as not utterly binding. The terminology employed in Matt. 5:19 would be thoroughly familiar to Pharisaic and Scribal circles, but Huber's effort to confine the reference in Matt. 5:17 f. to their traditional interpretation of their Law cannot be carried through.

IV

In the previous pages we have questioned two attempts at by-passing the contradiction involved, in our judgment, in Jesus' attitude to the Law in Matt. 5:17 f. Because neither source criticism nor recourse to a rigid distinction in the mind of Jesus between the written Law and the oral Law provide us with a satisfying explanation of Matt. 5:17 f. we shall attempt in what follows to examine, very tentatively, certain lines of thought which might account for the contradiction concerned.

We saw above that Huber [31] interprets Matt. 5:17 f. as very

[28] *Idem.*
[29] See the commentaries.
[30] See G. D. Kilpatrick, *The Origins of the Gospel according to St. Matthew*, London, 1946, pp. 25 f. He transposes Matt. 5:19 f. to a place after Matt. 5:41 and makes τῶν ἐντολῶν τούτων refer to the revised commandments in verses 21, 27, 33, 38. Thus the words, according to Kilpatrick, do not refer to the Law at all. This is to cut the Gordian Knot: but we are not convinced that this is legitimate.
[31] *Op. cit.*

intimately bound up with Matt. 5:13 f. and this to some extent leads him to neglect the equally close relationship which it has with what follows, because Matt. 5:17 f. is concerned not only to deny any iconoclasm on the part of Jesus but also, as we have argued, to assert His positive attitude to the Law. Matthew, as we saw, has cast around Jesus the mantle of a new lawgiver, whether as New Moses or Son of Man or Messiah we need not here determine. And it is as the inaugurator of a New Torah which He Himself proclaimed while on earth and the promulgation of which He, as Lord, entrusted to His emissaries after His death that Jesus appears to Matthew as fulfilling the Law (Matt. 28:16-20).

But there can be little doubt that this understanding in its developed form is Matthew's own. The evidence suggests that Jesus refused to regard Himself, or to allow others to regard Him, as having legislative functions. To a request that He should divide an inheritance, His answer was an unequivocal negative, and His immediate warning against covetousness points to what was His essential concern, that is, to penetrate to what lies behind disputes about inheritances, as about other things (Luke 12:13 ff.). And this concern enables us at least to go behind Matthew's presentation in 5:17 f. to some degree. The most satisfying treatment of this passage is that of Albertz,[32] who distinguished two kinds of Antitheses (to which we have already referred above) within the complex Matt. 5: 21 ff. In the first group, which consists of verses 21, 22 a, 27 f., 33, 34 a, 37, the Antitheses take the form of a deepening of the demand of the Law as it were to the nth degree. In the second group, which consists of the remaining Antitheses, in verses 31-2, 38 f., 43, we have not a radicalizing of the pertinent demands of the old Law, as in the first group, but the contravention of them. We suggest that it is the first 'original' Antitheses which reveal the essential attitude of Jesus to the law. He came not to annul but to fulfil in the sense that He revealed the ultimate intention of the Law or uncovered its radically absolute meaning. This means that Jesus brought the Law to its eschatological or ultimate fulfilment. Πληρῶσαι in Matt. 5:17 thus has an eschatological connotation. The verb πληρόω and its

---

[32] Martin Albertz, *Die Synoptischen Streitgespräche*, Berlin, 1931, *ad rem.* and *Botschaft des Neuen Testaments*, Zürich, 1947-1952, *ad rem.*

cognates have such associations elsewhere in the New Testament.[33] And the eschatological associations of the term are found in Dan. 5:26 in Theodotion's translation. The verse Dan. 5:26 is rendered in the R. S. V. as follows: 'This is the interpretation of the matter: MENE, God has numbered the days of your kingdom and brought it to an end.' The Aramaic is as follows: *denâh pešar millitâ' mené' menâh 'elâhâ' malkûtâk wehašlemah*. The LXX renders the last two words by συντέτμηται καί συντετέλεσται ἡ βασιλεία σου. But Theodotion translates ἐμέτρησεν ὁ θεὸς τὴν βασιλείαν σου καὶ ἐπλήρωσεν αὐτήν. Here ἐπλήρωσεν means 'to bring to its destined end', an end which here has an immediate connotation of destruction. Perhaps, behind πληρῶσαι in Matt. 5:17 lies the same Aramaic word, but with a different immediate application. In possible support of this we may refer to the last verse of what Albertz regards as the original complex in Matt. 5:48, which reads ἔσεσθε οὖν ὑμεῖς τέλειοι, ὡς ὁ πατὴρ ὑμῶν ὁ οὐράνιος τέλειός ἐστιν. Torrey [34] suggested as the original Aramaic form underlying τέλειοι the term *gmyryn*. But we have seen that in the LXX the verb *slm* was rendered by τελειόω and it is not impossible that τέλειοι in Matt. 5:48 translates some form of *slm*. The disciples are exhorted to achieve their destined end. Possibly, in the original Aramaic unit of the tradition, πληρῶσαι in the first verse would find an echo in the τέλειοι of Matt. 5:48. But whether this suggestion concerning Matt. 5:48 be acceptable or not, it is highly probable that in its original context πληρῶσαι in Matt. 5:17 had an eschatological force. Jesus brings the Law to its final end; He does this, as we stated, by utterly radicalizing it.

How did Jesus achieve this radicalizing of the Law? How did He penetrate the tradition of the Fathers and the written Law itself to that perfect will of God which lay behind them and beyond them? Certainly He was rooted in the Law and the Prophets, and full recognition must be given to His appeal to Scripture itself against Scripture, although this must not be taken to mean, as Schoeps and Huber seem to imply, that He was bound by Scripture. Nurtured as He was on the Law and the Prophets, Jesus passed beyond His

---

[33] Consult any concordance of the New Testament. On Matt. 5:48 see Matthew Black, *An Aramaic Approach to the Gospels and Acts*, Oxford, 1955, pp. 138 f.
[34] C. C. Torrey, *Our Translated Gospels*, London, no date, pp. 92 f.

nurture to what we can only call an intuitive awareness of the will of
God in its sheer nakedness. We cannot doubt that Jesus followed the
immediate deliverances of His own conscience.[35] But this means that
the attitude of Jesus to the Law implies His Messianic awareness or
consciousness.[36] We cannot without extreme caution speak of any
claim that Jesus made to be the Messiah: what claim He made was
not explicit but implicit in His words and works. It is implicit in His
treatment of the Law not only in His use of what we must still be
allowed to call the Messanic 'I' of Matt. 5:21 f., but also, and possibly
even more so, in His appeal to *creation*.[37] The Messianic Age was to
be a return to the beginning: it would inaugurate a new creation
comparable to the first creation.[38] It is in the light of this that we are
to understand the teaching of Jesus on divorce in Mark 10:1 f.,
where He appeals to the order of creation as supplying a deeper and
truer clue to the intention of God than the Law, as it is in the same
light that we are to understand much in the parables of Jesus and in
such passages as Matt. 5:45 f.

Here, however, we are particularly concerned with the question
how the old Law fares under this radicalizing Messianic process,
which Jesus introduces in terms of creation, which is the theme of
Matt. 5:17-20. Clearly this radicalizing meant not merely the
deepening of some parts of the Law but the annulling of others. As
we saw the attempts of Schoeps and Huber to confine the critique
of the Law by Jesus to the tradition cannot be substantiated. Nevertheless, according to Matt. 5:17 f., the radicalizing of the Law by
Jesus still leaves room for the validity of the Old Law in all its force,
not only in parts. We shall now explore further the total situation
in the Ministry of Jesus in an attempt to understand why this could
be the case. Are there any considerations of history or of 'dogma',

[35] Even Isa. 53 may not have been the original source of Jesus' understanding
of Himself as the Servant-Messiah; so Charles F. D. Moule, *Studiorum Novi Testamenti
Societas*, Bulletin III, Oxford, 1952, p. 53, citing in support Vincent Taylor, *The
Atonement in New Testament Teaching*, London, 1940, p. 97, and Joachim Jeremias,
Aux Sources de la Tradition Chrétienne, Paris, 1952, p. 113.
[36] On this see H. J. Schoeps, *op. cit.*; W. G. Kümmel, 'Jesus und der jüd. Traditions
—gedanke,' *Zeitschrift für N. T. Wiss.*, 33, pp. 105 f. In our judgment their emphasis on
the Messianic consciousness of Jesus as governing His attitude to the Law is essentially
sound.
[37] See H. J. Schoeps, *Aus Frühchristlicher Zeit*, Tübingen, 1950, pp. 271 f.
[38] W. D. Davies, *Paul and Rabbinic Judaism*,[2] London, 1955, pp. 37 f.

if we may so express it, in the Ministry of Jesus, which might account for this contradiction?

The following considerations of history are pertinent. First, is it conceivable that there could arise during the Ministry of Jesus certain conditions in which what we may call 'sweet reasonableness' might demand an assertion such as Matt. 5:18? It will be recalled that one of the criticisms of Jesus which the late C. G. Montefiore [39] levied was that He who demanded the perfection of love from His followers was Himself uncharitable in His criticism of His Pharisaic opponents; and this criticism is hard to answer if we can only go by the conflict stories of the Gospels and Matt. 23. But, in this connection, it is well to recall that the sources we possess for the Ministry of Jesus emerge from a period when the Church and the Synagogue were increasingly diverging, so that many aspects of the relations between Jesus and the Pharisees and Scribes have either been hidden from us by silence or misinterpreted by partial and manipulated information. One of the services of W. L. Knox was that he detected certain passages in the Synoptics which suggest that Jesus, for a period which we cannot now determine, tried to maintain friendly relations with the Pharisees. The passages to which he refers are 'preserved in isolated sayings which are entirely contrary to the general attitude of the early Palestinian Church, as represented by the dominant tradition'.[40] Knox noted the following:

(1) Matt. 23:23. 'Woe unto you scribes and Pharisees, hypocrites, for ye pay tithe of mint and anise and cummin and have omitted the weightier matters of the law, judgment, mercy, and faith: these ought ye to have done and not to leave the other undone ($\tau a \hat{\upsilon} \tau a$ $\delta \hat{\epsilon}$ $\check{\epsilon} \delta \epsilon \iota$ $\pi o \iota \hat{\eta} \sigma a \iota$ $\kappa \dot{a} \kappa \epsilon \hat{\iota} \nu a$ $\mu \dot{\eta}$ $\dot{a} \phi \epsilon \hat{\iota} \nu a \iota$)'. Here $\check{\epsilon} \delta \epsilon \iota$, a strong term, even though we may not here take it to be a '$\delta \epsilon \hat{\iota}$ of divine necessity', is used in reference to the minutiae of the Law as much as to $\kappa \rho \acute{\iota} \sigma \iota \varsigma$, $\check{\epsilon} \lambda \epsilon o \varsigma$, $\pi \acute{\iota} \sigma \tau \iota \varsigma$: this is in agreement with Matt. 5:18. A parallel to $\tau a \hat{\upsilon} \tau a$ $\delta \hat{\epsilon}$ $\check{\epsilon} \delta \epsilon \iota$ $\pi o \iota \hat{\eta} \sigma a \iota$ $\kappa \dot{a} \kappa \epsilon \hat{\iota} \nu a$ $\mu \dot{\eta}$ $\dot{a} \phi \epsilon \hat{\iota} \nu a \iota$ occurs also in Luke 11:42. Schniewind holds that the sentence is here ironical: he compares the irony of Matt. 22:21 (Gott und Cäsar: vergesst Gott nicht!)[41] But

---

[39] See *Some Elements of the Religious Teaching of Jesus*.
[40] Wilfred L. Knox, *Sources of the Synoptic Gospels*, Cambridge, 1953, p. 16.
[41] *Op. cit., ad loc.*

Klostermann's comment is more apt than this sentence 'Klingt aber unerwartet konsiliant'.[42] Branscomb regards the words as scarcely possible on the lips of Jesus for reasons which we may gather together thus: (1) the statement appears to be a later addition designed to defend Jesus against criticism; it seems to belong to a later period of reflection in the Church rather than to the heat of the conflict of Jesus' Ministry; (2) it is unlike Jesus' method 'to follow His utterances with qualifying phrases and interpretative additions'; (3) the content of the utterance is against its authenticity. 'It is', writes Branscomb, 'historically and psychologically unbelievable that one of the demands which he made was that the tithes be paid with the most minute and detailed accuracy'.[43] On this last point we need only remark that the conservative practice of Jesus Himself, to which we have previously referred, can be perhaps enlisted as much against it as for it. And, as for the first point, the ascription of a verse to a late date on *a priori* grounds must be carefully scrutinized. Here the presence of the sentence in Q forbids our taking it to be merely a correction by the later Church of Jesus' extreme attitude. It is difficult to imagine that a saying such as this, which was contrary to the convictions which the Church increasingly came to cherish, should have been invented. Moreover, it is precisely the kind of indiscriminate condemnation of His opponents, which Branscomb apparently finds customary in Jesus, which Montefiore rightly condemns.

(2). Luke 5:39. καὶ οὐδεὶς πιὼν παλαιὸν θέλει νέον λέγει γὰρ ὁ παλαιὸς χρηστός ἐστιν. Knox here finds Jesus' wistful recognition of the difficulties which the Scribes and Pharisees must have found in abandoning their established outlook in favour of the 'new wine' of his teaching.[44] The textual evidence against the verse is weak: its sole omission by D can be explained as due to the influence of Marcion. Luke is hardly likely himself to have ascribed to Jesus a saying which is so contrary to the contest.

(3) Luke 13:31, where Pharisees warn Jesus of the danger from Herod, bespeaks a friendly attitude towards Him. The same appears in Luke 7:36 where Simon the Pharisee is host to Jesus. We

[42] Ernst Klostermann, *Das Matthäusevangelium*, Tübingen, 1937, *adl oc.*
[43] *Op. cit.*, pp. 212 f.
[44] *Op. cit.*

may perhaps add to these passages cited by Knox the attitude of Jesus to Jerusalem which was one of sorrow over the city of the Scribes and Pharisees rather than of indignation. The last word of Jesus to the city—following on His woes on the Pharisees—is sorrow not anger. (Matt. 23:37 f.)

(4) Luke 17:20; Mark 12:28 f.

In addition to the above Knox pointed out that the conflict stories which are usually deemed to begin at Mark 2:1 may well have begun at Mark 1:40, the object of the pericope beginning there being to show that it was Jesus' intention to keep the Law. (The interpretation offered by Lohmeyer [45] of Mark 1:44 is too involved though not impossible.) But it should be pointed out that Jesus may here be merely conforming to the Law in its civil aspects and that too much should not be made of this.

In any case the chronological incidence of the conflict stories in Mark 2:1-3, 6 cannot be historical, and it has had the unfortunate result of giving the impression that Jesus and the Scribes and Pharisees were at daggers drawn from the very opening of the Ministry. The evidence provided by Knox makes it clear that there was a period when such was not the case, and the story of Nicodemus in the Fourth Gospel supports this view.

Here it will be profitable to turn to Paul, who was not un-influenced both by the words and works of Jesus,[46] because fortunately we possess discussions by him on the attitude which Christians, who did not observe the Law, should take towards those who had scruples on this and other similar matters. Dodd has recently dealt with one such discussion, that in 1 Cor. 9:19 f.[47] Here Paul takes loyalty to what he regards as the Law of Christ to be not incompatible with the observance of the Jewish law for the sake of the weaker brother. The Law of Christ for Paul is in part at least the explicit words of Jesus as found in the Sermon on the Mount and elsewhere and echoes of which recur in Paul's discussion.[48] This Law is, moreover, fulfilled in love (ἀγάπη). The point

---

[45] Ernst Lohmeyer, *Das Markusevangelium*, Göttingen, 1937, *ad loc.*

[46] Archibald M. Hunter, *Paul and His Predecessors*, London, 1940.

[47] C. H. Dodd, *Studia Paulina in Honorem Johannes de Zwaan*, Haarlem, 1953, pp. 96 f., ENNOMOS ΧΡΙΣΤΟΥ.

[48] C. H. Dodd, *op. cit.*, p. 106.

here to be emphasized is that this Law of Christ in certain circumstances itself demands the observance of the very Jewish Law which it has transcended. Whence did Paul derive this view? Even if we hold that the phrase ἔννομος Χριστοῦ here, as the phrase νόμος Χριστοῦ well may, bears no reference to the life of Jesus, there is still one place where Paul specifically refers to the practice of Jesus as justifying accommodation to the scruples of the weak. This is in Rom. 15:7 f. διὸ προσλαμβάνεσθε ἀλλήλους, καθὼς καὶ ὁ Χριστὸς προσελάβετο ἡμᾶς εἰς δόξαν τοῦ θεοῦ. λέγω γὰρ Χριστὸν διάκονον γεγενῆσθαι περιτομῆς ὑπὲρ ἀληθείας θεοῦ κ. τ. λ. The submission of Christ to the Torah was both for the truth of God and so that the Gentiles might glorify God, but the phrase διάκονον γεγενῆσθαι περιτομῆς occurs in the context of a discussion concerning the strong and the weak. With what is almost certainly a side glance at Matt. 7:1 Paul has urged in Rom. 14:13 f. that Christians should not judge each other in the matter of eating: each Christian stands or falls by his own conscience before God: the important thing is that he should walk in love. In a sentence which recalls Luke 6:5 (D) Paul asserts that πᾶν δὲ ὃ οὐκ ἐκ πίστεως, ἁμαρτία ἐστίν. To walk κατὰ ἀγάπην is not to please ourselves, just as Jesus did not please Himself. But this means that Christians, like Jesus Himself, may be called to submit to the Law for the sake of the weaker brethren. For our purpose the significant thing is that Paul appeals to the example of Christ as 'minister of circumcision' in dealing with consideration for those who observed the Jewish Law. To be ἔννομος Χριστοῦ could demand submission to the Law of Moses. Thus Paul, the apostle of freedom, must as a Christian also say διόπερ εἰ βρῶμα σκανδαλίζει τὸν ἀδελφόν μου, οὐ μὴ φάγω κρέα εἰς τὸν αἰῶνα, ἵνα μὴ τὸν ἀδελφόν μου σκανδαλίσω (1 Cor. 8:13). Paul could find warrant for his tolerant attitude to weak Jewish Christians and others in the Ministry of Jesus, διάκονος περιτομῆς. All this points to an attitude of tolerance towards the observance of the Law in the Ministry of Jesus which must be given its full force, and indeed it agrees with Matt. 23 where the validity of the observance of the Law is recognized, its hypocritical abuse alone being condemned.

Nevertheless, caution is necessary here. The recognition that Paul could base his lenient tolerance on *imitatio Christi* does not necessarily

mean that we can take Matt. 5:18 as expressing Jesus' attitude. There
the permanency of the Law as a principle is asserted, whereas in Paul
the permanency and primacy of love is in mind.

But, in the second place, the relation of Jesus to the populace of
His day must be borne in mind if we are properly to assess His
attitude to the Law. The multitudes are seldom far from Jesus: if we
accept the claim of Knox that there was a period when Jesus attempted to conciliate the leaders of Jewry, it is more certain that His main
appeal was to the multitudes. The common people heard him gladly.
Jeremias [49] has rightly emphasized recently that the salvation Christ
brought was for the poor, and that Jesus came as the Saviour of
Sinners. Because of this the risk of antinomianism was real: but
Jesus was not afraid of this risk: He took it gladly. But while allowing
full force to Jeremias' position, fear of antinomianism among the
'am ha-aretz was not a peculiarity of the later Church or of Paul.
The freedom with which Jesus apparently dealt with the Law—this
friend of sinners—might have created among the multitudes the
impression that here was the end of all law. 'Ανομία would be
attractive to the many during the Ministry, as later, and Jesus could
not but have recoiled against it. Thus the story of the woman taken
in adultery reveals not only the compassion of the Lord but also
His demanding sternness, and especially pertinent here is the story
given by the Western Text (D) at Luke 6:5, and the excellent
discussion of it by J. Jeremias in his Unbekannte Jesusworte.

The relation of Jesus to the 'am ha-aretz [50] of His day is a matter
of debate, but we are justified in assuming that because apparent
indifference to the demands of the Law often marked the activity
of Jesus, certain of the common people who heard Him gladly might
misunderstand Him as breaking down the fence. It is not beyond
probability that in the face of such an attitude Jesus, in certain
circumstances, might be tempted to assert the validity of the Law—
this assertion He might well feel preferable to the unrestrained
encouragement of indiscipline which might be mistakenly, on
occasion, ascribed to Him. May it not be conceivable then that

[49] Joachim Jeremias, The Parables of Jesus (English translation), London, 1954.
[50] On this see S. S. Cohen, in The Journal of Biblical Literature, vol. XLVIII,
pp. 82–108.

Matt. 5:18 should find its *Sitz im Leben* in the Ministry of Jesus? It may have emerged from His contacts with irresponsible iconoclastic elements among the crowds who followed Him. It was to the sheep without a shepherd that He perhaps first uttered these words, in a spirit, no doubt, of hyperbole.[51]

Thirdly, the possibility has to be noticed that the attitude of Jesus towards the Law both in thought and practice changed during the course of His Ministry, a fact which might account for the contradictory attitudes that our sources reveal. But this possibility is hard to substantiate. Although we may reject the view that we are not to seek for any development in the mind of Jesus,[52] and although Taylor [53] and others have been able to detect changes in other respects in Jesus' thought and Ministry, e.g., in His expectation of the End, nevertheless, the chronology of the ministry is so confused that it would be hazardous to trace developments and changes too confidently.

We have seen above that from two sides at least it would be natural for Jesus to seek as far as was at all possible an affirmative attitude to the Law. The desire to conciliate or to enlist the support of the Jewish leaders, Pharisaic and other, would tend to this, at least in the earliest stages of the ministry, as would also the necessity, which probably became more and more clamant, to curb or control antinomian tendencies among the *'am ha-aretz*. At the same time it must be recognized that neither of these two very general factors can be regarded sufficient to account for the explicit assertion of the validity of the Law, while heaven and earth lasted, which we find in Matt. 5:18.[54] We are, therefore, driven further to ask, in the absence of external compulsions, whether there were inner compulsions in Jesus' understanding of His mission which might have led to this

---

[51] On the term 'shepherd', see the illuminating remarks of T. W. Manson, *The Servant-Messiah*, Cambridge, 1953, pp. 70 f. On the rejection of revolutionary methods by Jesus, see Cecil John Cadoux, *The Historic Mission of Jesus*, London, 1941.

[52] See e.g., Joseph Bonsirven, *Théologie du Nouveau Testament*, Paris, 1951; also R. H. Lightfoot, *The Gospel Message of St Mark*, Oxford, 1950, p. 34.

[53] V. Taylor, *The Life and Ministry of Jesus*, Nashville, 1955, pp. 179 f.

[54] It is not enough to assert with John Martin Creed, *The Gospel according to Saint Luke*, London, 1930, p. 207, that 'the attitude of a great personality . . . may often appear equivocal to outsiders. . . .'

assertion, i.e., considerations of what we here loosely call a 'dogmatic' kind.

At this point let us recall the situation in the early Church. The earliest Christians did not understand Jesus to have demanded the abandonment of the Law: on the contrary, the admission into the Church of Gentiles who did not observe the Law provoked pro-longed controversy which centred particularly in the activity of Paul. And it is of the utmost significance that the Apostle to the Gentiles was not able apparently to appeal to any specific word or act of Jesus during His ministry which would justify His champion-ing of Gentile Christians. On the contrary, he is constrained to refer to Jesus as a διάκονος τῆς περιτομῆς. His epistles reveal that it was not from anything in the life and teaching of Jesus that Paul argued to the freedom of Gentile Christians and indeed of all Christians from the Law. But those same epistles do reveal that he did this, from one event, the death of Jesus. The following passages are relevant.

Gal. 3:13.

Christ hath redeemed us from the curse of the Law, being made a curse for us; for it is written, Cursed is every one that hangeth on a tree.

Gal. 2:21 and 2:19 f.

I do not frustrate the grace of God: for if righteousness come by law, *then Christ is dead in vain.*

Eph. 2:13 f. (See also Col. 2:14).

13 But now in Christ Jesus ye who sometimes were afar off are made nigh by the blood of Christ. 14 For He is our peace who hath made both one and broken down the middle wall of partition between us. 15 Having abolished in his flesh the enmity even the law of command-ments contained in ordinances for to make in himself of twain one new man, so making peace. 16 And that he might reconcile both unto God in one body on the cross, having slain the enmity thereby.

Gal. 5:11.

And I, brethren, if I yet preach circumcision, why do I yet suffer persecution? Then is the offence of the cross ceased. (cf. Gal. 6:12.)

These verses make it unmistakably clear that it was the Cross, which, it must be noted in passing, was never in his thought separated from the Resurrection, that for Paul ended the dispensation of the

Law and thus made free the way for the Gentiles into the Israel of God.

The question now prompts itself how Paul came to make this connection between the death of Jesus and freedom from the Law: did he derive this connection from the expectations of Judaism concerning the Messianic Age? There are two possibilities to be examined. First, there were certain Rabbinic speculations about the role of the Law in the Messianic Age which might have influenced Paul in his claim that Christ was the end of the Law. But apart from the uncertainty of our knowledge about such speculations, Paul makes no explicit reference to them. Moreover, although it is not now everywhere certainly claimed, as it used to be, that Judaism in pre-Christian times knew nothing of a suffering and dying Messiah, Rabbinic speculations such as have come down to us about the Law in the Messianic Age did not specifically connect this with the death of the Messiah even when they did speak of the cessation of the commandments in the time to come.[55] Secondly, Paul would be familiar with the view that death brought freedom from the Law, so that he would naturally have drawn the conclusion that Jesus through death was made free from the Law, as were also, in consequence, those who were joined with Him, who were 'in Christ'. And in Rom. 7:1 Paul does refer to the freedom from the Law that death brings, but the section is very difficult to assess exactly. Not only is what he asserts about the law being effective only during a person's lifetime applicable both to Roman and Jewish law (and it is equally difficult to determine whether the phrase $\gamma\iota\nu\dot\omega\sigma\kappa o\upsilon\sigma\iota$ $\gamma\dot\alpha\rho$ $\nu\dot o\mu o\nu$ $\lambda\alpha\lambda\hat\omega$ is meant as a compliment to Roman readers or to Jewish Christians who knew the Law of Moses), but Paul has made his illustration very obscure; we need not here enlarge upon this obscurity.[56] The point relevant to our purpose is that Paul's reference to freedom from the Law, through death, even if we take the term $\nu\dot o\mu o\varsigma$ here to refer to the Jewish Law, as indeed is most likely, occurs only as an illustration. It emerges not so much as the ground of Paul's doctrine of the death of Christ, as the end of the Law, so much as a means of illuminating it. Rom. 7:1 f. in itself does not justify

[55] See W. D. Davies, *Torah in the Messianic Age*, etc.
[56] Compare C. H. Dodd, *The Epistle to the Romans*, London, 1932, *ad loc.*

us in regarding Rabbinic speculation on the relation of the Law to death as the source of Paul's teaching in this field.

But if so, we may now ask whether in connecting the end of the Law with the death of Jesus, Paul was at one with the Lord Himself: had Jesus already made this connection? The extent to which we are to regard the Synoptic Gospels as preserving a chronologically accurate sequence of the historical Ministry of Jesus is a matter of acute debate.[57] But what we cannot regard as a matter of dispute is the fact that at some point in the Ministry Jesus became convinced of the necessity of His death. It is possible that Jesus regarded Himself from the beginning of His Ministry as the Servant of the Lord destined to pour forth His soul unto death: the narrative of His Baptism at least suggests that the Church so interpreted the case. At any rate He did come to regard Himself before the close of the Ministry as the Suffering Servant of the Lord predicted by Deutero-Isaiah and therefore called upon to die in the fulfilment of His vocation.[58] And the question with which we are concerned is whether this awareness of the necessity of His death influenced the attitude of Jesus to the Law.

That, as Servant, Jesus would have to come to terms with the Law can be regarded as certain. As I have argued elsewhere,[59] the figure of the Servant of the Lord in Deutero-Isaiah is in part that of a *Toralehrer*, this on the ground of Isaiah (42:4 c),—'And for his torah the far coasts wait eagerly.' As Servant Jesus would expect to bring His *torah*—and not only as Servant. With the figure of the Servant Jesus combined that of the Messiah, and the Messiah, like the Servant, was to bring His *torah*. Whether he was merely to bring with Him a deeper interpretation of the existing Torah or a New Torah cannot certainly be determined, because of the late date of the pertinent passages and their ambiguity. But it was incumbent upon one who was the Servant-Messiah to define His attitude to the Law, as it was also requisite that He should come to terms with death,

---

[57] For two recent different emphases contrast R. H. Lightfoot, *The Gospel Message of Saint Mark*, Oxford, 1950, pp. 33 f.; and R. H. Fuller, *The Mission and Achievement of Jesus*, London, 1954, p. 54.

[58] It would take too long to buttress the position adopted here and it is sufficiently familiar not to need such, although not all accept it.

[59] *Op. cit.*, pp. 29 f.

because the Servant was predicted to die. And it is our hesitant suggestion that in the Ministry of Jesus these two elements are closely related: His attitude to the Law is conditioned by His attitude to His death. If Jesus lived in the awareness that as Servant He was destined to die, and more, that only in death would He and could He be fully the Servant, then until that death had occurred there was of necessity a certain reserve, if we may so express it, about the claims that He might make about Himself and also, in consequence, about His relation to the Law. This reserve has been noted in relation to the Person of Jesus in a significant article by C. F. D. Moule.[60] We cannot recapitulate his argument here: suffice it to state his careful conclusion that the lesson that the Son of Man and the Messiah were the Servant came home to the Church not through what Jesus *said* but in what He *did* in His death.

Here Moule recognizes an important principle of reticence in the Ministry of Jesus. This is not to be confused with anything like an economy of truth which may have marked the Ministry because His disciples were not prepared for all things and were not able to bear them. The reticence about which we write is determined, not by the condition of the disciples, but by Jesus' awareness of the supreme sacrifice which He had to pay, His awareness, namely, that only through death could He justify Himself as Servant and thus bring into being a New Torah to transcend the old. Until His blood had been shed, His New Covenant could not be ratified and His New Commandment could not be proclaimed with authority to all. This implies that Jesus would not assume the full right to annul the Old Law until He had proved His right to do this in death. This is a kind of dogmatic reason, we suggest, why there is no explicit or unequivocal *public* annulment of the Law on the lips of Jesus but only an implicit one: there were some things that His death alone could utter about the Law as about His own person. It remains merely to add here that this dogmatic reason for reticence coincides with those demands of sensitivity which Jesus, we cannot forget, must have known to a far greater degree than we can measure. No iconoclast or

[60] C. F. D. Moule, *art. cit*, p. 53. Like Moule, I here make no attempt to relate all the above to the problem of the Messianic Secret.

revolutionary, considerations of refinement would not easily enable Jesus to dismiss the impressive tradition of Judaism until He was assured of His right to stand above it. And it was death alone that fully gave Him this right.

The principle of reticence to which we have referred, emerges in the following ways:

(a) In His own practice Jesus seems to have been conservative. While some of what is usually taken as evidence for this may be due to Jesus' desire to comply with necessary civil laws, nevertheless, His personal conservatism is noteworthy. The evidence for this is familiar: it need not be repeated here.

(b) Where He or His disciples break the Law, as we have previously seen, this is justified not in any spirit of iconoclasm or of undisciplined or unprincipled 'liberalism'. Either this happens in the interests of the emerging Messianic community, as in Mark 2:23 f.,[61] where no impatience with the Sabbatarianism of Judaism is shown by Jesus but rather a desire to convince His opponents, or Jesus reacts to certain situations in immediate response to the will of God, thereby recognizing the supreme claims of that will without consideration of the effect of this response on the Law, as in Mark 3:1 f. In any case in Mark 3:1 f. we are dealing not with an irresponsible, sweeping libertinism, but with a matter of principle. Possibly we are to find here both the immediate response of Jesus to human need which swept aside for Him all considerations of legality and the assertion of His Messianic right to judge the Sabbath Law, and it is not irrelevant to note that W. L. Knox has claimed that this pericope originally formed, in Mark's source, at this point, an immediate prelude to the passion narrative.[62] We can be sure that it was no mere anti-Sabbatarianism that governed Jesus' action. Similarly it is Jesus' inability, even against Himself, to resist the priority of human needs or, in other words, the claims of the Rule of God, that governs Jesus' action in Luke 13:10 f., rather than mere frivolous anti-Sabbatarianism. What this last called forth from Him we see in the story preserved in the Western Text at Luke 6:5. The way in which both here and in Luke 14:1 f. the Pharisaic objection to His act is

---

[61] See T. W. Manson, in *Coniectanea Neotestamentica*, Lund, 1947, pp. 138 ff.
[62] *Op. cit.*

effectively silenced in itself shows that here was no mere iconoclasm.

The Ministry, then, reveals that the Law was broken by Jesus in the interests of the overriding claim of God's demand as He conceived it and in the interests of the Messianic Community which He was gathering around Him. Does not this, however, contradict the claim which we made above that the Death of Jesus alone would annul the Law? Was it not clear that already during His Ministry the Law was being annulled? This is the case. During the Ministry itself the powers of the Age to Come were already present for those who had eyes to see, there were already 'signs' taking place that the Law's dominion was coming to an end. But that these 'signs' were not as explicit as we are led to think by the sources is clear from the fact that the Church did not take them to mean the end of the Law. They were not sufficiently unambiguous to convince even the Messianic Community, in whose interests they were often performed, that the Law no longer ruled over it. Those very acts in which human need or the claims of the Messianic community transcended the Law themselves were not intended by Jesus to annul the Law in fact, although they did so in principle.

(c) This last is further attested by the striking fact that, although He felt free, when utterly necessary in the interests of the Rule of God, to break the Law, Jesus probably never *explicitly* asserted the annulling of the Law. The discussion of things clean and unclean, with which we dealt above, illustrates this. The discussion is concluded in Mark 7:19 with the words καθαρίζων πάντα τὰ βρώματα. There is no parallel to the section in Luke but Matthew has such: he, however, omits the phrase καθαρίζων πάντα τὰ βρώματα. Here Matthew virtually asserts by implication that during the Ministry the principle of 'clean and unclean' was not explicity annulled. Moreover, as is the case with the annulling of the law on divorce in Mark 10, so also in Mark 7, the explicit annulment of the Law is announced not in public but in private to the disciples: this is the case both in Matthew and Mark.

If our understanding of the Ministry of Jesus be correct, we have in it, therefore, two seemingly contradictory elements pertaining to the Law. First, an awareness, possibly going back to the very beginning of the Ministry, that He was the Servant-Messiah who, as such, would bring His Torah and who did, therefore, proclaim God's perfect will; and, secondly, a reticence in explicitly annulling the Old Law even while His acts and words transcended it. We have suggested above that this is so because Jesus had the further awareness that only when He had completed His service in death would He be justified in replacing the Old Torah by His own New Torah. The death of Jesus must not be too rigidly separated from His ministry: they were both of a piece, and that is why there were implicit and—for Jesus and His own gathered community—explicit contraventions of the Law during the Ministry itself. Nevertheless, it is highly significant that the καινὴ ἐντολή of the Fourth Gospel only emerges in the Farewell Discourses; it is the death that makes the new commandment explicit, as also in the Fourth Gospel it is this that chiefly gives that same commandment its real content.[63] We suggest that there were two facets to Jesus' relation to the Law, which account for the complex nature of the material in our sources. Before His death He could, by word and deed, give signs that there was now a deeper Torah to be obeyed than the old, and in private, among His disciples, He could explicitly annul parts of the old Torah, but He would not explicitly state this in public: although the sheer pressure of human need sometimes led Him to break the Law openly. But after His death the principle of freedom from the Old Law would ultimately be established. When this happened the Gentiles, who during His Ministry had been only sporadically touched by Jesus, would be free to join God's people: the ground for the transcending of the Law would have been laid.

This reference to the Gentiles can illumine for us the thought of Jesus on the Law. The same kind of contradiction or inconsistency which we have studied in Jesus' attitude to the Law marks also His attitude to the Gentiles. Fortunately Jeremias has surveyed the ground for us.[64] The proselytizing activity of Judaism is severely condemned

[63] See especially C. H. Dodd, *The Interpretation of the Fourth Gospel*, Cambridge, 1953, pp. 40 ff.

[64] It is pertinent to note here that the Gentile world plays a part in the context of Matt. 5:17 f. This is particularly noted by Karl Bornhauser, *Die Bergpredigt*, Gütersloh, 1923, *ad loc.*; J. Jeremias notes the view of von Rad that Matt. 5:14 refers to the eschatological city on the holy mountain, the light of which is to be an ensign to the Gentiles. See J. Jeremias in *Studiorum Novi Testamenti Societas*, Bulletin III, Oxford, 1952, *The Gentile World in the Thought of Jesus*, pp. 18 f.

by Jesus; He confined His own Ministry to Israel and forbade His
apostles to go outside it to the way of the Gentiles. This is the
testimony of the Synoptics, the Fourth Gospel and Paul. But, on
the other hand, as Jeremias points out, this does not mean that Jesus
was unconcerned with the Gentiles: but their hour is reserved,
according to the Fourth Gospel, Paul and the Synoptics, to the period
after the Resurrection. All these sources are agreed that (1) in the
future God would deal graciously with the Gentiles; that (2) the
distinction between Jew and Gentile was not to be valid for ever;
physical descent from Abraham was not for ever to be decisive for
salvation; that (3) God is not bound to Israel but can call Gentiles in
its stead to fulfil His purposes. The evidence for what we have here
summarized is given by Jeremias and need not be repeated. The
question we have to concentrate on is: what makes possible the
incursion of the Gentiles into the 'Israel' of God? The answer is that
it is the death of Jesus for 'many'. It is beyond that death that the
Law no longer holds to separate Jew and Gentile. Jeremias' study
thus leads to the same conclusion on Jesus' attitude to the Gentiles
that we drew on His attitude to the Law: two aspects of it are to be
distinguished. Jesus 'came' only to the lost sheep of the House of
Israel; He observed the Law. But beyond His completed obedience—
His death—Gentiles would enter the Kingdom and the Law would
no longer be in force. And, as in the case of the Law, so in the case
of the Gentiles, there are anticipatory signs or proleptic events of
what was to be made explicit after the death during the Ministry
itself.

We now suggest, with some hesitation, that it is in the light of the
place which His death had in His thinking that we are to understand
Jesus' words in Matt. 5:18. It is our very tentative view that we are
to recognize here a distinction in the thought of Jesus Himself
between the period before His death, which is the *final* culmination
of the old order, and the period which fully comes to birth through
that death. The phrase ἕως ἂν πάντα γένηται refers on this view to the
Cross and what was to follow τὰ εἰς χριστὸν παθήματα καὶ τὰς μετὰ
ταῦτα δόξας (1 Pet. 1:11). The significance of the phrase ἕως ἂν πάντα
γένηται would then be that while this present order endures (ὁ οὐρανὸς
καὶ ἡ γῆ) the old Law remains in force (although signs that it is to

pass are already given during the Ministry and, indeed, for the new Messianic community it was already in process of passing), but once the obedience of Jesus has finally issued in death and the New Covenant has thus been fully inaugurated (because the Ministry itself is its partial inauguration) then the old Law ceases to have authority.

The main burden of our suggestion falls on the interpretation of the phrase ἕως ἂν πάντα γένηται. The possibility has often been noticed that this phrase, which is absent in the corresponding verse in Luke 16:17, may be merely an editorial gloss which has no significance. There is no obvious support for this view, however, apart from the difficulty that the phrase presents to interpreters. That Luke has a form which is simpler to understand should not be taken as an argument in favour of the originality of Luke at this point: indeed, it almost certainly suggests the contrary. But if we accept the phrase as an integral part of Matthew's verse, does it not merely state, in other words, what has already been asserted in the words ἕως ἂν παρέλθῃ ὁ οὐρανὸς καὶ ἡ γῆ κ. τ. λ?[65] In answer to this we can only insist that such loose tautology is not customary in Matthew whose usage is well knit and architectonic.[66] The phrase must not only be taken as it stands but treated with seriousness as more than a tautologous addendum. Two possibilities have been suggested hitherto.

First, it is possible to connect ἕως ἂν πάντα γένηται very rigidly with the preceding phrase ἕως ἂν παρέλθῃ κ.τ.λ. This is the position brilliantly stated by Lagrange, who [67] appeals for support to Jerome on the one hand and Loisy on the other. Taking Matt. 5:17 to refer

---

[65] This is the view recently defended by A. M. Honeyman, in *New Testament Studies*, ed. Matthew Black, Cambridge, 1954, pp. 142 f. *Matthew V. 18 and the Validity of The Law*. He takes the whole of Matt. 5:18 to assert the eternal validity of the Law. He suggests that ἕως is used in two different senses in this verse as an equivalent of ʿd, ʾšr, ʿd š and the Aramaic ʿd d which can be used of time but also of degree, manner or extent. He writes: 'The structure of Matt. 5:18 is elucidated by these usages. The clause ἕως ἂν πάντα γένηται, reproducing an Aramaic, ʿd dyt q y y m k l h (or k l ʾ) expresses in positive terms what is negatively expressed in the previous clause. The force of ἕως is inclusive and not temporal but modal,—ʿ . . to the extent, so that (on the contrary) all (of it) will be fulfilled'. Honeyman does not recognize the difficulty of translating γένηται as 'will be fulfilled'.

[66] Cf. E. Klostermann, *op. cit., ad loc.*

[67] *Op. cit., ad loc.*

to a perfecting of the Law which Jesus is to introduce, he refers
ἕως ἂν πάντα γένηται to the complete realization of every part of the
Law. 'Le contexte montre,' writes Loisy,[68] 'qu'il s'agit des choses
qui sont dans la Loi'; and Lagrange adds: 'Les moindres traits
doivent parvenir à leur terme . . . le ciel et la terre passeraient
plutôt que les moindres traits de la Loi ne réalisent leur fin, et c'est
bien ce qu'a compris Luc, εὐκοπώτερον. . . .' But this requires us
to place on γένηται a weight which it can hardly bear. The use of a
form of γίνεσθαι suggests a more particularized event than the general
concept of the fulfilment of the Law. Were this last Matthew's
meaning the term γένηται would hardly have been used. A more
convenient verb, employed by Paul, was to hand in πεπλήρωται.
Moreover, it must be conceded that Lagrange's interpretation,
although familiar, is subtle to a degree, and even more so is
Schweizer's [69] view that πάντα refers to the advent of the Golden
Rule as the fulfilment of the Old Law. Josef Schmid [70] has further
criticized the position represented by Lagrange as follows: ' "Bis alles
geschieht" kann sich nicht auf die Erfüllung des Gesetzes beziehen
und damit der Geltung des Gesetzes mit dem Anbruch der Neuen
Heilsordnung eine zeitliche Grenze setzen; denn damit würde der
Satz in sich selbst widerspruchsvoll. Es muss damit vielmehr das
Ende der gegenwärtigen Weltzeit gemeint sein.' This judgment, to
which we shall refer below, in criticism, conveniently leads us to
the second possible approach to ἕως ἂν πάντα γένηται.

Secondly, then, the phrase has been made to refer to the end of
the present age, the winding up of all things in the cosmos. Perhaps
this view is best expressed by Schniewind [71] who interprets ἕως ἂν
πάντα γένηται thus: 'So lange, bis alles sich erfüllt was vorhergesagt
ist, Gottes Weltenplan, Gottes Gericht und die neue Ordnung aller
Dinge in Gottes zukünftiger Welt, in Gottes Reich und Herrschaft,
bis das Geschick des Judenvolkes zu seinem eigentlichen Ziel
kommt, . . . bis der Menschensohn kommt in der Herrlichkeit
seines Vaters mit seinem Engel. . . .' As have others before him,
Schniewind contrasts Matt. 5:18 and Mark 13:31. The words of

[68] Cited by J. Lagrange, op. cit.
[69] Op. cit., ad loc.
[70] Josef Schmid, Das Evangelium nach Matthäus, Regensburg, 1952, ad rem.
[71] Op. cit.

Jesus persist into the Age to Come while the Law only persists to the end of this world. This as we saw was the interpretation accepted by Schmid. He urged that ἕως ἂν πάντα γένηται must refer to the end of all things, not to an event in the present order, because this latter would make the verse self contradictory. The words ἕως ἂν παρέλθῃ ὁ οὐρανὸς καὶ ἡ γῆ mean that as long as this world lasts the Law in all its details remains in force so that no point within this present order of heaven and earth could be the end of the Law.

Now if this view of Schmid's is correct then our reference of ἕως ἂν πάντα γένηται to include the Cross is ruled out. But at this juncture we have to be careful to define our terms. The phrase 'heaven and earth' taken literally means, as in Gen. 1:1, this present physical world. But may it not also be a figurative expression for this present age or world order? In this sense the 'present age' could come to an end before the passing of the physical order of heaven and earth. We have the authority of Paul that although heaven and earth in a physical sense had persisted beyond the death of Christ, yet the new creation or the new age had come—εἴ τις ἐν χριστῷ καινὴ κτίσις· τὰ ἀρχαῖα παρῆλθεν ἰδοὺ γέγονεν καινά. In a similar way it is difficult to assess exactly how Jesus Himself conceived of His death καὶ τὰς μετὰ ταῦτα δόξας. Did He conceive the order which His death would inaugurate as a physical continuation of this present order, of this heaven and earth, or not? Schmid's view is tenable only if we apply a scientific exactitude to phrases like 'heaven and earth' and refuse to allow for their figurative character. Indeed, he himself later on insists, perhaps too much, on this figurative character of the words. Thus he comments on Matt. 5:18 '(Der Satz) muss aber trotz seiner bewussten Anlehnung an die Aussagen der Rabbinen über das Gesetz nicht buchstäblich gedeutet werden, sondern nur als bildlicher Ausdruck dafür versteht, dass Jesus die Autorität des Gesetzes anerkennt und nicht weniger ernst nimmt als sie.' It is our contention, however, that the words in Matt. 5:18, while not to be taken with wooden literalness, are to be interpreted (as, indeed, Schmid also elsewhere in the same connection himself recognizes) with utter seriousness in the light of the eschatological awareness we find in Jesus and elsewhere in the New Testament.

In this particular, while not endorsing his position otherwise, we

agree with Schoeps.[72] But he explains ἕως ἂν πάντα γένηται as an
addition to the previous words ἕως ἂν παρέλθῃ ὁ οὐρανὸς καὶ ἡ γῆ,
which assert the permanence of the Law till the Age to Come arrives.
He does not here clarify the relation between the Age to Come and
the Messianic Age, but he regards the addition as due to Matthew's
desire to resume Pauline speculations on the abrogation of the Law in
the Messianic Age. But this is unnecessary, as it is erroneous to
introduce into the passage any distinction between *Gesetz* and *Gebot*—
the Law being regarded as temporary and the commandment as
permanent, as is done by Schniewind.[73] The conceptions which
Schoeps finds it necessary to trace to Pauline influences, as we
suggested above, may go back to Jesus Himself.

Is there any evidence that Jesus was concerned with such speculation on the Law? The extent to which Jesus indulged in apocalyptic
speculation is a matter of debate: that he discouraged the calculation
of the times is clear. The saying in Mark 13:31 has been so variously
regarded that it would be precarious to place too much weight
upon it. But there is one passage the authenticity of which cannot
be questioned where Jesus ponders and declares the role of the Law
and the Prophets: it is in Matt. 11:12–13a and its parallel Luke
16:16.[74]

Fortunately we need not for our purpose decide on the exact

---

[72] *Op. cit.*   [73] *Op. cit.*

[74] The Matthean form is generally taken to be original. Two things are clear:
(1) that the advent of John the Baptist stands at the beginning of a new epoch; the
exact interpretation of the words 'the Kingdom of Heaven suffereth violence and men
of violence take it by force' need not for the moment detain us; suffice it to say that
the Rule of God has become active since the advent of John the Baptist: this eschatological significance of John the Baptist is made further explicit in the identification of
him with the Elijah who was to appear as the Forerunner of the Messiah in 12:14.
(2) Not only so but the dispensation of the Law and the Prophets pointed to this.
Is this the meaning of the words ἕως 'Ιωάννου 'επροφήτευσαν or is it rather what
emerges in the Lukan text ὁ νόμος καὶ... μεχρι. 'Ιωάννου, the dispensation of the
Law and the Prophets ceased with John the Baptist? Probably Luke truly expresses
the meaning, of ἕως 'Ιωάννου ἐπροφήτευσαν. As Huber, *op. cit.*, has expressed it:
'mit des Messias mit Jesu Kommen fallen Tora und Propheten dahin, weil sie Norm
nur für die alte Weltordnung sind'. Dodd, *The Parables of the Kingdom, ad loc.*, interpreted the verse to mean that with the coming of Jesus the Kingdom of God had
come. Fuller's interpretation is that this difficult saying does not necessarily imply a
realized eschatology. 'The Reign of God is already breaking in proleptically in the
proclamation and Signs of Jesus (that is the difference between the time of Jesus'
Ministry and the time of John the Baptist) but it would be to overstate the case to
say that with Jesus the Kingdom of God has actually come.' *Op. cit.*, p. 32.

interpretation of the two passages. What is for us significant is that they do prove that speculation on the duration of the validity of the Law such as we have traced in Matt. 5:18 goes back to Jesus Himself and this would be tied up, as we have elsewhere suggested, with the attitude of Jesus to the Gentiles.

We may now recapitulate. For Jesus it seems clear that it was only beyond His death that the distinction between Jew and Gentile could be openly declared to have become secondary, although there were anticipations of this during the actual ministry in Jesus' dealings with men in their need. This was so because only through that death could Jesus establish His right to be above the Law, so that only beyond His death would the Law in fact be annulled as that which governed the relations between man and God, when neither circumcision availed anything nor uncircumcision but a new creature. To ask whether that new creation to which the new creature was to belong implied that the present heaven and earth was to pass away or that it was to be a continuation of the present order is to touch on the extremely complex problem of how precisely Jesus conceived the future, a problem which would take us too far afield in this essay. The nature of the consummation which Jesus expected beyond His Cross He described in symbolic terms which present no rigid consistency. We can only certainly say that it was a consummation, whatever its exact nature, when the Law separating Jew and Gentile no longer ruled. It is to this consummation, wrought through His death, that Matt. 5:18 looks in the phrase ἕως ἂν πάντα γένηται and we suggest that in its present Matthaean form the verse may well go back to Jesus. Moreover it is not irrelevant to point out that the interpretation of πάντα here proposed does not exclude a reference within it, by implication, to the fulfilment of the Law, such as Lagrange desiderated, because in the consummation envisaged by Jesus, through His death, the final torah would prevail, while it would preserve all that was valid in the Old Torah; but this reference must not be made the primary one.

Finally, we emphasize that the solution to the contradiction in Matt. 5:17 f. which we here suggest—an eschatological one—is very tentative. But at least it serves the important function of insisting that it is not necessarily the Jewish-Gentile conflicts of the early Church that are responsible for it, but the complexity of the actual Ministry and purpose of Jesus: it is to be understood over against the wider eschatological understanding of His own Ministry and Person that Jesus Himself cherished.[75]

[75] Since the above was completed I have been referred to the illuminating articles by A. Feuillet, *Revue Biblique*, Paris, 1949, on *Le Discours de Jésus sur la ruine du Temple* and *La Synthèse eschatologique de saint Matthieu*. His conclusions on Matt. 5:17–20, expressed in *Revue Biblique*, no. 1, p. 85 and no. 2 p. 85, are very similar to ours. He takes the phrase ἕως ἂν πάντα γένηται to mean 'until the new world has come': this new world he connects closely with the Fall of Jerusalem but he recognizes in *Revue Biblique*, no. 3, pp. 36 f., that it was His death that, in part at least, constituted the 'Hour' of Christ, the 'Hour' of the coming of the new order. I deeply regret that I did not see H. Ljungman's study, *Das Gesetz Erfüllen*: Matt. 5:17 ff. *und* 3:15 *untersucht*, Lund, 1954, in time to use it here.

REFLECTIONS ON
ARCHBISHOP CARRINGTON'S
'THE PRIMITIVE CHRISTIAN
CALENDAR'

For some time criticism has been concerned to understand the documents of the New Testament not only in the light of their setting in life, conceived in a broad sense, but also especially in the light of the worship of the Church from which they emerged. A slight but stimulating volume by the Archbishop of Quebec, *The Primitive Christian Catechism* (Cambridge, 1940), brilliantly and fruitfully exemplified and served this concern. Primitive Christian baptismal and other practices he there exploited to illumine certain patterns of ethical exhortation which often recur in the New Testament. In a recent volume, *The Primitive Christian Calendar* (Cambridge, 1952), the same author has turned to what he considers to have been the lectionary needs and practices of the early Church as a key to the compilation and structure of some of the New Testament and other early Christian documents; in particular, he has sought to prove the relationship of the Gospel of Mark not only with the Jewish lectionary tradition but also with the primitive Christian calendar.

Since it was not likely that Christians should remain uninfluenced by their religious environment (any more than Carrington himself by the contemporary 'Myth and Ritual School', indebtedness to which he acknowledges), the tradition of evangelical teaching was moulded in such a way that it reflected the festal tradition of the surrounding Jewish community (this in turn was influenced by age-long mythological forms which thereby entered the Christian tradition itself: it is here that Carrington shows the influence of the

'Myth and Ritual School').[1] Not less than fifteen years after his death,[2] the tradition about Jesus became fixed in its main outlines around certain central days such as the Passover, Pentecost, Tabernacles, the New Year, the Day of Atonement. Carrington begins by pinning down the Feeding of the Five Thousand to Passover activity, in the light of John 6:4. With this as a starting-point,[3] he is able to fit the rest of Mark into a lectionary scheme arranged to cover one whole year. The Passion narrative proper, which he takes to begin at Mark 13:1, he regards as a distinct lectionary unit for reading at the annual Christian Passover. It is preceded by what Carrington calls Mark I[4] or the Galilean Mark, which was not primarily an account of the life and teaching of Jesus, but of the origins of Christianity in Galilee,[5] in emphasizing the importance of which Carrington follows Lohmeyer. But Mark I and the Passion narrative are interlocked by an intricate system of triadic key-words, a triadic structure which is also apparent, in a minor pattern, in the various pericopae both of Mark I and the Passion narrative.[6] What is here to be emphasized, however, is that Carrington regards the whole of Mark, i.e., the Galilean Mark, and the Passion narrative, as through and through liturgical in its structure and intention. It is not merely that Mark has certain liturgical characteristics, but that it *is* a lectionary.[7] That this is the case, it is claimed, is supported by the fact that the lectionary units from which Mark was composed are reflected in the lectionary and script divisions of some of the oldest manuscripts of the New Testament.[8] It is not claimed that these divisions preserve the original lectionary arrangement of Mark; indeed, the text of Mark which we now have does not represent the original Mark, which was fitted into the Hebrew calendar of agricultural festivals, but a revised Mark which was made to fit the Julianic calendar at Rome.[9] Nevertheless, Carrington claims that the manuscripts enable him to underpin his thesis with factual evidence which he regards as mathematical in its cogency. This understanding of Mark as

---

[1] *The Primitive Christian Calendar*, pp. xiv, 8 ff.
[2] p. 85. Direct page references in these notes are to Carrington's book.
[3] p. 15.   [4] See pp. 18 ff.
[5] p. 81.   [6] pp. 9 ff., 80.
[7] p. 87.   [8] pp. 23 ff.
[9] pp. 78–80.

originally composed to serve as a lectionary, according to Carrington, explains why Form-Criticism has been able to isolate self-contained units of the tradition, which retained their opening and closing formulae *after* their inclusion in a full-length Gospel. This was so because they were intended as lectionary units in the services of the Church.[10]

Finally, the structure of Matthew is to be understood in the same light as that of Mark. It came into being, probably at Antioch or at any rate some other Syrian city, on the arrival of the Gospel of Mark from Rome. Mark was combined with Q and an old Aramaic Matthew, which was now translated into Greek and was itself a full liturgical gospel like Mark,[11] as is shown, according to Carrington, by the evidence of Papias.[12] Thus there emerged the canonical Matthew to form a kind of omnibus volume, a new lectionary which in its main divisions followed those of Mark. We shall deal with the details of Carrington's argument as we proceed. His study, which is marked by learning, ingenuity and a massive industry, raises, in an acute form, the question whether it was through the medium of a Christian lectionary that the Christian tradition was most transmitted. We shall now examine his thesis in order to discover whether it helps us to assess the significance of the lectionary factor in the transmission and formation of that tradition. It rests on what we can conveniently call a triad, namely, certain underlying assumptions, certain secondary supports, and, lastly, a certain external mathematical confirmation of these, derived, Carrington claims, from the manuscript evidence.

The main assumption behind Carrington's work is that the very early evolution of a fully developed lectionary, immensely complicated in its inner connections, was probable and possible in the early Church. This in turn rests, implicitly if not always explicitly, upon his view of that Church as a well-organized community which was so closely parallel to the Synagogue that the lectionary practice of the Synagogue found a natural counterpart in a lectionary concern within the Church. To Carrington it has become 'clear that the vigorous organization of the Christian ecclesia was not a new

[10] p. 18.   [11] pp. 59 ff.
[12] pp. 58 f.

creation which evolved slowly out of nothing, but *simply the normal organization of the old Jewish Synagogue transformed by the injection into it of the Christian gospel and apostolate with its faith in Jesus and its possession of the Holy Spirit*' (my italics).[13] Insisting on the 'system of readers, teachers, evangelists and so forth' in the Church, he holds that among other things the Church would certainly observe all the festivals of the Jewish liturgical year, so that its literature would be connected with the sacred Jewish calendar and thus subserve a lectionary purpose.[14] Nor is it necessary or possible to deny outright the synagogal connections upon which Carrington thus so strongly insists. The Jewish year doubtless continued to be followed for calendrical purposes at least by Christians who had once been Jews; the Jewish festivals supplied the Church with a wealth of imagery or symbolism,[15] features of synagogal worship reappeared in that of Christians;[16] it has been possible to claim that the organization of the Synagogue was the pattern for that of the Church.[17] It is not for nothing that in some parts the Church was actually designated a synagogue,[18] and we know that the separation of Church and Synagogue was a gradual process.

Nevertheless, certain factors must be recognized. First, at this point, it is highly pertinent to note the difference between the ethos of Christian and synagogal worship. The Synagogue was primarily a *beth midrash* which centred in the reading and interpretation of the

[13] p. 17. It should be noted that to many who do not share Carrington's view of the early Church, but who regard it as a society altogether more free in its forms than Carrington would probably concede (see, for example, the salutary article by H. J. Cadbury in *The Crozier Quarterly*, vol. xxi (1944), pp. 246 ff., on 'The Informality of Early Christianity'), it may seem sufficiently cogent to reject his thesis on general grounds. We have here attempted, however, to deal with specific points without prejudging the general issue as to the character of the early Church; see W. D. Davies, *A Normative Pattern of Church Life in the New Testament*, on the broad outlines of this problem, pp. 199 ff. below.

[14] p. 17.

[15] This need not be illustrated because it is so obvious.

[16] See, for example, C. W. Dugmore, *The Influence of the Synagogue upon the Divine Office* (1944), pp. 1 ff. For details see W. D. Davies, *op. cit.*, pp. 218 f., where the debt to the Synagogue is recognized.

[17] e.g. *The Ministry and the Sacraments,* ed. R. Dunkerley, 1937, pp. 368 ff., E. J. Palmer on 'A New Approach to an Old Problem: The Development of the Christian Ministry'.

[18] See the evidence for this in C. W. Dugmore, *op. cit.*, p. 5; K. L. Schmidt, *Theologisches Wörterbuch*, Bd. iii, p. 521.

Torah,[19] so that for the Synagogue the eventual evolution of some kind of lectionary system was a necessity, although, even so, that evolution, as far as we can gather, proceeded very slowly over centuries.[20] In the earliest days, to accept Carrington's dating,[21] these would last up to the sixties of the first century, but we can safely think of them as lasting longer, Christians frequently participated in the synagogal services with their concentration on the lessons. But it is easily possible to exaggerate how far they transferred any such concentration into their own services. The Church, it must be remembered, was not always imitative of the Synagogue; there was not only assimilation to synagogal forms of worship among Christians but also a deliberate cultivation of differences.[22] The multiplicity of forms which the specifically Christian services developed should warn us against elevating any lectionary concern to any such place as would demand a fixed lectionary as early as Carrington maintains.[23]

An assessment of the references to the reading of documents in the services of the Church confirms this warning. That there was much lectionary activity in the services is very probable;[24] nevertheless, the explicit references to this are surprisingly few. In his lengthy

[19] See, for example, T. W. Manson in *Christian Worship*, ed. N. Micklem, pp. 35 ff.

[20] The early lectionary practice of the Synagogue is wrapped in obscurity. Büchler's treatment in *J.Q.R.*, vols. v, pp. 420 ff., vi, pp. 1–73, is now antiquated; see Jacob Mann, *The Bible as Read and Preached in the Old Synagogue*, Ohio, 1940, p. 6. In addition consult Elbogen, *Der Jüdische Gottesdienst* (1931).

[21] p. 17.

[22] On the caution necessary in dealing with the relations between Church and Synagogue see O. S. Rankin, *Journal of Jewish Studies*, vol. i, No. 1 (1948). The history of fasting in the Church, of the recitation of the Decalogue in the Synagogue, the *Birkath ha-Minim*—to note only the most obvious factors—show how the Church and Synagogue reacted against each other; I hope to deal with this problem elsewhere. Cf. C. W. Dugmore, *op. cit.*, p. 6.

[23] On this see, for example, O. Cullmann, *Early Christian Worship* (Eng. trans. 1953), pp. 12 ff.

[24] W. L. Knox, *The Sources of the Synoptic Gospels*, Cambridge, 1953, p. 5, ' "In the beginning was the sermon" (Fascher) needs to be supplemented by the words, "The lesson was a close second. . . ." ' Knox is writing of specifically Christian lessons. R. M. Grant, *The Bible in the Church* (1948), is not concerned with lectionary activity; A. Harnack, *Bible Reading in the Early Church* (Eng. trans. 1912), deals specifically with the private reading of Scripture. Although he does not find much evidence for this in the period before Irenaeus (p. 47), nothing that he writes suggests that the Gospels could have been intended primarily for public reading.

discussion of the necessity for order in worship, Paul never once refers in 1 Cor. 11 ff. to the reading of the Scriptures. This is a difficulty for Carrington's theory whose emphasis is that such reading was from the first κατὰ τάξιν. At least in the Gentile churches of Paul's acquaintance this was not so. That Paul could expect his own Epistles to be read at length in the services points to much flexibility.[25] Such reading for the Sabbath, i.e. our Saturday, as we find in the lectionaries at a far later date than Paul may well be a direct inheritance from the Synagogue,[26] but not the reading of the Epistles of a living person like Paul. Moreover it is difficult to imagine that a fixed lectionary comports in any way with such scenes as are implied in 1 Cor. 11 or Acts 20. The reference in 1 Tim. 4:13 is probably to the public reading of documents in the Church, but it does not provide any evidence as to *how* such reading was conceived.[27] The first fairly full description of a church service comes to us from Justin Martyr. Carrington has not noticed the point that the implications of this passage are directly opposed to this theory. The passage, the *First Apology*, 1:67, reads: 'And on the day called Sunday, all who live in cities or in the country gather together to one place, and the memoirs of the apostles or the writings of the prophets are read, as long as time permits; then when the reader has ceased, the president verbally instructs, and exhorts to the imitation of these good things. . . .' It seems to us that the phrase μέχρις ἐγχωρεῖ, which

---

[25] 1 Thess. 5:27; Col. 4:16. Too much, however, should not be made of this point. It would be customary for a *shaliach* to read letters from Jerusalem and elsewhere at various synagogues (cf. Acts 9:1), (see Rengstorf, *Theologisches Wörterbuch*, Bd. I, p. 416), and a similar custom would of necessity develop in the Church, though we need not, therefore, take the *shaliach* to be the strict prototype of the *apostolos* (see T. W. Manson, *The Church's Ministry* (1948), pp. 31 ff.). Professor Nock also pointed out to me the very significant fact that 'in the fixed pattern of the Roman Mass the Pastoral Letter of a Bishop is read'. So too M. Goguel, *L'Église Primitive,* Paris, 1947, pp. 292 ff., insists that it is erroneous to find in Col. 4:16 a reference to such a strictly lectionary practice as we find in the Synagogue. He connects the introduction of the Gospels into the public reading of the Church with its edificatory needs and with the necessity of establishing its authority. The desire to see in the Christian cult no improvised novelty but a transcendent reality, which had been prefigured in the cult of the Old Israel, led the New Israel to seek conformity between its cult and that of the Old. This, Goguel thinks, contributed to the establishing of lectionary activity in the Church. But we have seen reason to question this emphasis on imitation, certainly in the early period in which Carrington finds it.

[26] See C. R. Gregory, *Canon and Text of the New Testament* (1912), p. 387. The whole section (pp. 384–393) is relevant to a discussion of Carrington.

[27] The context of 1 Tim. 4:13 favours making it refer to public reading.

Cullmann renders *so lange es die Zeit erlaubt*, i.e. as long as time allows, makes the conception of any fixed lectionary improbable.[28] The length of the reading would depend not on a prearranged *schema* but on the exigencies of time. Had Justin Martyr had a fixed lectionary in mind he would have used some such phrase as κατὰ τάξιν. Notice also that the Old Testament prophets were read, how it is not stated, but this points again, however, to the *varied* character of lectionary activity, as of other forms, in the services. The whole section in Justin does not suggest rigidity of any kind. 'The president *verbally* instructs' probably implies that he instructs freely according to his own discretion; similarly he 'offers prayers and thanksgivings according to his ability'. In 1:65 it is not stated, that the prayers are of a fixed length but of a 'considerable length' (εὐχαριστίαν ὑπὲρ τοῦ κατηξιῶσθαι τούτων παρ' αὐτοῦ ἐπὶ πολύ). Again the evidence of I Clement XL:1 ff., to which Carrington appeals,[29] equally points not to a fixed or formalized order of worship, however much the author may have desired such, so much as to a disorder or form- lessness which needed to be corrected. (We shall return to this below.) It is pertinent, finally, to point out that Cullmann is probably to be followed in rejecting the older view that gatherings for the pro- clamation of the Word and gatherings for the Lord's Supper, were to be sharply distinguished as were in Judaism the synagogue service and the temple cult.[30] There was little that Christianity took over neat from Judaism, and particularly in its worship is this the case. His- torical probability does not favour Carrington's lectionary emphasis.

To illustrate further how, by implication at least, Carrington exaggerates the parallelism between Church and Synagogue, we turn to his treatment of the development of the Christian Calendar. His contention—as it applies to Jewish Christians, at least—that the Church took over the Jewish Calendar would seem to be probable.[31] (How far the bulk of Gentile converts to the Church would be

---

[28] So too L. Pautigny, *Justin, Apologies*, Paris, 1904, p. 143, translates 'autant que le temps le permet'.

[29] p. 41.

[30] *Op. cit.*, pp. 26–32.

[31] Carrington's use of I Cor. 16:8, Acts 20:16,; 27:9 is pertinent and valid here, *op. cit.*, p. 17. It should be noted, however, that the festivals of the Gentiles attracted some Jews very strongly (see Mishnah, Abodah Zarah), as indeed Carrington is fully aware.

sufficiently familiar with the Jewish year to 'take it over' for their own use is more questionable; it is probable that the Church became increasingly full of people who had little awareness of the Jewish festal tradition.) But it is probably erroneous to regard this as a deliberate process as if Christians formally decided to do so; rather there was among the earliest Jewish Christians at least an unconscious or quite natural maintenance of the calendrical tradition of Jewry.

Carrington's over-emphasis appears in his treatment of the emergence of the Lord's Day.[32] He searches for a parallel to, or precedent for, the celebration of the day we term 'Sunday' and early Christians 'the first day of the week' and later 'the Lord's Day', in the Jewish Calendar and finds it in the Firstfruits when it was traditional to bring offerings. It is in the light of the Firstfruits that the Christian Sunday, he seems to imply, is to be understood; this in turn explains why Paul arranged for the collection of money for the poor of Jerusalem on the first day of the week. But it is far more probable that the Christian Sunday, which was designed above all to commemorate the resurrection of the Lord, emerged not indeed in parallelism to any Jewish observance like Firstfruits, but actually in conscious opposition to or distinction from the Jewish Sabbath.[33] Nor need we find any deeper motif for making arrangements for the collection of money on the first day of the week than that of simple convenience: probably it had nothing to do with the custom of offering Firstfruits, any more than with the Temple tax.[34]

[32] Op. cit., pp. 38 ff. But see now his According to Mark, 1960, pp. 20 f., 140.

[33] Compare O. Cullmann, op cit., pp. 10–12, where the evidence is sifted. There seems to be little, if any, evidence that the Christian Sunday was, for instance, a day of rest, as was the Jewish Sabbath. On this point contrast Cullmann, who (op. cit., pp. 87, 91) suggests that the first day of the week (our Sunday) was a day of rest for early Christians according to John 5; it replaced the Jewish Sabbath as such. He finds support for this view from the Epistle of Barnabas xv. 9. But here the eighth day is stated to be kept in joyfulness not in rest, it being implied that the true rest can only be regarded as a future gift at the Son's coming again. (Cullmann finds an eschatological idea analogous to this in John 5:17 and compare also Heb. 4:10.) The tone of the Epistle to Diognetus IV, does not suggest that Christians observed any day as a sabbath, as Professor H. J. Cadbury pointed out to me. See also C. H. Dodd in Journal of Ecclesiastical History, vol. III, no. 3 (Oct. 1952); J. Daniélou, Bible et Liturgie, Paris, 1951, pp. 305 ff.; B. S. Easton, The Apostolic Tradition of Hippolytus (1934), p. 5 n. 2; R. Bultmann, New Testament Theology, vol. I, p. 123; A. D. Nock, St Paul, pp. 58 f.

[34] See K. Holl, 'Der Kirchenbegriff des Paulus in seinem Verhältnis zu dem der Urgemeinde', in Sitzungsb. Preus. Akad. Wiss., vol. LIII (1921), and the discussion in R. N. Flew, Jesus and His Church (1938), ad loc.

So too in Carrington's treatment of the Christian Passover he has rightly recalled us again to the debt of early Christian sources to the festal tradition of Judaism, but that debt has to be carefully assessed. Paschal imagery does invade 1 Corinthians, and so too 2 Corinthians may well reflect Pentecostal and Tabernacle motifs, as Carrington and T. W. Manson have affirmed; and it may well be that other New Testament documents are to be illuminated by reference to Jewish festivals, as is Romans, for example, by the Day of Atonement.[35] But it is quite another thing to ascribe to such imagery as we have referred to any strictly calendrical intention. Thus to take 1 Cor. 5:7 as implying a deliberate calendrical adherence to the Jewish Passover in a new Christian dress is to press the imagery too far. Paul's intention here is to emphasize that the *whole* of the Christian life is a Passover, Christ, the Passover Lamb, having been slain; he is not thinking of a specific Christian Passover day but of the Christian dispensation as such as a feast.[36] Again that the Pentecostal imagery in 2 Cor. 1–5 must not too certainly be taken to indicate the Pentecostal dating of that section appears from the fact that in 2 Cor. 5 the imagery may be interpreted as suddenly changing to that of Tabernacles.[37] All this means that the strictly calendrical significance of the festal symbolism or imagery of the New Testament documents should not be over-emphasized. What the imagery shows is that early Christians exploited the festal tradition of Judaism for their own evangelistic and hortatory ends; with its calendrical import they were not consciously concerned, and still less were they seeking to base a Christian calendar upon it. Much as a modern poet, Dylan Thomas, made use of images born of the Christian tradition, because they were his *necessary* medium of communication in his own particular environment, which had been largely conditioned

[35] For references see *Paul and Rabbinic Judaism*, pp. 240 ff., 313. See also J. Munck, *Paulus und Die Heilsgeschichte* (1954), pp. 137 ff.

[36] It is important to realize that *every* Sunday commemorated Easter. How soon did the Church fasten on one day to commemorate the death of Jesus? There is no real evidence for thinking that Jesus intended His death to be commemorated annually. On the interpretation of 1 Cor. 5:7, see J. Weiss, in Meyer, *Kommentar: Der Erste Korintherbrief* (1924), *ad loc.*; A. D. Nock, *St Paul* (1938), p. 53.

[37] It is to be noted that T. W. Manson does not find Pentecostal motifs in 2 Cor. 5 but Tabernacle ones: see *Journal of Theological Studies*, Jan.–April, vol. XLVI (1945), pp. 1–10; Carrington, p. 43.

by Christianity, even though he himself had never embraced that tradition, so too early Christians could use Jewish festal imagery without being aware in any way that they were thereby contributing to the establishment of a Christian calendar.

For example Carrington takes the passage I Clem. XL:I ff. to prove that 'a liturgical year of the Hebrew type must have been well established in Rome and in Corinth by the 90's. The passage reads: πάντα τάξει ποιεῖν ὀφείλομεν, ὅσα ὁ Δεσπότης ἐπιτελεῖν ἐκέλευσε[ν] κατὰ καιροὺς τεταγμένους· τάς τε προσφορὰς καὶ λειτουργίας ἐπιτελεῖσθαι, καὶ οὐκ εἰκῆ ἢ ἀτάκτως ἐκέλευσεν γίνεσθαι, ἀλλ' ὡρισμένοις καιροῖς καὶ ὥραις κ.τ.λ.[38] Carrington notes that it is a feature of the style of I Clement to avoid precise detail: this makes it difficult to determine the exact connotation of his words. What do the phrases κατὰ καιροὺς τεταγμένους, ὡρισμένοις καιροῖς καὶ ὥραις, and προστεταγμένοις καιροῖς (XL:4) mean? Because of the reference to the high priest, priests, Levites and laymen, Carrington interprets them to refer to a liturgical year of a Hebrew type, i.e., the seasons refer to Passover, Tabernacles, etc. But this is to draw far more rigid a parallelism between the Old and the New Dispensation than is intended by I Clement. Doubtless there is a parallelism to be seen between the 'ministers' of Judaism, the high priest, priests, Levites and laymen and those of the Church, apostles, bishops, deacons; but, as Lightfoot[39] long since pointed out, no *direct* reference to or identity with Christian ministers is suggested: it is only by *analogy* that they are referred to. Not only is a direct reference made improbable by the fact that while the high priest, priests and Levites constitute three orders, the Epistle recognizes only two, presbyters and deacons, but any attempt to identify Jesus with the high priest, and presbyters with the priests and the deacons with the Levites must fail, because this would be to blur the distinction between the high priesthood of Christ and any other. Just as the offerings, sacrifices and gifts presented by the presbyters are not a literal reference to Jewish sacrifice but are to be understood as prayers, thanksgivings, alms, eucharistic elements and gifts,[40] so too there is no identification of

---

[38] The text used is from Hippolyte Hemmer, *Clément de Rome* (1926), pp. 83 f.
[39] *The Apostolic Fathers*, vol. II, pp. 122 ff.
[40] See Lightfoot, *op. cit.*, pp. 134 f.; H. Hemmer, *op. cit.*, p. 85 n., notes on the use

the appointed seasons of I Clem. XL with the Levitical seasons: they refer rather to the Lord's Day, the first day of the week. Carrington's understanding of I Clem. XL is far too literal. Moreover, in any case, even if I Clement did intend to refer to a fixed Christian calendar following the pattern of the Hebraic, which is most improbable, as we saw, what the text points to is a disorder and formlessness in the Corinthian Church, a formlessness which must have ignored such a calendar, if it was intended to be followed, and demanded correction. Such evidence as we have in the New Testament, to which Carrington refers in the Pauline Epistles, does not point to a desire for such a calendrical imitation of Judaism. Rom. 14:5 and Gal 4:10, 11 certainly lend no support to this. In both we know Paul's attitude; he himself doubtless failed to achieve logical consistency in his life, and continued to observe days, but he is far from wanting Christians to follow any calendar. To see Christians, taught by him, insisting that days, months and years should be observed, prompts him to fear that he has laboured in vain in Gal. 4:10, 11. It is true, as Carrington points out, that he is more tolerant in Rom. 14:5, and the same tolerant attitude lies behind Col. 2:16 f., but he makes no secret of the fact that he himself is 'among the strong' in such matters as meats and, by implication, the calendar. Justin's *Dialogue with Trypho*, X is very explicit in its assertion that Christians observe no festivals or Sabbaths: both Justin and Trypho refer to this. Nor is it irrelevant to point out in this connection that were the calendrical interests of the early Christians as strong as is suggested by Carrington it is unlikely that the controversy on matters of chronology to which he refers, the Quartodecimian controversy, would have arisen at all. Surely such interests would have helped to preclude the development of any such.[41]

The same hesitation arising from historical probabilities makes it difficult to believe that early Christians were concerned to set forth the life and teaching of Jesus in the intricate triadic form discovered

[41] pp. 39 f.

of προσφέρονται in I Clem. XLI:2, 'Clément de Rome emploie le présent pour décrire une institution demeurée dans son souvenir; mais il ne trace de parallèle entre les deux sacerdoces que parce que la disparition de l'un fait valoir l'autre.' He cites a parellel usage of the present tense in Josephus, *Antiquities*, III:7–11; Barnabas, VII–IX; *The Epistle to Diognetus*, III; Justin, *Dialogue*, CXVII.

by Carrington in Mark, which he makes quite integral to his lectionary theory.[42] Apart from the difficulty of accepting the view that the Gospel which found its way into the canon is the product of what Carrington seems to regard as a kind of esoteric and poetic group in the early Church,[43] this hesitation is amply sustained by an examination of the facts.

Let us first take what Carrington calls the Major Triads in Mark.[44] His most important triad is that of the three mountains at 3:13 ff., 6:30 f., 9:2 f. At the first mountain 3:13 ff., the death and resurrection of the Son of Man is announced in parables. Carrington takes all the three parables in 4:1–20, 26–9, 30–2, to be concerned with this one theme. But, if they were intended to be triadic, why should 4:21–5 be inserted to break their continuity? Moreover, the explanation of the parable in 4:1–8 is appended in vv. 13 ff. where the experience of the Church in its missionary activity is reflected. Whether or not this is the correct explanation of the parable, it *is* the one accepted by Mark and it does not coincide with Carrington's. Is it really conceivable that Mark had an explanation other than the one he provides in his text? In any case, the close connection of these parables, even if Carrington's explanation of them be accepted, with the mountain mentioned in 3:13 f. is doubtful. Thus 4:1 does not follow immediately after 3:19. Carrington ignores the intervening material in 3:20–30 and 3:31–35. The parables are uttered not at the mountain but by the sea; they do not follow directly the choice of the Twelve.

The episode of the so-called second mountain, where the death and resurrection of Jesus is claimed to be enacted sacramentally is equally misrepresented by Carrington. It is only *after* the feeding of the five thousand that the Lord goes up to a mountain, there to pray. No mountain is mentioned in connection with the feeding at all: we have to wait till 6:46 for it, and there it is more closely connected with the walking on the sea than the feeding of the five thousand. Equally significant is the fact that in the feeding of the four thousand

---

[42] pp. 8 ff. On p. 9 Carrington writes: 'A recognition of the triads is equivalent to a recognition of the structure of the Gospel.' He reiterates this in the *Church Quarterly Review* (April–June 1953), no. 311, vol. CLIV, p. 216.

[43] pp. 92 f.

[44] These Major Triads are listed on pp. 94 ff.; see also the whole section in pp. 6 ff.

in 8:1–10, which Carrington regards as a lectionary duplicate of 6:30–44, designed for Pentecost, there is no reference to a mountain, which is inconceivable if that phenomenon was as central as Carrington insists.

When we turn to the third mountain, when the death and resurrection of Jesus is revealed openly, Carrington finds even more points of triadic significance. He takes the episode of the third mountain to open at 8:27 ff. where the reference to John the Baptist (8:28) looks back, Carrington thinks, to 6:14 ff. which precedes the feeding of the five thousand, whilst the reference to Herod in 6:14 ff. similarly looks back to the reference to the Herodians in 3:6. Assuming that the episode of the first mountain begins at 3:7, of the second mountain at 6:7—although Carrington does not always make it clear where the various episodes begin; thus on p. 6 it seems to begin at 6:7, but on p. 7 at 6:14 ff., where we read of 'echoes of those words of Herod which open the Episode of the Second Mountain'—and of the third mountain at 8:27, it will appear that within these episodes the references to the Herodians and Herod do not constitute a triad. The term Herodians at 3:6 occurs *outside* the first episode.

The Major Triad to which Carrington attaches most importance, in the light of the above, cannot be regarded as very convincing; indeed only by a *tour de force* can it be established as a triad at all. Nor are his other Major Triads more convincing. He himself admits that there are difficulties in identifying them because 'we often have to distinguish the significant uses of a word from the non-significant'.[45] Since this virtually amounts to an admission that what Carrington treats as triads are actually not triads, the difficulty he mentions is a real one indeed. In a list of Major Triads given on pp. 94 ff., there are seventy-three cases mentioned in all; of these six are regarded by Carrington himself as dubious and seven as merely significant repetitions, not triads, and by any strict triadic standard twenty-five other cases, it seems to me, on examination, must be rejected. This means that of the seventy-three cases only thirty-five are admissible. More important still is it that the Major Triads on which Carrington places the greatest emphasis—the Three

Mountains, the Three Predictions of the Passion, the Three Parables—are all inadmissible.[46]

The same negative verdict follows an examination of the minor triads isolated by Carrington in the various lections.[47] He divides Mark into sixty-two lections plus a supplemental Resurrection and Ascension lection (the spurious ending of Mark 16:9–20). In some of these he finds no minor triads, namely, in lections 7, 22, 23, 27, 39, although this last is a very important lection, though short (Mark 9: 30–32). No reason is given why these particular lections should be thus devoid of minor triads. An examination of the other lections where Carrington finds such reveals, in my judgment, only nine cases where straightforward minor triads are admissible, in lections 8, 17, 19, 30, 32, 33, 36, 50, 51. In the remainder it is only by special pleading that the minor triads proposed by Carrington can be established at all. It can be asserted that Carrington's understanding of the structure of Mark, if it rests only on the recognition of the triadic structure which we have above examined, must be rejected. We can only regret that he has confused his discussion of the lectionary character of the Gospel with an improbable and unproven theory of its literary character.

Were that theory accepted, it is further to be stated that Carrington's work then suffers from a deep inner contradiction which arises from the last assumption which we note. Throughout his treatment Carrington emphasizes the deliberate and highly intricate artistry with which the Gospel units and the total structure of Mark have been composed, this artistry, triadic in pattern, being linked to a specific liturgical purpose. In this last section, however, he describes the origin of what he calls the Galilean Gospel.[48] Accepting Lohmeyer's claim that there was a Galilean Christianity which is to be sharply distinguished from that of Jerusalem, Carrington pictures the convocations of Galilean Christians, which, it is suggested, in a phrase which it is difficult to understand precisely, 'came into being

---

[46] It should be noted that the employment of various sources by Mark, which might account for the frequent incidence of certain words, is not seriously considered by Carrington; for example, contrast the use made of the incidence of the term 'Twelve' by W. L. Knox, *op cit.*, pp. 17 ff., with that by Carrington.

[47] The minor triads are noted after each lection, which Carrington isolates, on pp. 118–230; this is a monument of industry.

[48] pp. 75 ff.

as a continuation of the ministry of Jesus in the churches which He had Himself created'.[49] At these convocations one or more of the Twelve would stand up to recite their memories of Jesus, and thus the liturgical Gospel was given to the world. This Carrington supports by the somewhat amazing statement, in view of his previous treatment, that 'the Gospel units have the *character of a local tale*, and are the work of someone who could tell a story effectively'[50] (my italics). Can anything be further from a local tale than the intricacies of the triadic structure of Carrington's units, not to speak of his lectionary? We cannot examine Lohmeyer's thesis here that there was a distinct and influential Galilean Christianity. Nor need we, because the importation of the Jerusalem-Galilee antithesis into the discussion of lectionary factors is not necessary. But we may at least safely assert that the popular Galilean activity of Jesus is not the only background to His ministry. Synagogal activity and other more private meetings all had their place. The festal element in the ministry cannot be made the dominant one.

Carrington supports the above broad assumptions with which we have dealt by certain secondary considerations which must now be examined. These are as follows.

(a) In a section entitled 'The Dodekad of Preaching' there is offered a thrice-twined argument. First, the view is stated that there could be only one gospel in a given Church. Mark was the Gospel for Rome and constituted a lectionary based on the Julianic calendar used there. Matthew was the one Gospel at Antioch.[51] Marcion clung to this principle and used a mutilated form of Luke which had been assimilated to Mark at some points and given a Marcan title.[52] Secondly, it is pointed out that Mark at an early date was the one Gospel in use at Alexandria. This is affirmed on the ground that the original theology of the Alexandrian heretics, such as Cerinthus (he is supposed by Carrington to have received an Egyptian education, although he taught in Asia), Valentinus and Basilides, who held that the Divine Christus became incarnate at the Baptism, must have depended on a Gospel like that of Mark which begins with the Baptism.[53] And, thirdly, because Mark had been read from the

[49] p. 87. [50] p. 88.
[51] pp. 44 ff. [52] pp. 46 f.
[53] pp. 48 ff.

earliest times in the Church as an annual cycle of liturgical lessons, the idea would naturally grow that the events which were thus chronicled had taken place within a single year.[54] Thus Mark became associated with the view that the ministry of Jesus lasted twelve months, a view also associated with the heretics and strongly attacked by Irenaeus.[55] In addition, this explains the famous reference to Mark in Papias.[56] Papias, Carrington points out, preferred to hear the Gospel orally transmitted. Nevertheless he did not criticize Mark for *what* he wrote but for the *order* in which he did so, and Carrington argues that the order here referred to is neither chronological nor topical nor historical but lectionary.[57] By implication he argues that the connection of Mark with Alexandrian Gnosticism would naturally predispose the Great Church against Mark and that Papias' disapproval of the twelve months' ministry which was, according to Carrington, as we have seen, closely connected with the arrangement of the Marcan lectionary, led him to look askance at the Marcan order.[58]

The position here adopted by Carrington is open to much doubt. First, does the evidence support the view that each Church had one gospel? Since Carrington himself regards his treatment of Marcion with uneasiness [59] we need not stay with it, except to point out that it is indeed hard to believe that we can make a list of its chapter divisions when we cannot satisfactorily reconstruct the Marcionite Luke itself.[60] The exclusive connection of Matthew with Antioch cannot be certainly established. While it is true that Ignatius was certainly acquainted either with our Matthew or with a Gospel very closely akin to it, he is also very probably dependent on the Fourth Gospel, and indeed emphasizes the Johannine doctrine of the pre-incarnate activity of the Logos.[61] Carrington supplies little evidence

[54] p. 53.

[55] On this see *Adv. Haer.* II, xxi. The passage is dealt with by G. Ogg, *The Chronology of the Public Ministry of Jesus*, Cambridge, 1940, pp. 48 ff.

[56] See Eusebius, *Ecclesiastical History*, III, 39.

[57] pp. 58 f.   [58] *Ibid.*   [59] p. 48.   [60] p. 47.

[61] See E. Massaux, *Influence de l'Évangile de Saint Matthieu sur la littérature chrétienne avant Saint Irénée,* Louvain, 1950, p. 134; *The New Testament in the Apostolic Fathers,* Oxford, 1905, p. 83, 'Ignatius' use of the Fourth Gospel is highly probable'—though it 'falls some way short of certainty'. G. D. Kilpatrick rejects the association of Matthew with Antioch; see *The Origins of the Gospel according to St Matthew,* Oxford, 1946, p. 134.

for the continued sole use of Mark at Alexandria as its one Gospel,[62] nor should he assume as settled the Roman provenance of Mark. *The Shepherd* of Hermas normally turns to Matthew rather than Mark; I Clement shows no trace of Mark.[63]

Again can we associate Mark so closely with Alexandrian Gnosticism as does Carrington? Had that association been very close it is difficult to understand why Mark so easily achieved canonicity. The case of the Fourth Gospel is instructive here: that Gospel's alleged *gnostic* affinities constituted a barrier to its canonicity.[64] Moreover, the arguments put forward by Carrington why Alexandrian Gnosticism would be specially drawn to Mark [65]—namely because it omitted a nativity story—would also apply to the Fourth Gospel. There seems no evidence for associating Mark peculiarly with Alexandria.[66] Nor need we turn to its Alexandrian Gnostic and calendrical affinities to account for the paucity of references to it. The incorporation of Mark into Matthew and Luke would sufficiently account for this.

[62] pp. 50 f. Carrington refers only to Eusebius, *op. cit.*, II, 16 (on which see Lawlor and Oulton, *Eusebius: translation, introduction and notes*, vol. II, 1928, p. 66). He writes: 'The form of the Alexandrian heresy which now begins to emerge is obviously Marcan, and is best explained by a theory of an early ascendancy of Mark in Alexandria, which went on later and was perhaps more influential there than elsewhere' (p. 51). It is difficult to follow Carrington in his understanding of Irenaeus and other authors here. The impression gained from Irenaeus is that it was the Simonians who were the well from which the rank growth of Gnostic heresy developed (see *Adv. Haer.* I, xxiii–xxv). Basilides is connected therewith although he promulgated his views in Alexandria: Valentinus, as Carrington himself points out (p. 48), is specifically connected with the Fourth Gospel (*Adv. Haer.* III, xi). Cerinthus according to the text preserved by Hippolytus was indeed trained in the wisdom of the Egyptians but the Latin text merely describes him as a 'certain man in Asia' (*Adv. Haer.* I, xxvi). Is there any real evidence for what Carrington calls a pre-Gnostic theology based on Mark in Alexandria? (p. 51). For Hippolytus, see W. H. Harvey, *Sancti Irenaei*, tom. I, p. 221.

[63] E. Massaux, *op. cit.*, pp. 324 f.; on I Clement Massaux (p. 65) writes: '. . . des évangiles seul celui de Mt. a exercé une influence littéraire certaine sur Clément de Rome: il ne dépend jamais des autres évangiles.'

[64] On this see B. H. Streeter, *The Four Gospels* (1926), pp. 13, 436 ff.

[65] How subjective such judgments can be emerges with peculiar force in S. G. F. Brandon, *The Fall of Jerusalem and the Christian Church* (1951), pp. 217 ff., who traces the origin of Matthew to Alexandria.

[66] See V. Taylor, *The Gospel according to St. Mark* (1952), p. 32. In a penetrating discussion R. P. Casey, *Theology*, vol. LV, No. 38 (October 1952), p. 366 n. 4, also dismisses Carrington's understanding of Alexandrian Gnosticism. This article came into my hands after I had long pondered Carrington's thesis and on all points independently reached the same conclusions. As will emerge from the above, I am not sure that we can dismiss the lectionary significance of the divisions in the manuscripts as surely as does Casey.

However, Carrington's speculations on Mark and Gnosticism need not further concern us because there is nothing in the context of Papias' statement to which he refers to support the view that Mark was necessarily a liturgical Gospel. The term τάξει refers to the things which had been spoken and done by Jesus. Mark had not been able to record these in the strict chronological order in which they happened because he himself in person did not always hear or follow Jesus, but had to rely on the account given to him by Peter. The context favours taking τάξει to refer quite simply to chronological order. (Compare how Luke uses a compound verb ἀνατάξασθαι, which is closely related to τάξις, to describe his method of compiling a gospel;[67] but Carrington does not take Luke as originally composed as a lectionary.)[68] Similarly Carrington's further identification of the λόγια to which Papias refers with an Aramaic lectionary Gospel [69] carries no conviction; two comments are apt at this point. First, it is by no means certain that the phrase τὰ λόγια refers to an Aramaic Gospel.[70] Secondly, the one thing about which many scholars seem to agree is that Papias at least meant by τὰ λόγια our canonical Matthew, which had been translated into Greek.[71] But if Papias meant by τὰ λόγια the Aramaic original of the canonical Gospel then Carrington is in difficulty because he has urged that the canonical Matthew follows more or less the lectionary order of Mark, so that if Papias rejected the lectionary order of Mark he would also have to reject Matthew (τὰ λόγια) for the same reason: that Papias meant another lectionary Gospel than Matthew the text probably does not indicate and so Carrington from the point of view of Papias himself is probably involved in a contradiction.

(b) Carrington refers to Irenaeus' quotation of a 'piece of traditional mysticism which assigns to each gospel as an interpretative symbol one of the four "beasts" or rather living things (ḥayyoth) of

---

[67] Luke 1:1.   [68] p. 48.   [69] p. 59.

[70] See, for example, the exhaustive treatment of τὰ λόγια by T. W. Manson, *Bulletin of the John Rylands Library*, vol. XXIX, No. 2 (February 1946), especially the appendix, pp. 22 ff. One of the most recent Roman Catholic treatments (A. Wirkenhauser, *Einleitung in das Neue Testament*, 1953) takes τὰ λόγια to refer to Q., i.e. the original Aramaic document translated into what is designated Q (I depend on G. D. Kilpatrick *J.T.S.* vol. IV, Part 2 (1953), p. 229, for this).

[71] T. W. Manson, *op. cit.*, pp. 4 f., points out that B. W. Bacon and J. Donovan who discussed τὰ λόγια recently agree on this, as does T. W. Manson himself, p. 5.

the Revelation; the face (πρόσωπον) of the man is assigned to
Matthew, the eagle to Mark, the calf or bull to Luke, and the lion
to John'.[72] He suggests that the four zodiac figures referred to may
'have denoted the seasons of the year to which the four gospels
were allotted in the new four-gospel lectionary which succeeded the
one-gospel lectionary'.[73] But a very strong argument against this is
the fact, pointed out by Carrington, that the order of the Gospels
which it attests is Matthew, Luke, John, Mark, but no list of the
Gospels gives this order;[74] and what is particularly damaging to
Carrington's view is that Irenaeus himself has the order Matthew,
Mark, Luke, John.[75] Moreover, in the lectionaries which later
emerged in the Church, Matthew is assigned for reading not to
25 December as is the case, on Carrington's theory, in Irenaeus'
intention, but to the period following Pentecost.[76] It is not likely
that the later tradition is radically different from the earlier in lectionary matters. Moreover, Pentecost, which was associated with the
giving of the Law,[77] is precisely the time at which we should expect
Matthew to be read. (Carrington himself points to the use of
Matthew after Pentecost in the Greek calendar.)[78] But apart from
this, to interpret the 'faces' in Irenaeus calendrically is to import into
his words an idea wholly alien to the context. Irenaeus is concerned
to emphasize the universal scope of the Gospel. In the relevant
passage, *Against Heresies* III, xi, 8, Irenaeus interprets for us the
cherubim in Ezek. 1:5 ff. and/or Rev. 4:7; their four faces were
images of 'the dispensation of the Son of God'. This means that each
face symbolized some aspect of the character or activity of the
Christ. Similarly each of the four Gospels were severally concerned
to express this in different ways. Thus the connection between the
Gospels and the various beasts has to do with their particular
emphases in presenting the life of Jesus, and by a logic strange to us
moderns these four emphases are somehow related in Irenaeus' mind
with the four zones, and the four principal winds of the world

---

[72] pp. 65 f.   [73] p. 66.   [74] p. 67.
[75] Irenaeus, *Adv. Haer.* III, i. I.
[76] See C. R. Gregory, *The Canon and Text of the New Testament*, New York,
1912, pp. 389 ff.
[77] See G. F. Moore, *Judaism*, vol. II, p. 48.
[78] p. 58.

which suggests the propriety of the fact that there should be four pillars (Matthew, Mark, Luke, John) for the Gospel. To find here an allusion to the calendar, even though the connection of the beasts with the Zodiac in Rev. 4:7 be established,[79] is to drag in an idea irrelevant to the context.

(c) There is a third minor point which remains to be noticed. Carrington argues that already in the New Testament the phrase 'to proclaim the Gospel' meant the delivery of a form of words with some solemnity in the Ecclesia, i.e. among other things it included the reading of a lection. He takes Mark 14:9, 'Verily I say unto you, wheresoever the Gospel shall be preached throughout the whole world, that also which this woman hath done shall be spoken of for a memorial of her,' to mean 'Wherever this lection is read'.[80] But this is hardly tenable. If this was Mark's meaning there was nothing to prevent his saying 'wherever the Gospel shall be *read*'. Moreover, Carrington's interpretation demands the pronoun τοῦτο (so Matthew) to make it at all possible that the meaning is 'wheresoever *this* lection is read'. Further, the words 'that also which this woman hath done shall be spoken (λαληθήσεται)' become tautologous if the reference is to reading *this* lection, nor is it appropriate to refer to a lection read in the Ecclesia as being directed to the whole world, εἰς ὅλον τὸν κόσμον. This is far better taken as a reference to the general evangelistic or preaching (κηρυχθῇ) activity of the Church.[81]

The passages to which Carrington appeals in support of this interpretation of τὸ εὐαγγέλιον in Mark 14:9, i.e. 1 Cor. 15:1–5 and 1 Cor. 11:23, are not strictly concerned with lections as such. The first, 1 Cor. 15:1–5, presents the Gospel in what is probably a kind of 'credal' summary of it; 1 Cor. 11:26 refers to the *recital* not the reading of the Passion narrative. Despite the close connection with the acts of breaking of the bread and taking of the cup, the verb καταγγέλλειν is probably best understood of the recital of the story of

---

[79] See R. H. Charles, *Revelation*, International Critical Commentary, *ad loc.* See also J. Lawson, *The Biblical Theology of St. Irenaeus* (1948), pp. 43 f. Irenaeus seems to have combined Ezek. 1:4 ff. and Rev. 4:7 in his thinking here.

[80] pp. 18 f.

[81] So V. Taylor, *ad loc.* For another view of Mark 14:9, different from Carrington's, see J. Jeremias, *Zeitschrift für die neutestamentliche Wissenschaft*, Band 44, Heft 1/2.

the death of Jesus,[82] not of the acts themselves, but Carrington goes too far in thinking of this recital in lectionary terms. The analogy of the Passover would seem to point to a procedure more elastic than the reading of a Passion narrative: it suggests rather free *haggadah*. Neither 1 Cor. 15:1-5 nor 1 Cor. 11:23 f. can be urged as evidence for an early lectionary or for early lectionary units.

We next turn to the use that Carrington makes of manuscript evidence in support of his theory. Having satisfied himself that he can divide Mark 1-9 into a series of lections beginning with the Jewish New Year (placing the Feeding of the Five Thousand at Passover and that of the Four Thousand at Pentecost), and further that the chapter divisions of the Vaticanus (B) fit in very well with this scheme, which he has imposed upon or discovered in Mark, Carrington concludes that the purpose of the chapter divisions was precisely to indicate the incidence of the lections.[83] He thus finds an 'external mathematical confirmation' of his theory.[84]

Two difficulties at least have to be noted. What is the exact purpose of the divisions in both the Vaticanus (B) and other Greek manuscripts of the New Testament? In all manuscripts Carrington, as we stated, takes their purpose to have been lectionary, and he assumes that the system of division in B is earlier than that found in non-B manuscripts.[85] But, as far as I am aware, students of the manuscripts of the New Testament have not found in the divisions of the text any lectionary significance. von Soden takes the divisions in the Vaticanus to be the work of some commentator [86] to mark passages in the Gospels merely for purposes of dividing the text satisfactorily;[87] the non-B divisions, on the other hand, he takes to be earlier than those of B and designed, as were the Eusebian canons and the Ammonian sections for purposes of synopsis.[88] He notes the

---

[82] See *Paul and Rabbinic Judaism*, p. 252, n. 3; J. Schniewind, *Theologisches Wörterbuch* (ed. Kittel), vol. 1, p. 70; H. Lietzmann, *Messe und Herrenmahl*, p. 222 n. 1.

[83] pp. 20 ff.

[84] p. xiii. Note that Carrington does not actually identify the lection system that he discovers in B in all respects with the original system.

[85] pp. xi, 27.

[86] H. von Soden, *Die Schriften des Neuen Testaments*[2], vol. 1 (1911), p. 440.

[87] *Op. cit.*, p. 432. The divisions in B arose because the divisions of the non-B manuscripts were unsatisfactory in the division of the material according to content.

[88] *Op. cit.*, pp. 432, 426 ff. Note that F. H. A. Scrivener, *A Plain Introduction to the Criticism of the New Testament*[4], vol. 1 (1894), p. 56, takes B to present the oldest

fact that in the Passion narratives of the Gospels only those sections which are peculiar to each Gospel seem to be noted by the division lines: and since it is likely that the Passion narratives in themselves constituted lectionary units, the peculiar sections marked probably served a synoptic purpose.[89] When we turn to the divisions in B, moreover, many of them delimit sections which are either too long or too short as lectionary units.[90]

But, secondly, even if it should be proved that the divisions of the Vaticanus were lectionary, this evidence refers merely to the fourth century. The divisions also occur in Codex Zacynthius, a palimpsest containing the greater part of Luke 1:1–11:33 which is dated in the eighth century and in Cod. 579 from the thirteenth century.[91] Carrington claims that they do not appear in the Sinaiticus (‭א‬), from the second half of the fourth century.[92] Kirsopp Lake, however, found that at least in the first seven pages of Matthew in the Sinaiticus we are to find 'either the same or nearly the same system of division'.[93] A. Schmidtke, cited by Kenyon, found traces of the divisions in the Sinaiticus and 579 and argued that the divisions went back to the Gospel harmony of Ammonius, which is to be dated in the third century.[94] It is specially noteworthy that the Chester Beatty Papyri, which may go back even to the beginning of the second century, show no traces of the divisions.[95] Carrington claims that the Diatessaron of Tatian, already in the second century, points to the existence of a strong tradition in favour of reading particular

[89] Op. cit., pp. 426 ff.
[90] Thus, for example, Mark 1:12–13 is taken as a lection by Carrington, p. 120. Again can a long discourse like the Sermon on the Mount have been a single lection? (See Carrington, pp. 20, 123.)
[91] See F. G. Kenyon, Handbook to the Textual Criticism of the New Testament[2], (1912), pp. 80 f.
[92] p. 23.
[93] Codex Sinaiticus Petropolitanus, Oxford, 1911; photographs by Helen and Kirsopp Lake, with description and introduction by Kirsopp Lake, p. xxi, col. a.
[94] See F. G. Kenyon, op. cit., pp. 80 f.
[95] The Chester Beatty Biblical Papyri, ed. F. G. Kenyon, London, 1933, etc.

divisions. On p. 55 Scrivener writes: '[The sections] seem to have been formed for the purpose of reference, and a new one always commences where there is some break in the sense.' For a convenient statement, see W. H. P. Hatch, Facsimiles and Descriptions of Minuscule Manuscripts of the New Testament (1951), pp. 22 ff. C. R. Gregory, op. cit., is very unsatisfactory in his treatment; indeed he largely ignores the problem (p. 469).

lections at a particular time and that time and time again the non-B order of lections appears in it.[96] But all this is built on the assumption that the divisions found in an eleventh-century Arabic version of the Diatessaron are a safe guide to divisions in the second-century original, and ignores the simple fact that the only fragment of the Greek Diatessaron which we possess, that from Dura-Europos, does not show any traces of chapter divisions.[97] Nor must it be forgotten that the date of the Diatessaron, even if it did contain the divisions, is about A.D. 160–70, whereas Carrington's thesis requires textual evidence in the first century to supply us with 'mathematical' proof.

In addition to the above two major difficulties there emerge other minor ones. One is that it is very surprising, if Mark was intended from the first as a lectionary, that there are no marks of this intention in the text itself. For example, in discussing lection 23 (Mark 6:7–13)[98] Carrington points out that in the parallel section in Q 'the sending out of the Twelve was preceded by a liturgical formula, "Pray to the Lord of the Harvest", etc.' It is curious that such formulas should be missing in Mark were its intention lectionary. Where Carrington discovers one such lectionary formula in Mark one must be sceptical. In Mark 13:32 Carrington is tempted to take the words 'Concerning that Day and that hour'[99] to be the title of the lection which has been incorporated into the text. Thus one of Schmiedel's foundation texts turns out in Carrington's view to be merely a lectionary title. Moreover, it may not be irrelevant to point out that in the Vaticanus and the Zacynthius chapter divisions occur in the text of Luke, but Carrington does not regard Luke to have been originally intended as a lectionary. But does not this mean either that the divisions are not lectionary or that they are much later than Carrington would have us believe?[100]

Finally, we have to point out that the divisions in the Vaticanus constitute a lectionary for one year of Sundays. Two factors are noteworthy. It follows, in the first place, that whatever the actual

[96] pp. 29 ff.
[97] See G. H. Kraeling, *A Greek Fragment of Tatian's Diatessaron*, London, 1935.
[98] pp. 150 f.
[99] p. 211. The title of the section given in the Codex Alexandrinus is περὶ τῆς ἡμέρας καὶ ὥρας; this has, according to Carrington, become the περὶ δὲ τῆς ἡμέρας ἐκείνης ἢ τῆς ὥρας of Mark 13:32.
[100] See p. 48.

length of the ministry of Jesus it is compressed on Carrington's theory to a year of lections. It is hardly likely that the ministry lasted only one year;[101] history would not, therefore, suggest the lectionary arrangement that Carrington finds in the Vaticanus and that arrangement had necessarily to do violence to history. On the other hand, the practice of the Synagogue which on Carrington's theory, as we saw, exercised a heavy influence on the practice of the Church would suggest not an annual cycle of lections but a triennial one; the Palestinian Jewish lectionary was almost certainly triennial.[102] Thus in the present state of our knowledge of the divisions of the manuscripts, it has to be asserted that it does not seem possible to accept Carrington's understanding of their purpose.

From all the above it will have emerged that the three supports upon which Carrington's lectionary or calendrical theory rests have all in turn failed to satisfy. Nevertheless, his study, by its thoroughgoing challenge and scope, has thrown into relief two necessities. First, it may be permitted to one who is not primarily a textual critic to voice a doubt. Casey, [103] in a review to which I am very greatly indebted and at all of whose conclusions I had independently arrived, has dismissed Carrington's understanding of the divisions in B outright. But von Soden pointed out that even in the case of the non-B manuscripts only an increased knowledge of the liturgical practice of the early Church can further enlighten us on the purpose of some of the divisions.[104] For example that the use of such lines as those found in B, etc., to divide the text may well go back to the earliest days of the Church, despite the lack of actual textual evidence in manuscripts of the New Testament, may be suggested by the Isaiah

[101] See G. Ogg, op. cit., p. 323. Only by concentration exclusively on a Galilean ministry can that of Jesus be reduced to a single year. Compare V. Taylor, op. cit., pp. 24 f.

[102] See J. Mann, op. cit., pp. 3 ff. On the other hand it is not impossible that even within Palestine the practice varied; see R. Marcus' introduction to his translations of Philo's Questions and Answers on Genesis (Cambridge, Mass., and London, 1953), p. xiii. (I owe this reference to Professor Nock.) How varied calendrical practice in general must have been emerges from the fact that the sages at Jamnia had to regulate the calendar. It is erroneous to speak of a single utterly fixed Jewish Calendar therefore before Jamnia; see, for example, Mishnah, Rosh Ha-Shanah, ii, 9, et passim; an astronomically fixed calendar was adopted only about the middle of the fourth century, see G. F. Moore, op. cit., vol. II, p. 23, n. 3.

[103] Op. cit., pp. 367 f.

[104] Op. cit., p. 428.

scroll from Qumrân. The dissident sect which used that scroll used lines in their text which are very similar, if not identical, with those found in B, etc. These lines were noted by Millar Burrows [105] who apparently takes them to refer to lections (as does Carrington the *paragrapha* [106] in B, etc.). The grounds on which Millar Burrows takes this view are not stated, but if his conjecture is correct that the lines in D S Isa. are meant to serve a lectionary purpose it is difficult to think that the somewhat similar lines found in B, etc., may not have served the same purpose at least at some stage. Until the lines in both the Isaiah scroll and in manuscripts of the New Testament have been more thoroughly examined all this must remain highly conjectural, but there is no justification for any outright dismissal of Carrington's understanding of the divisions concerned.

But in the second place, not only is it necessary to examine the textual evidence more thoroughly than has hitherto been done, but also the influence of liturgical practice must still further be considered in the formulation and transmission of the tradition, although Carrington's study suggests that this is to be traced more along the lines pursued by G. D. Kilpatrick in his work on *The Origins of the Gospel According to St Matthew*, where there is intensive examination of the text itself, than by the more mechanical method of Carrington. That that influence is a real factor in the process referred to can hardly be questioned, but it is not likely to have dominated the creation

[105] *The Dead Sea Scrolls of St. Mark's Monastery*, vol. I (1950), p. xvi. The lines in the Isaiah scroll are short and horizontal; some bend slightly on the left: they are placed at the edges of columns. I counted—including doubtful cases—about sixty-one instances of their use. In some instances their incidence coincides with a break in the sense, i.e. they mark new sections, but in others they break across the sense of a passage. They do not cover the whole of the text but only certain sections. Bleddyn J. Roberts (*Bulletin of the John Rylands Library*, vol. XXXVI, no. 1, September 1953, p. 91) claims that there are 'open' and 'closed' paragraphs in D S Isa. It has been customary to regard the identification of 'open' and 'closed' paragraphs as due to lectionary interests (see Bleddyn J. Roberts, *The Old Testament Text and Versions*, Cardiff, 1951, p. 36), in which case there would be no need for a special line to mark lectionary divisions, and it may be that the lines under consideration in D S Isa. were merely designed to draw attention to certain particular passages frequently used. It should be noted, however, that the significance of the 'open' and 'closed' sections in manuscripts is not fully established. (See M. Gaster, *Hebrew Illuminated Bibles of the Ninth and Tenth Centuries* and *A Samaritan Scroll of the Law*, London, 1901, pp. 32, 34.)

[106] For these see Fig. 1 in Carrington, p. 121. It should be borne in mind that the Vaticanus is a far more finished manuscript than D S Isa.

of the Gospels of Mark and Matthew in the way that Carrington implies.[107]

In the course of his argument, p. 15, Carrington refers to the work of P. Levertoff in *A New Commentary on Holy Scripture*, ed. Gore (London, 1928), pp. 128 ff.; and, since Levertoff's work was an early attempt to trace a connection between the Gospels and the Jewish year, it may be well to examine it. He claimed in particular that Matt. 3:1–7:13 is to be interpreted in the light of the liturgical seasons of the Synagogue. Apart from those places where he obviously follows Mark, it is these liturgical seasons, according to Levertoff, which determine the sequence of events for Matthew. Moreover, this is so not because Matthew happened to be concerned so to arrange his material, but because of the simple fact that the material was, as a matter of history, connected with certain pivotal points in the liturgical schema of the Synagogue, i.e. the liturgical sequence of the material is historical and not merely editorial.

Nor can it be denied that the Synoptics make it clear that the Jewish festivals did play a significant part in the ministry of Jesus. It was at the Passover season that Jesus did set Himself to die at the geographic and spiritual centre of the nation's life (Luke 22:15, cf. 13:33). As for the Fourth Gospel, it has been possible to claim that it presents the ministry of Jesus as a series of circles, so to speak, revolving round various Jewish festivals. (Thus J. Lowe in an unpublished paper communicated at Oxford, 1949.) The connections between these last and the Fourth Gospel have been forced (the identity of the various feasts referred to in the Gospel is by no means always clear), but at least they do serve as a reminder that the possibility is a real one that much of the course of the ministry would be influenced, if not determined, by the incidence of the important Jewish festivals.

With this preliminary let us examine Levertoff's case. He begins by placing the ministry of John the Baptist in the 'month' of Elul (i.e. in the end of August and the beginning of September). At this time of the year preparation was being made in the Synagogue for the New Year's Day on the first of Tishri (i.e. about 14 September); following this there were ten days of penitence leading, on the tenth of Tishri, to the Day of Atonement, which again was followed on the fifteenth of the same 'month' by the Feast of Tabernacles. During the period when the Baptist is presumed to have begun his ministry, Levertoff finds certain emphases in the Synagogue liturgy—on repentance, the Kingdom of Heaven, the descent of Jewry from Abraham, in short, on those elements which according to Matthew were prominent in the Baptist's teaching; moreover, what Levertoff calls the Baptist's allusion to Isa. 40 (Matt. 3:3) is due

---

[107] Compare the restrained treatment of the problem in G. Delling, *Der Gottesdienst im Neuen Testament* (1952), p. 91.

to his familiarity with the synagogal lessons of the time which were derived from Deuteronomy and Deutero-Isaiah; the very act of baptism itself is connected with another synagogal lection, namely, Mic. 7:19 which reads 'and thou wilt cast all their sins into the depths of the sea'. Thus the activity and the message of the Baptist were, according to Levertoff, directly moulded by the synagogal practice at the time at which presumably he began his ministry.

The criticisms of this position are fairly obvious. First, Levertoff's assumption that John the Baptist began his ministry in Elul cannot in the nature of the case be proved or disproved. It is probable that the ministry took place between Nisan A.D. 28 and Nisan A.D. 29, but even this is not universally accepted.[108] Even if it were proven that Elul was the month which saw the beginning of the Baptist's ministry, there still remains the twofold problem: (1) whether we can with certainty establish the synagogal lessons for the months of Elul and Tishri, and (2) whether the Matthaean account of the ministry of the Baptist justifies the assumption that it was these same lessons which governed the particular time and form which that ministry assumed.

To deal with (1) first. We can be fairly confident that the Pentateuchal and Prophetic lessons were in use in the first century (see J. Mann, *op. cit.*, pp. 4 ff.; so Büchler, *J.Q.R.*, vol. v (1892–3), pp. 420 ff.; vol. VI (1893–4), pp. 1 ff.; Elbogen, *op. cit.*, p. 176). In the *J.E.*, vol. VI, pp. 136 f., the view is given that the *Haftaroth* for the feast days were first determined in the middle of the second century, and that there followed *Haftaroth* for the special sabbaths and later still those for ordinary sabbaths only a few of which were fixed). Levertoff claims that Deutero-Isaiah was the source of the prophetic lessons for the period following Elul when John the Baptist appeared. According to *J.E.* vol. VI, *ibid.*, Isa. 57:14–58:14 was a *Haftarah* for the Day of Atonement in the second century when the *Haftaroth* for the various festivals were formally fixed and was probably also on this supposition the *Haftarah* for the same day in the first century, but this is conjectural. We cannot be as certain as Levertoff assumes as to the exact *Haftaroth* used in the first century. (Thus the use of Isa. 40–61 for the *Haftaroth* of consolation on the sabbaths extending from the ninth of Ab to the Day of Atonement is later than the early first century according to Thackeray, *The Septuagint and Jewish Worship* (1923), p. 83. Unfortunately Mann's work, cited frequently above, was not completed.)

The other problem (2) demands an answer equally unfavourable to Levertoff. He claims, as we saw, that John applied to himself a passage which was one of the current *Haftaroth*, namely Isa. 40:3. Assuming that we know that Isa. 40:3 was a *Haftarah*, is this position of Levertoff's likely? One thing we may safely assume, that the name, the Baptist, by which John came to be known probably affords the best clue to what historically was most noteworthy about his activity, namely, his emphasis on baptism.[109] With this agrees the contrast found in

---

[108] Ogg, *Chronology of the Public Ministry of Jesus* (1940), p. 300.
[109] Lohmeyer, *Das Evangelium des Markus* (1937), p. 13.

Mark and Q between his baptism which was with water and that of the coming
One which was to be with Holy Spirit and fire.[110] Note, however, that the
emphasis supplied by the quotation from Isa. 40:3 is not upon the ministry of
baptism at all, so much as upon the significance of John as an eschatological
figure, the forerunner of Christ. Moreover this emphasis, as Dibelius has shown,
is the outcome of the Church's reflection on the meaning of the Baptist's
ministry: the presentation of John in all the Four Gospels is coloured by the
desire to clarify the mutual relationship of John and Jesus. It was this desire that
probably occasioned the juxtaposition of Isa. 40:3 with the ministry of John:
it supplied scriptural support from the Church's understanding of John the
Baptist as the forerunner of Jesus, the beginning of the Gospel.[111] Levertoff
fails to perceive that Isa. 40:3 does not really illumine John's understanding
of his own ministry; historically it was possibly not particularly relevant to that
ministry; rather does it reflect the understanding of it which the early Church
came to cherish. We may further suggest that if, as Levertoff holds, John saw
a direct connection between his activity and the Synagogue lectionary, he had
to hand a most pertinent quotation from Ezek. 36:25 which was used in the
liturgy of the Day of Atonement; and which reads: 'Then will I sprinkle clean
water upon you and ye shall be clean.'[112] This rather than Isa. 40:3 we may
surmise would have been used by John were he himself responsible for any
quotation from Scripture. One thing is indeed suggested by our treatment
of John, that the tradition probably came to be formulated under the impact
of the Scripture reading in the Church and its exegesis. Thus the emphasis on the
location of John's baptism in the desert probably reflects the influence of Isa.
40:3;[113] and Lohmeyer[114] sees the same influence at work in the statement in
Mark 1:5 that 'there went out unto him all the land of Judaea, and they of
Jerusalem', which is further expanded in Matt. 3:5; this insertion was dictated
by the necessity to fulfil Isa. 48:20, and 52:11. In Mark the account of the
Baptist's ministry is largely derived from a traditional exegesis of Scripture,
what Lohmeyer calls 'ein altes Stück urchristlicher Schrifttheologie', and
although Matthew, like Luke, has redressed this by giving the actual teaching
of John as presented in Q, he too has retained this exegetical matter. This is the
element of truth in Levertoff's position, that the 'lectionary' activity of the
Church—not as he thinks, however, of the Synagogue—has left its mark on
the tradition. But his attempt to determine the chronology and character of
John's ministry by means of the synagogal lectionary must be rejected.[115]

He carries the same method through to Matt. 17:1-13, but it is only by the

[110] Mark 1:8 and parallels.
[111] *Die Urchristliche Überlieferung von Johannes dem Taufer* (1911), p. 47.
[112] See Abrahams, *Studies in Pharisaism and the Gospels*, second series, p. 35; Danby,
The Mishnah, p. 172.
[113] Bultmann, *Geschichte der Synoptischen Tradition*, p. 261.
[114] *Op. cit.*, p. 15.
[115] New light on the *Schrifttheologie* of the early Church has probably been supplied

same kind of violence to his sources that he manages to do this. We need not further examine his position in any detail. Let us note only one point by way of illustration. According to Levertoff behind the Sermon on the Mount we are to see the influence of the Synagogue lectionary such as we saw behind the account of the Baptist's ministry; if we understand him aright he would seem to connect the 'Sermon' with the lections of the period around about Tabernacles; but his argument really demands that the Sermon on the Mount which contains what we may be allowed to call 'the New Law' should be connected with Pentecost, which was the festival of the giving of the Law, as we argued above.

---

by the Qumrân Scrolls; see K. Stendahl, *The School of Matthew*, Uppsala, 1954; on Matt. 3:3 f., see pp. 47 ff. If Stendahl is correct in tracing in parts of Matthew a method of Biblical interpretation similar to that found in the DSS, this perhaps gives added force to our suggestion above that the textual works in *D S Isa. may* be relevant to our understanding of New Testament manuscripts. On this see further my forthcoming work on the Sermon on the Mount; Carrington has published *According to Mark: a running commentary on the oldest Gospel*, Cambridge, 1960, in which he applies his calendrical theory exegetically and considers many of the above criticisms.

V

THE DEAD SEA SCROLLS
AND CHRISTIAN ORIGINS

There is an old saying that a new broom sweeps clean. Certain it is that the Dead Sea Scrolls, although old, are new; and that they have been claimed to sweep the musty, cobwebby house of New Testament scholarship very clean. But let me begin by claiming that because the Dead Sea Scrolls are new, and insufficiently examined and assessed, their significance for New Testament studies can be easily exaggerated. The attention being paid to them at the moment is very reminiscent of the spate of books and articles which the publication, for example, of the *Didache* called forth at the end of the last century. Today it is safe to assert that ninety-nine per cent of those books and articles have long been forgotten; and the New Testament teacher now usually merely refers in passing to what was once urged to be a quite revolutionary document. Time not only heals wounds but tames, and sometimes re-inters, revolutionary documents. It behoves us, therefore, not to rush to conclusions about the Scrolls.

On the other hand, there is also another equally grave danger—the danger born of an excess of caution. It is this, it seems to me, that lies behind the slight reaction toward underestimating the Scrolls which now appears in some quarters. An excellent example of this emerges in Kingsley Barrett's footnote to his very important work on the Fourth Gospel. He writes: 'It is now much clearer than it was when I completed the manuscript of this book [on 31 December 1951] that . . . the Dead Sea Scrolls call for consideration as part of the background of the Fourth Gospel. I regret that I have not been able to incorporate such consideration, but it would not have substantially modified my work.'[1] This last sentence is hardly credible. I do not doubt but that a study of the Dead Sea Scrolls might have substantially modified parts of Barrett's treatment. Similarly, it is not enough cautiously to claim that all the parallels between the Scrolls and the New Testament can be explained in terms of their common dependence on the Old Testament and on Judaism; the parallels cannot be so easily dismissed. We have, therefore, to guard against an excess of enthusiasm and an excess of caution; against claiming too much and claiming too little. I shall suggest that the Scrolls are more important than some scholars have grudgingly admitted and less revolutionary than has been claimed by others.

In the notes which follow I shall assume the fascinating account of the discovery and contents of the material which Professor Millar Burrows and others have given us, and merely seek to assess its relation to the New Testament, without undue elaboration, as it presents itself to me. In the first part I shall discuss the way in which the Dead Sea Scrolls greatly enrich our understanding of the background of the New Testament. From this point of view the significance of the Scrolls can hardly be exaggerated. Let me suggest the following points.

The Problem of Sources for the New Testament

First, the Scrolls reopen the problem of the sources of the New Testament. The documents of the New Testament were written in Greek, or more accurately, in *Koinê* Greek. In one sense this is far easier to translate and to understand than classical Greek, because it is simpler. But this simplicity is altogether deceptive; and, in another sense, it is far more difficult fully to appreciate and even to translate New Testament Greek than classical. This is mainly because so often, while the vocabulary of the New Testament is Greek, its idiom and inner substance is Semitic or at least Septuagintal. This fact has led during the present century to all sorts of theories to account for these Semitisms. These theories were particularly

[1] C. K. Barrett, *The Gospel According to Saint John*, London, 1955, p. viii, note 1; also p. 33, n. 3.

associated with the distinguished American scholar, Professor C. C. Torrey of Yale. Torrey went so far as to suggest that all the Four Gospels, as well as Acts 1 to 15, were originally written in Aramaic.[2] Similarly C. F. Burney of Oxford urged an Aramaic original for the Fourth Gospel,[3] and, in particular, DeZwaan and others [4] have traced written Aramaic sources in various parts of Acts, especially in Acts 1 to 5. The point to emphasize is that it is in part on the assumption of the early nature of these chapters that it has been possible to reconstruct the early Christian preaching, the isolation of which has been one of the most fructifying forces in recent New Testament scholarship.[5]

But how much credence should we place upon theories of Aramaic sources underlying the Gospels and Acts? Some scholars rejected these theories with something like contempt, because we had no contemporary Aramaic or Hebrew sources which would make it natural or reasonable for us to assume that there could be such Christian sources. Edgar J. Goodspeed is typical. I quote from his *New Solutions of New Testament Problems*.[6]

> In weighing the arguments of Professor Torrey [he writes] one is hampered by the difficulty of finding any Hebrew or Aramaic documents definitely referable to the first century with which to compare the supposed Hebrew or Aramaic manners of speech in the Gospels and Acts. The fact is there is next to nothing in the way of contemporary written Semitic materials by which to test the Hebrew or Aramaic documents postulated by Professor Torrey. . . .
>
> Looking broadly at early Christian history, it would seem that it was the impact of the Christian movement upon Greek life that resulted in the literary precipitate we find in early Christian literature. That Christianity had found literary expression in Aramaic or Hebrew is by no means a matter of course. We should have first to show that Aramaic or Hebrew populations of the time had a bent for literary expression. But it is precisely here that evidence is strikingly meagre. Over against the steadily rising tide of Greek literary expression of Christianity, Palestinian Judaism and Christianity are all but mute.

[2] For details on this and other problems, see C. C. Torrey, *The Four Gospels: A New Translation*, 1933; 'The Composition and Date of Acts,' *Harvard Theological Studies*, 1916.

[3] C. F. Burney, *The Aramaic Origins of the Fourth Gospel*, Oxford, 1922.

[4] See J. Dupont, *Les Problèmes du Livre des Actes*, Louvain, 1950.

[5] See especially C. H. Dodd, *The Apostolic Preaching and Its Developments*, Chicago, 1936.

[6] Chicago, 1927, pp. 69–70.

According to Goodspeed there is no evidence that Palestinian Aramaic-speaking people in the first century were a reading people, nor had they the instinct for contemporary historical composition. Professor Albright made the same point as late as 1949.[7] He emphasized that there was no trace of an Aramaic literary tradition between the early Hellenistic period and the second century A.D. In such a condition it was exceedingly unlikely that Aramaic-speaking Christians should reveal a strong literary instinct, and the search for Aramaic sources to the New Testament would appear to be a wild goose chase.

It is here that the Dead Sea Scrolls (DSS) introduce a new factor. We now do have literature in Hebrew and Aramaic produced by a community which was alive in the time of Jesus. This must not be exaggerated, because the Hebrew texts discovered far exceed the Aramaic ones in number and extent. Nevertheless, the DSS do supply us with greater justification for thinking that early Aramaic-speaking Christians lived in a milieu where there was far more literary awareness than Goodspeed and others have allowed. I cannot enlarge on this here, but it is odd how at a moment when the source criticism of the New Testament is, in some quarters at least, under a cloud,[8] the DSS should have made the practice of source criticism far more reasonable.

Matters of Grammar and Vocabulary

Let us now go on to the second point, Apart from its relation to the source criticism of the New Testament, the new sources provide us with material which may have been familiar to some early Christians and which is therefore highly pertinent to the interpretation of what they wrote. In two ways we may note their helpfulness in detailed interpretation. First, in matters of *grammar*. The DSS supply us with much new material in the light of which we can test the alleged Semitisms of the New Testament.

[7] The problem is illuminated by W. F. Albright in his essay, 'Recent Discoveries in Palestine and the Gospel of St. John,' in *The Background of the New Testament and Its Eschatology*, ed. by W. D. Davies and D. Daube, Cambridge, 1956.

[8] In particular Austin Farrer of Oxford has rebelled against it in his many works; cf. *Studies in the Gospels*, ed. by D. E. Nineham, Oxford, 1955, pp. 55 ff.

An example will illustrate this. In Rom. 12 Paul uses the Greek participle to express the imperative. The slight parallels to this usage in the Greek papyri are not convincing. In the Mishnah and other post-Christian Hebrew sources, however, the participle is regularly used as an imperative. Daube, therefore, suggested that Paul was drawing upon Hebrew or Rabbinic codal material in Rom. 12.[9] But he could not prove this conclusively because the imperative participle was post-Christian, as far as we knew. But in the DSS we find the participle on its way, at least, to being used as an imperative. They reveal Hebrew at a stage between Classical Hebrew and Mishnaic Hebrew, and supply something like a proof of a theory which previously could at best be only a conjecture.[10]

But secondly, the *vocabulary* of the New Testament is in many ways illuminated by the Scrolls. To illustrate this in detail would take too long, we refer briefly only to a few examples. The vocabulary of the Fourth Gospel has been particularly illuminated by the DSS.[11] Phrases like 'Eternal Life', for example, which have been often taken to point directly to a Hellenistic and even Platonic milieu, are now seen to be perfectly compatible with Hebrew or Palestinian circles. See the following passages:

John 17:3	CDC 3:20 has the exact phrase
And this is life eternal	'eternal life'.
that they know thee	DSD 2:3 has 'eternal knowledge'.
the only true God:	DSD 9:3-4 'eternal truth'.
John 8:12	DSD 3:7 'the light of life'.
I am the light of the world.	

So, too, when we turn to the Synoptics. For example, in Mark 10 we have Jesus' discussion of divorce where He declares that monogamy is, as it were, part of the order of creation itself. 'But from the beginning of the creation male and female made he them' (10:6). As Teicher has recently pointed out, the Sect's literature provides us with an almost exact counterpart of the Greek of Mark 10:6 in Hebrew. In CDC 4:21 we have the phrase, 'the principle of nature

[9] Daube's work is now published on pp. 90 ff. of his *The New Testament and Rabbinic Judaism*, The Jordan Lectures, London, 1956.

[10] See my *Paul and Rabbinic Judaism*, New York, 2nd ed. 1955, pp. 329, 367.

[11] Consult F. M. Braun, 'L'arrière fond judaïque du quatrième évangile et la Communauté de l'Alliance', Revue Biblique, No. 1, January 1955, pp. 511 ff.

is: a male and female He created them'. Mark 10:6 merely seems to reproduce in Greek what is expressed in Hebrew in CDC 4:21, and in both passages the same appeal is made, implicitly at least, to Gen. 1:27. For completeness we may also further point out that the vocabulary of Paul, for example, and particularly the Pauline use of the term 'flesh', is much illuminated by the Scrolls.[12]

IDEOLOGY

Thirdly, passing beyond matters of grammar and vocabulary, we find that much in the *theology* or, more loosely, the *ideology* of the New Testament is paralleled in the DSS. This is to be expected, because the Scrolls are the literary products of a community expecting its Messiahs soon, and the New Testament the product of one looking both backwards to a Messiah who had come and forward to His coming again. In the terms in which the Sect thinks of itself we can find a close parallel to the way in which the early Church thought of itself.[13]

Just as the early Church did, so did the Qumrân Sect apply to itself and to its leaders various apocalyptic, eschatological Scriptures.[14] Thus the Qumrân community is conceived as the faithful remnant, the true Israel, the community of the New Covenant; it seems to have experienced a divine sprinkling with cleansing water, the outpouring of a new Spirit—a kind of baptism of water and the Spirit. The community looked forward to a new Jerusalem and a new temple, where acceptable sacrifices would be offered by an acceptable priesthood. In countless ways the thought of the Sect helps us to understand anew and better how early Christians came to think of themselves as they did.[15]

To turn to another field, in *The War of the Sons of Light and the Sons of Darkness* we find an irreconcilable opposition between the

[12] K. G. Kuhn, *Zeitschrift für Theologie und Kirche*, 1952, pp. 200 ff. For further references see *Paul and Rabbinic Judaism*, 2nd ed., p. 325; and pp. 148 ff. below.

[13] Matthew Black of St. Andrews has paid particular attention to this in unpublished papers.

[14] C. H. Dodd, *According to the Scriptures*, Charles Scribner's Sons, 1953.

[15] A clear and careful statement is given by James Muilenberg in 'The Significance of the Scrolls', in *Union Seminary Quarterly Review*, vol. XI, No. 3, March 1956; pp. 6 f. especially for our purpose.

darkness and the light: the sons of men are divided as they belong to either of these two forces. The same antithesis appears in DSD 3:13 through 4:26, a section which gives us in a brief compass the theology of the Sect. A comparison of this with the Fourth Gospel reveals a striking similarity. In John (12:36) Christians also are the sons of light, and the dualism of the Scrolls finds an echo in the Gospel.

DISCIPLINE

Not only in the terms in which the Sect describes itself but also in the *discipline* which it imposed on itself are we recalled to the New Testament. Here again I can only refer to the most striking instance. In Matt. 18:15-17, where we have a discussion of church discipline, we find rules laid down which have almost an exact equivalent in DSD 5:26 ff. The passages are as follows:

DSD 5:25 f.

One shall not speak to his brother in anger or in resentment, or with a stiff neck or a hard heart or a wicked spirit; one shall not hate him in the folly of his heart. In his days he shall reprove him and shall not bring upon him iniquity; and also a man shall not bring against his neighbour a word before the masters without having rebuked him before witnesses.[16]

MATT. 18:15-17

Moreover if thy brother shall trespass against thee, go and tell him his fault between thee and him alone: if he shall hear thee, thou hast gained thy brother. But if he will not hear thee, then take with thee one or two more, that in the mouth of two or three witnesses every word may be established. And if he shall neglect to hear them, tell it unto the church; but if he neglect to hear the church, let him be unto thee as an heathen man and a publican.

As we shall have occasion to note later, much in the practice of the Sect is very similar to what emerged in the early Church.

THE USE OF SCRIPTURE

But now, I come to what is probably both the most striking and the most important point of affinity between the Sect and the New Testament, namely, its *use of Scripture*. Apparently the Teacher of

[16] Millar Burrows' translation. See the note in W. H. Brownlee, *Bulletin of the American Schools of Oriental Research, Supplementary Studies*, Nos. 10-12, New Haven, 1951, p. 23.

Righteousness who led the community at one early period taught a new interpretation of the Scriptures, which gave to his followers an understanding both of their present experiences and of their future role in the purposes of God. This Scriptural interpretation was developed. Somewhere around 63 B.C., perhaps, one of the members of the Sect expounded the Book of Habakkuk as applying to his own day. By 'Chaldeans', he said, Habakkuk really meant Kittim—the name by which the expositor signified the Romans. Again, in Cave Four at Qumrân a leaf containing a short selection of texts from the Old Testament was found. These texts were used as *testimonia*, to refer perhaps to the coming prophet, the Davidic and the Priestly Messiahs, whom the Sect expected. The term used to describe the interpretation carried on by the Sect was *pesher*. To judge from the so-called 'commentary' on Habakkuk, they gave a *pesher* to a whole book or books, i.e., a kind of continuous exegesis. A contemporary application was found or sought for each item in the text.

Now in the New Testament the interpretation of Scripture is a major element. Throughout all its strata there is a constant attempt to set the life, death, and resurrection of Jesus of Nazareth over against the setting of the Old Testament. The method by which this is done has been exhaustively examined by scholars in our time. Rabbinic sources in particular have been exploited to illumine New Testament exposition of the Old. But it seems possible that the closest parallel to New Testament usage is the *pesher* of the Scrolls; the early Church like the Qumrân Sect should be thought of probably, in some of its aspects at least, in terms of a school. To substantiate the similarity between early Christian and Qumrân interpretation would take me too far afield. I shall, therefore, merely refer to the work of Krister Stendahl of Harvard, who has argued that behind the Gospel of Matthew, in particular, there is a school of exegesis very similar to that at Qumrân. The significance of the light thus thrown for us on the early Christian interpretation of Scripture is evident, when we recall that it is the interpretation of Scripture that perhaps supplies us with the best clue to the meaning of primitive Christian thought.[17]

[17] See Dodd, *op cit.*; K. Stendahl, *The School of Matthew*, Uppsala, 1954.

The Problem of Christian Origins

I have thus briefly, and inadequately, indicated how very greatly the Dead Sea Scrolls enrich our understanding of the New Testament in all sorts of ways. The words of Professor W. F. Albright [18] can most certainly be confirmed, that 'perhaps the most important service of the Dead Sea Scrolls will be the demonstration which may be brought from them that John, the Synoptics, St. Paul, and various other books draw from a common reservoir of terminology and ideas which were well known to the Essenes and presumably familiar also to other Jewish sects of the period'.

Nevertheless, I must point out that I have concentrated on the parallels between the DSS and the New Testament, and such concentration may distort and magnify the significance of the DSS. Parallels such as those indicated can be found sometimes in other documents. It must be recalled that we already had before the recent discovery a considerable knowledge of the Essenes, and, in particular, we possessed the *Zadokite Fragments* which had been extensively used in the elucidation of the New Testament by many scholars. Nor have I pointed out differences between the Qumrân material and the New Testament. We have now, therefore, to ask—while fully recognizing that the literary remains of the Sect, which was so like the Early Church in so many ways, are of very great value in illuminating the background of the New Testament—whether they also affect radically our understanding of Christian origins.

The problem of Christian origins may be considered under three heads. First, what was the nature of the matrix within which Christianity arose: do the DSS radically alter our understanding of it? Secondly, how did primitive Christianity develop into the great Church of the second and subsequent centuries: do the DSS illumine the emergence of Catholicism? Thirdly, how did Jesus of Nazareth come to be the object of worship of a universal community, the Church: can the DSS illumine the Christological problem?

I

First, then, do the Scrolls radically alter our understanding of the

[18] *Op. cit.*, p. 169.

Judaism within which Christianity arose? To appreciate the force of this question we have to recall the case urged by George Foot Moore in his classic work, *Judaism in the First Centuries of the Christian Era* (1927). According to him, what we call Judaism remained substantially the same from pre-Christian times, past the Fall of Jerusalem in A.D. 70, which did not affect Judaism fundamentally, down to Mishnaic and Talmudic times. There existed what Moore called a 'normative Judaism' throughout these periods, and this 'normative Judaism' we are to judge by its own specifically Rabbinic sources. Sectarian literature, apocalyptic and other, is not a true indication of the character of this Judaism and is, therefore, largely to be ignored in its understanding. By Judaism before and during and after the first century is meant 'Pharisaic' or 'Rabbinic' Judaism.

Many students had long questioned this position.[19] What the Dead Sea Scrolls have done is not to initiate this questioning but to justify it still further; they have not initiated any revolution in our understanding of first-century Judaism, but they have made the classic position of Moore still more untenable than it was already known to be. In two ways they help to change our estimate of first-century Judaism.

First, they supply added proof to the view that Judaism before A.D. 70 was very different from the developed Rabbinic Judaism of Jamnia and subsequent periods. It was far more variegated. They reveal more clearly to us a virile sect which must have had considerable influence on Judaism before A.D. 70. Secondly, and more important, the Scrolls further attest that Judaism was not merely very divided in the time of Jesus, but also far more open to outside influences than Moore allowed. In short, they help further to destroy the view that pre-Christian Judaism was almost a monolithic structure. I discussed the nature of Judaism in the first century before the discoveries of the Scrolls in 1948, when I argued against too rigid a separation between Hellenism and Judaism in the first century. The same position was strongly maintained by Albright, and Daube

---

[19] We have now the fascinating treatment by E. R. Goodenough, *Jewish Symbols in the Greco-Roman Period*, Bollingen Series, New York, 1953, and an unpublished paper by Morton Smith on 'The Simultaneous Hellenization and Judaization of Palestine'.

has recently argued that even Rabbinic methods of exegesis were Hellenistic in origin.[20]

Now this approach to first-century Judaism is confirmed to the hilt by the Dead Sea Scrolls. It is tempting to see in the Qumrân Sect the representative of a syncretistic Judaism: was it a Hellenized Judaism? Scholars have been sharply divided at this point. The problem revolves chiefly around the concept of *gnosis* in the DSS. According to some, this points to a pre-Christian Jewish Gnosticism which can be compared with Hellenistic Gnosticism. I myself have argued against the application of the term 'Gnosticism' to the beliefs of the Sect on several grounds, which I cannot here enumerate.[21] Nevertheless, one has to agree, I think, that terms with a 'gnostic connotation—terms which we had previously been tempted to connect at once with Hellenistic movements—here appear in Hebrew documents.

To quote one obvious example, the term *mustêrion* has constantly in the past been taken to indicate Hellenistic, i.e., specifically extra-Palestinian influences. It now appears in Hebrew dress, used very frequently by this Sect. Indeed one of the finds published by Barthélemy and Milik in *Discoveries in the Judaean Desert I, Qumrân Cave I*, is entitled *The Book of Mysteries* (p. 102), which speaks for itself.

The Scrolls, therefore, have brought a much stronger light to bear on Judaism in the first century. While they have not perhaps revealed anything strictly new, at least they have brought into prominence elements in the first-century scene which hitherto could be easily overlooked. For example, it has been frequently emphasized that, by the first century, experience of the Spirit was regarded as almost extinct in Judaism, the activity of the Spirit having ceased with the last of the Old Testament prophets.[22] We now see that there were groups in first-century Judaism which had a vivid awareness of the Spirit, over against which the 'spiritual' outbursts of song in Luke 1 and 2 become more and more understandable. The Qumrân Sect placed great emphasis on the Spirit.

[20] W. D. Davies, *op. cit.*, 1 ff. and additional note, p. 354 on p. 16 for bibliographical details.

[21] See below, pp. 119 ff.

[22] W. D. Davies, *Paul and Rabbinic Judaism*,[2] pp. 208 ff; also pp. 145 ff. below.

In particular, the Scrolls have further shown that much that has been labelled Hellenistic may well have been native to Judaism. The results of this in New Testament studies are manifold, particularly in the Fourth Gospel and possibly, through perhaps not to the same extent, in Paul, and, for other reasons, in Matthew. The Semitism of most of the New Testament is more than ever established, as long as we recall that possibly this Semitism itself has been partially Hellenized and Persianized; and with this, the customary dating of many New Testament documents falls to be re-examined, albeit with due care.[23]

How shall we assess all this? Let me express it roughly as follows. The New Testament in modern scholarship has been approached along four main highways—from Hellenism, from the Old Testament, from Apocalyptic, from Rabbinism. The Essenes were known, and a few scholars had approached Christianity as if it were Essenism 'which had succeeded on a broad scale'; but for most scholars up till now, Essenism remained a little insignificant lane along which we might approach Christian origins. The Scrolls seem to justify the claim that this little lane has become a highway. For some parts of the New Testament, indeed, the conceptual climate of the Sect may provide the best approach. This is particularly true, possibly, of Matthew and John.[24]

II

Let me move to another problem of Christian origins. How can we account for the emergence at so early a date of the fully developed hierarchical system of the Catholic Church? In other words, how did the Christian community come to develop its later rigid constitution?

Broadly speaking, there are two classic answers to these questions. Protestants have tended, on the whole, since the time of Sohm, to

[23] W. F. Albright claims that 'In general, we can already say emphatically that there is no longer any solid basis for dating *any* book of the New Testament after about A.D. 80, two full generations before the date between 130 and 150 given by the more radical New Testament critics of today.' *Recent Discoveries in Bible Lands*, New York, 1955, p. 136.

[24] W. F. Albright, in *The Background of the New Testament and Its Eschatology* (*op. cit.*).

think of the primitive Christian community as a loosely knit fellowship of the Spirit, a kind of glorified company of enthusiasts, which,
to use a phrase made familiar by President John Mackay, was filled
with ardour but had little sense of order. From this pristine purity
and freedom and spirituality it fell into the neo-legalism of the
second century, and thus radically departed from its original character
as a spiritual society; it ceased to be an organism and became an
organization. On the other hand, Catholic scholars, of Roman and
other persuasions, have always maintained that order as well as
ardour existed in the Church from the beginning, the Church being
from the first an apostolate, a creed, an institution.[25]

The bearing of the Dead Sea Scrolls on the problem arises from a
very simple fact: namely, that so much of the structure of the Catholic
Church finds a parallel in the Sect that the question is inevitable
whether the organization of the Church has been directly influenced
by the Sect, and whether, indeed, it is the influence of the Sect that
supplies us with a clue to much of the organizational development of
the Church.

The chief parallels are clear. Just as in the Church participation in
the Eucharist became the final stage in the initiation of a person into
the fellowship, so in the Sect the final term of initiation was participation in a sacred meal. Baptismal rites were practised by both the
Church and the Sect. The liturgical practices which the Church later
came to adopt bear many close parallels with those of the Sect; for
example, the *Didache* urges prayer three times a day as do the DSS.
It has been argued that the community of goods practised by the
early Church, as described in Acts, finds its origin and exact parallel
in the same practice among the Essenes. In the Essene milieu, the
Christian ideal of poverty naturally took the form of a community
of goods. The Christian emphasis on hospitality in Matthew 10,
and elsewhere, is like that of the Essenes; and the emergence of
celibacy in the Church, which is difficult to understand against the
background of what Moore called 'normative' Judaism, becomes
more understandable against the background of a semi-monastic
Essenism.

These parallels, and there are others, have been strongly urged by

[25] For a survey and bibliography, see Chap. 9, pp. 199 ff. below.

Catholic writers especially.[26] Although they are almost all, on examination, not as exact as appears on the surface, nevertheless they seem to me persuasive enough to justify the question whether at some stage the influence of the Sect penetrated the Church and gave to it a strong organizational impulse. A point of particular note is that the Sect supplies us with just that combination of order and ardour, Law and Spirit, which hitherto we had found wanting in Judaism, and had concluded to be unique in the early Church.

But, we may now ask, at what stage did this influence make itself felt? How conjectural and how very uncertain is the relation of the Essene sectarians to the early Church appears at this point. Some have claimed that John the Baptist, who can hardly have failed to be familiar with the sectarians, had at one time been a member of the Sect, so that sectarian influences were already at work during the ministry of Jesus Himself.[27] On the other hand, Cullmann, who tends to belittle the role of John the Baptist at this point, has the suggestion that the Hellenists in the early chapters of Acts, who have usually been regarded as Greeks or more probably as Greek-speaking Jews, were closely related to the Qumrân Sectarians, so that from the earliest days of the Church they were a very considerable factor in its evolution.[28] At the other extreme to Cullmann's theory, which I find very difficult to accept, we have that of Schoeps that it was the primitive Palestinian Ebionite Christians who were open to Essene influences.[29] Thus, whereas Cullmann tenuously connects the *Hellenistai* with influences similar to those at Qumrân, Schoeps connects their opponents, the *Hebraioi*, with the Qumrân community. A third possibility is that it was after the collapse of Qumrân about A.D. 68 that incipient Catholicism crept into the Christian movement.

I mention these views to show how uncertain the whole problem is. It does seem, however, that at some point the Sect may have had a real influence on the form which Christianity assumed. Some

[26] See especially J. Schmitt, 'Sacerdoce judaïque et hiérarchie ecclésiale dans les premières communautés palestiniennes', in *Revue des Sciences Religieuses*, July 1955, pp. 250 ff.; J. Daniélou, 'La Communauté de Qumrân et l'organisation de l'Eglise ancienne', in *Revue d'histoire et de philosophie religieuses*, t. XXXV, 1955, pp. 104–116.

[27] W. H. Brownlee, in *Interpretation*, vol. IX, 1955, pp. 71 ff.

[28] *Journal of Biblical Literature*, vol. LXXIV, Pt. IV, December 1955, pp. 213 ff.

[29] His latest treatments are in *Urgemeinde, Judenchristentum, Gnosis*, Tübingen, 1956.

scholars have pointed to a radical opposition between the organization of the later Church and the Qumrân Sect.[30] The Church, it is claimed, rejected the Jewish sacrificial system and with it the Levitical conception of priesthood. On the other hand the Qumrân Sect preserved the categories of priests and Levites and looked forward to the restoration of a new Jerusalem with a purified sacrificial system. This, I think, is to oversimplify the matter. The Church did not simply take over neat the Levitical forms of the Sect, but the various degrees of ministries that it came to recognize, e.g., the distinction between cleric and lay, may perhaps go back to the distinctions of the Sect.

But lest we exaggerate the significance of the DSS as such at this point, we have to bear in mind that as far back as 1912[31] use was made of the *Zadokite Fragments* in this connection by Jeremias. Moreover, we have also to recognize that other Jewish institutions played their part in the evolution of Church order, notably the Synagogue.[32] It does seem to me, however, not unlikely that Essene influences played their part in the emergence of Catholicism: this the DSS have reinforced. They are not the only influences that did so, but in any case the possible importance of the Sect for understanding the organizational development of the Church cannot be ignored, and will have to be considered in future discussions of early Church order.[33]

III

Albert Schweitzer wrote as follows: 'The great and still undischarged task which confronts those engaged in the historical study of primitive Christianity is to explain how the teaching of Jesus developed into the early Greek Theology . . .'[34] In other words,

[30] F. F. Bruce, 'Qumrân and Early Christianity', in *New Testament Studies*, vol. No. 3, February 1956, pp. 187 f.; A. N. Wilder, in *The New Republic*, 9 April 1956, p. 17a.

[31] See J. Daniélou, *op. cit.*

[32] See, for example, W. D. Davies, *op. cit.* The possibilities of synagogal influence on Church organization are numerous. For example, A. Guillaume has argued that the Christian *episkopos* derives from the synagogal *chazan*.

[33] I here find myself in full agreement with F. M. Cross, Jr., in *The New Republic* (*op. cit.*), p. 19b. 'They [the Scrolls] will aid us in recovering more fully the primitive meaning of Christian institutions.'

[34] *Paul and His Interpreters*, Eng. Trans., London, 1912, p. v.

what was the pathway leading from Jesus to the *History of Dogma*? Do the Dead Sea Scrolls radically influence our understanding at this point, apart from supplying us with an enriched general background to which we have already referred? At this point let me retrace my steps.

I pointed out above that the claim has been made that there is a real parallel to the two Sacraments of the Church, Baptism and the Eucharist, in the lustrations and meals of Qumrân. Since these two Sacraments are at the heart of Christianity from the first, then if the Qumrân Sect has exerted an influence here, it has indeed entered into the very lifeblood of Christianity. But let us look at the Sacraments more closely.

First, let us recall the process of admission into the Sect. He who desired to enter the community had first to be inspected by the *mebaqqer* (Superintendent), whom many have thought corresponds to the Christian bishop.[35] If satisfactory in morals and intelligence, the candidate was admitted for instruction for one year. At the end of this period he was presented to the community, which deliberated over his case. If suitable, he was then granted admission, on which he was allowed to undergo lustrations and to participate in the community of goods. At the end of yet another year a further examinaton was held. Should this be favourable (DSD 6:13-23), the candidate was inscribed among the brethren and admitted to the common meal. Josephus adds a few details such as that a white vestment was given to the initiate and that fearful vows of love to the brethren and hate to those outside accompanied the admission.

With minor variations this recalls vividly the later initiation of Christians into the Church. Baptism, the Eucharist, the white vestments, the oaths reappear in the practice of the Church. Is Christian baptism, however, a real parallel to that practised in the Sect? Apart from the very many other possibilities of explaining the emergence of Christian baptism, it must be pointed out that the Sect, as far as we know, practised ritual lustrations and not a single rite of initiation, such as the Church did. Christian baptism by its

---

[35] For references see J. Schmitt, *op. cit.*, p. 257, 257 n. 2. Those who accept the position include Jeremias, Benoit, Kuhn, and now Albright (*Recent Discoveries in Bible Lands*, pp. 134 f.).

nature is a 'once and for all' event, not one lustration among others; moreover, it was not one among other initiatory acts but *the one act* of initiation. It is thus precarious to see in baptism a parallel to the Essene practice; this is especially so because of the Christological significance of Christian baptism.

Christian baptism, while it is rooted in the history of religion, and has, therefore, affinities with various aspects of first-century Judaism, nevertheless is something new.

> The members of the *ekklesia* are consecrated neither through rites of lustration, prescribed by the law, nor by an inner, moral purification of the soul, for which the outward rites are but the symbol. The essential consecration of the people of God is brought about once for all, through the expiatory death of Jesus (which is His baptism), His own initiation into heavenly Lordship. By baptism in the name of Jesus, this consecration by grace is applied to the individual believer, who is initiated to be a member of the church of God on earth, and to whom the risen Lord gives the gift of the Holy Spirit.[36]

There is no real parallel in the Scrolls to Christian baptism, because they lack any real counterpart to the dying and rising with Christ which Paul and other early Christians took to be the essence of baptism.

The same is the case, on examination, with the parallel drawn between the Eucharist and the sacred meal of the Sect. As we saw, participation in a sacred meal was the final term in the initiation into the Qumrân Sect, as was participation in the Eucharist the final stage of initiation into the Christian community. Moreover the meals described in the DSS do seem to offer *formally* perhaps the nearest parallel we have to the Eucharist. The following elements are common to the meal of the Sect and to the Eucharist: the elements of the bread and wine, the Prayers of Thanksgiving, the arm stretched forth in benediction. Obviously the meals of the Essenes were sacred or religious, and this would explain how in Jewish Christian churches there was a natural connection between the Eucharist and the common meal.

But there are again certain basic points to remember. Sacred meals were not peculiar to Essenes within Judaism, and the Essene meals

---

[36] N. A. Dahl, 'Interpretationes', in *Norsk teologisk tidsskrift* (vol. 56, 1–2), Oslo, 1955.

may have been derivative. More important, Daniélou [37] has urged strongly that, while the Essene meal was merely religious, the Eucharistic meal in the early Church became a cultic one. Indeed, one of the marks of Essenism as we find it in the Scrolls was precisely the absence of any *cultic* acts (for which was substituted, for the present evil time, the praise of the lips). Thus, even if the Church had borrowed the outward form of the eucharistic rite from the Essenes, it poured into it a sacramental content which was rooted in the Person of Christ Himself, who Himself transformed a religious meal into a sacramental one.

The description of the Messianic meal in the texts contains no reference to a broken body or to blood shed forth. Here is the essential difference between the Essene meal and the Eucharist. The Sect looked forward to Messiahs to come. The Church looked back to One who had come, but had suffered and died, and was now alive for evermore and to return. Thus the Christology of the early Church has transformed the affinities that its Eucharistic meal may have had with the Essene repast. Moreover, we must not forget that the connection of the Eucharist with the other contemporary Jewish meals has still to be considered.

In the light of the Sacraments, are we to conclude that the Messianic ideas of the Sect afford us no clue to the ultimate problem of Christian origins—the fact of Christ? Let us recall that the Sect was in many ways like the Church. Like the Church it believed that the appointed time for God's final intervention in human history had appeared. It had used very much the same passages as did the Church to expound to itself the meaning of its experience. Does its strictly Messianic expectation illumine the New Testament?

Here we enter a maze of theories. Up till the publication of Barthélemy and Milik's edition of *Discoveries in the Judaean Desert: Qumrân I*,[38] there was only one passage in the newly discovered texts which explicitly referred to a Messiah. This particular text in DSD 9:10–11 constituted a great problem. It reads thus: 'And they shall not depart from the whole counsel of the Torah to walk in all their hardness of heart but they shall be ruled by the first laws with which

[37] *Op. cit.*
[38] Oxford, 1955.

the men of the community began to be disciplined until the coming of a Prophet and the Messiahs of Israel and Aaron.'

What do the terms 'Messiahs of Israel and Aaron' mean? The many answers given to this question need not detain us. Fortunately the more recently published material makes it more or less certain that the Sect did in part look forward to two Messiahs. This becomes clear in what is already a famous passage, giving an ideal description of the whole of the new Israel at the end enjoying the eschatological or Messianic banquet:

> This is the sitting of the distinguished men invited to the communal council. When God begets [sic!] the Messiah with them the priest will come as head over all the congregation of Israel and all the fathers of the sons of Aaron, the priests who are invited to the feast . . ., and they shall take their place, each according to his rank. And afterward shall enter the Messiah of Israel. . . . When they solemnly unite at the communion table or to drink wine, and the communion table is arranged and the wine (mixed) for drinking, no one shall stretch out his hand on the first portion of the bread or of the wine before the (Messiah) priest, for he shall bless the first portion of the bread and wine, and (stretch out) his hand on the bread first of all. Afterwards the Messiah of Israel shall stretch forth his hands on the bread; and (having given a blessing) all the congregation of the community (shall partake) each (according) to his rank. And they shall follow this prescription whenever the meal is arranged, when as many as ten eat together.[39]

Note the presence of two Messiahs; a priestly Messiah of the stock of Aaron, a Levitical Messiah if we may so call him, and a political Messiah, the Messiah of Israel. But this expectation of two Messiahs is not inspired by a hope for a future ideal separation of 'church and state'. The priestly Messiah takes precedence over the political; 'the state' is subordinated to 'the church'.

Now as we have already indicated, one fundamental difference between the Qumrân Sect and the Church was that one looked forward to two Messiahs while the other looked back to Jesus of Nazareth as the Messiah who had come. Does the expectation of the two Messiahs help us to understand Jesus? In one respect, it may be argued that it does not. As Kuhn has urged,[40] the Messiah-

---

[39] Translation by James Muilenberg in *Union Seminary Quarterly Review, op. cit.,* p. 10.

[40] K. G. Kuhn, *New Testament Studies,* vol. I, No. 3, February 1955, pp. 168 ff.

ship of Jesus in the New Testament connects with the more traditional expectations of a single Davidic Messiah than with the expectations of the Scrolls. Nevertheless, later the Church did come to see that Jesus combined in His person the functions divided by the Sect between two Messiahs. Christ came to be regarded in the Church as Priest and King. He is both the Messiah of Aaron and the Messiah of Israel.

There is a further point to notice. In DSD 9:10-11 the Sect is also said to look forward to a figure called 'the Prophet', who was to appear along with the two Messiahs. The expectation of a Prophet reappears time and time again in the New Testament, and the Church came to see in Jesus the Prophet who was to come. Thus Jesus came to combine in a striking manner in His one Person the three persons anticipated by the Sect, and elsewhere. He became for the Church the Prophet, Priest, and King. Like much other literature, therefore, the Scrolls help us still better to place Jesus in His setting in contemporary Judaism.

Can we go further? Do the Scrolls help us to understand better what most scholars have regarded as the uniqueness of the Messiahship of Jesus—that is, His combination in His own Person of the Servant and the Messiah? Do the Scrolls help us to penetrate the mystery of the redemptive suffering of Jesus? As Brownlee and Black have shown, that the Qumrân Sect had pondered over its peculiar mission and destiny in the light of the Book of Daniel and of the Suffering Servant of Deutero-Isaiah is clear. The sectarians regarded themselves as the successors of the 'wise' of Dan. 12:3. Brownlee has urged that the Sect had given a Messianic interpretation to the Servant, and the community as a whole was thought of as having expiatory work (DSD 5:6 ff., 9:3 ff.), but the whole discussion of this problem is still too fluid to supply us with any solid answers. This much, however, is fact, that we have in the Scrolls further evidence at least of certain tentative anticipations of the suffering mission of the Messiah which we later encounter in the New Testament.[41]

[41] For details of W. H. Brownlee's work consult the various bibliographies. A paper by G. Friedrich emphasizes how the DSS illumine the emphasis on the High Priesthood of Christ in Hebrews, see 'Beobachtungen zur messianischen Hohepriesterwartung in den Synoptikern', *Zeitschrift für Theologie und Kirche*, 53, 1956, pp. 265-311.

But here we must stop. These anticipations must not be over-estimated. The measure of their merely anticipatory character can be gauged only when we contrast the Qumrân Community with the Church: the temper of the former, despite much that is congenial, remains far removed from that of the Church. Like the Church, the Sect had heard a voice calling it to the wilderness (Isa. 40:3):

> In the wilderness, prepare ye the way of the Lord,
> Make straight in the desert a highway for our God.

But the voice, at one point, called it to preparation for a Holy War. This is the degree of its distance from the Christian community. We miss in the Sect the concern for the lost, for the 'world'; the land for which it offers propitiation is the 'land of Israel'. The Sect remains a Jewish community: the Church is, in origin, a Jewish community called into being by Christ, and He has made all things new. The difference between the society created by Christ and that untouched by Him leaps to the eye. We have only to read the Gospels to recognize this. Indeed, there is much material to support the view that there may even be polemic in the New Testament against the narrowness of the Sect; but this is a subject in itself.

To sum up, then, the Scrolls make much more clear to us the world into which Jesus came; and the patterns which the early Christian movement assumed, both ecclesiastically and theologically, are thereby illumined in a most enriching manner. But the Scrolls also make more luminously clear the *new* thing which emerged with the coming of Christ, so that they emphasize even while they clarify the mystery of the gospel. As Amos N. Wilder has so well put it in the symposium in *The New Republic*, already referred to, 'The Scrolls add to our understanding of backgrounds and influences but do not revolutionize the basis of Christian doctrine. Christianity as an "episode of human history" must be seen in terms of depth as well as of horizontal links. Here the idea of revelation has its rights.'[42]

---

[42] For the theme, see *The Scrolls and the New Testament*, ed. K. Stendahl, New York, 1957, and F. L. Cross, *The Ancient Library of Qumran and Modern Biblical Studies*, New York, 1958, pp. 146–184; K. G. Kuhn, *Qumran*, RGG., pp. 751–754, forthcoming.

VI

'KNOWLEDGE' IN THE DEAD SEA SCROLLS
AND MATTHEW 11:25-30[1]

Interpreters of Matthew 11:25-30 have fallen roughly into two classes. On the one hand, there are those who have been content to explain the passage solely in the light of the Old Testament,[2] and, on the other, those who have traced in it a common pattern, ultimately deriving from Eastern theosophy, which emerges in Ecclus. 51, and elsewhere, and reappears in Matt. 11:25-30, through the agency of certain primitive Christian *thiasoi* of a 'mystical' type.[3] Not far removed from this is the view that, both on account of style and content, the passage is to be understood in the light of Hellenistic Gnosticism.[4] These different interpretations revolve chiefly around the nature of the *gnosis* revealed in the passage, and we shall here seek to show that the recently discovered Dead Sea Scrolls (DSS), along with the Damascus Fragment (CDC),[5] introduce us to a milieu

[1] I should like to acknowledge the helpfulness of my former colleague Professor W. H. Brownlee in all matters pertaining to the relevant literature on the Dead Sea Scrolls, and in the interpretation of the texts themselves.

[2] So among others, A. H. McNeile, *The Gospel According to St. Matthew*, 1918, p. 166; Vincent Taylor, *Jesus and His Sacrifice*, 1937, p. 37; W. Manson, *Jesus the Messiah*, 1943, pp. 71 f.; C. H. Dodd, *The Interpretation of the Fourth Gospel*, 1953, *ad loc.*; the most recent treatment strongly supports this view, see Julius Schniewind, *Das Evangelium nach Matthäus*, 1950. For a full discussion see also B. S. Easton, *The Gospel According to St. Luke*, 1926. On its relation to 'Wisdom' passages in the New Testament, see W. D. Davies, *Paul and Rabbinic Judaism*, 1948, *ad loc.*

[3] E. Norden, *Agnostos Theos*, 1913, *ad loc.*; also Tomas Arvedson, *Das Mysterium Christi, eine Studie zu Mt. 11:25-30*, Uppsala, 1937.

[4] M. Dibelius, *From Tradition to Gospel*, Eng. Trans., 1935, pp. 279 ff.; R. Bultmann, *Die Geschichte der synoptischen Tradition*², 1931, pp. 171-2.

[5] Except where otherwise stated I have used the translations of W. H. Brownlee, *Bulletin of the American Schools of Oriental Research, Supplementary Studies*, Nos. 10-12, 1951 for DSD and his translation of DSH in *BASOR*, Nos. 112-114 for December 1948 and April 1949; other translations are used as mentioned in the

which throws much light on the *gnosis* concerned. The existence of such a milieu has indeed been long suspected and even recognized but is now, if we accept the dating of the DSS which seems acceptable to most scholars,[6] even more clearly established. The nature of this milieu will appear as we proceed.

But in the first place it is well to mention three points of possible similarity between Matthew and the DSS which make it reasonable for us to seek illumination from these in elucidation of problems in Matthew. Too much weight should not be placed upon them, but they at least supply some justification for our procedure. They are as follows:

1. In DSD v:26–vi:1 there are certain regulations for the treatment of offenders which, as Brownlee has noted, recall unmistakably those in Matt. 18:15–17.[7] It is questionable whether we are to take Matt. 18:15–17 as the words of Jesus. More likely we are to see in them a bit of primitive Church Order which Matthew has incorporated into the tradition.[8] Moreover, since Paul appears to be familiar with somewhat similar regulations, 1 Cor. 5 ff., it is precarious to connect Matthew too closely with the kind of milieu from which the DSS emerged on this ground alone.[9]

---

[6] We cannot here enter into the already vast literature on this question: for this consult H. H. Rowley, *The Zadokite Fragments and The Dead Sea Scrolls*, 1952, where the exhaustive footnotes supply invaluable guidance.

[7] *BASOR*, Supplementary Studies, Nos. 10–12, 1951, p. 23 n. 3.

[8] A. H. McNeile, *op. cit.*, p. 266, although he thinks that some genuine sayings of Jesus lie behind the passage; E. Klostermann, *op. cit., ad loc.*, following Bultmann, *op. cit.*

[9] On the multiplicity of groups in Judaism in our period (even the Pharisees were divided into seven groups) with somewhat similar formulae of admittance and probably of regulation, see Saul Lieberman, *Journal of Biblical Literature*, vol. LXXI, Dec., 1952, pp. 199–206. C. H. Dodd points to the similarity in the ecclesiastical tradition in Paul and Matthew as one example of their dependence on a common and primitive tradition, *Expository Times*, vol. LVIII, 1947, pp. 294 ff. H. Strack-P. Billerbeck, *Kommentar zum Neuen Testament*, I, *ad loc.* suggest that such regulations as are found in Matt. 18:15–17 do not emerge so fixedly in the later Rabbinic sources although their forms are found: were they more typical of the sects than of the more 'normative' Judaism? For the catechesis of sects in Judaism and primitive Christianity, see W. D. Davies, *op. cit.*, pp. 129 ff.

---

text. For the Hebrew texts themselves I have used *The Isaiah Manuscript and the Habakkuk Commentary*, 1950, *The Dead Sea Scrolls of St. Mark's Monastery*, 1951, both edited by Millar Burrows with the assistance of J. C. Trever and W. H. Brownlee, and E. L. Sukenik, *Megilloth Genuzoth*, vol. I, II, Jerusalem, 1948, 1950. For the CDC I used Solomon Schechter, *Fragments of a Zadokite Work*, edited from Hebrew MSS in the Cairo Genizah Collection, Cambridge, 1910.

2. Of all the four gospels Matthew alone employs the term *teleios* and that only twice—in Matt. 5:48 and 19:21. In the DSS the Hebrew equivalent or its cognates occur frequently, and it may be urged that the usage of the DSS illumines that of Matthew. Thus DSD i:13 which reads: 'To direct their strength according to the perfection of His ways' recalls directly Matt. 5:48. So in DSD ii:2 the priests are those 'who walk perfectly in all His ways'. Indeed to walk perfectly in all things is the express aim of the community (DSD i:9, viii:1, 10b, 26, ix:2, 5, 6, 8, 9, 19, x:21): in these passages it is true that perfection is not directly thought of in terms of the *imitatio Dei*: it is rather complete obedience to the Law as understood by the community, a community which is itself designated 'a house of perfection' (DSD viii:9). But always the keeping of the law is itself rooted in the concept of *imitatio Dei*.[10] In several passages degrees of perfection appear to be recognized. Thus DSD v:24 implies that there is a yearly examination to ascertain the degree of perfection achieved: 'And they shall examine their spirit and their deeds, year by year to promote each according to his understanding and the perfection of his way.' (See also DSD ix:2, x:21.) The attainment of 'perfection' envisaged in these passages is clearly a matter of works and yet it is a gift of God (DSD xi:2).

The other passage, Matt. 19:16–23, deals with the story of the rich young man who failed to achieve 'perfection' because he refused to give up his all to the poor. Matthew alone calls the enquirer a *neaniskos*[11] and he alone, as stated, introduces the idea of perfection

[10] See I. Abrahams, *Studies in Pharisaism and the Gospels*, Second Series, pp. 246 f.: H. J. Schoeps again has shown how the concept of perfection in Matt. 5:48 (Luke 6:36 is secondary) connects with the Hebrew *tamim*: see *Aus Frühchristlicher Zeit, Von der 'imitatio Dei' zur Nachfolge Christi*, pp. 286 ff. See also A. Marmorstein, *Studies in Jewish Theology*, 1950, pp. 106 ff.

[11] The term *neaniskos* frequently occurs in the LXX; see E. Hatch and H. A. Redpath, *A Concordance to the Septuagint*, vol. II, where it does not appear at any time to refer to 'novitiate' in the technical sense but merely to youth. So too in 1 John the use of *neaniskos* is probably not technical, see commentaries by A. E. Brooke, *ICC*, and C. H. Dodd, Moffatt Series, *ad loc*. The significant thing in the Matthean passage is the distinction drawn between 'entering the Kingdom', which in Matthew tends to mean 'entering the Church', and being perfect, which, as in the DSS, involves the surrender of wealth to the poor—the poor meaning in the DSS the community itself; while in Matthew it may mean this, see Matt. 5:3, it probably means the literally poor. The 'being perfect' in Matthew would roughly seem to correspond to becoming 'a professed' in the DSS, and the professed were

into the narrative. Now it is noteworthy that in the DSS distinctions are drawn between the novitiates in the community and those who have actually professed membership.[12] The change from the novitiate to full profession coincided with the abandoning of all property, not to the literally poor, but to the community, which, in another sense, constituted the poor.[13] While this obviously cannot be pressed in view of the veneration of the 'Lady Poverty' in many religious circles in the period,[14] it is not impossible that the conception of perfection which breaks through in Matt. 19:21 reflects the same spiritual climate that we find in the DSS.[15]

3. In one passage in Matthew there emerges what may be taken as an esoteric motif which is commonly found in the mysteries and in apocalyptic and also appears, however, in the DSS. Matt. 7:6 reads: 'Give not that which is holy to the dogs neither cast pearls before swine, lest they trample them under their feet, and turn again

[12] See A. Dupont-Sommer, *The Dead Sea Scrolls*, Eng. Trans., 1952, pp. 50 f. In DSD i:11-12 we have regulations dealing with the novitiates; these are to bring 'all their intelligence and their strength and their power into the Community of God': on the other hand, the professed are to submit themselves to it 'in matters of the Law and goods, and rules', DSD v:2. Now the word translated 'power' in DSD i:11 is that which is translated 'goods' in DSD v:2. And although the Hebrew underlying both translations i.e., *hôn*, can mean 'power', see M. Jastrow, *Dictionary of the Talmud, ad loc.*, there is no justification for A. Dupont-Sommer's distinction on the ground of language alone: W. H. Brownlee renders *hôn* by 'property' in both places, so too J. T. Milik: H. E. Del Medico, *Deux Manuscrits Hébreux de la mer morte*, 1951, p. 34 translates *richesses* in i:11 and *la richesse* in v:2. G. Lambert gives *les avoirs* in both places. Nevertheless the distinction pointed out by A. Dupont-Sommer does hold, as appears from DSD v and vi where, although the novitiate does bring his property with him to the community on his entry therein, it is clear that the property is only abandoned to the community after probation, when the novitiate becomes a professed.

[13] See DSH on ii:17 Col. 12:2 ff. On the basis of this J. L. Teicher, *Journal of Jewish Studies*, II, No. 2, 1951, pp. 91 ff. and No. 3, 1951, pp. 115 ff. identifies the sect with Ebionite Christians.

[14] See especially H. J. Schoeps, *Theologie und Geschichte des Judenchristentums*, 1949, pp. 196 ff.

[15] This cannot, however, be pressed. The distinction which Matthew introduces is that between the merely good and the perfect. This, it may be argued, is not that between the novitiate and the professed. Nevertheless, distinctions such as these made in the DSS do perhaps help to illumine that drawn by Matthew.

'perfect'. On the term 'poor' in the Early Church see K. Holl, *Der Kirchenbegriff des Paulus in seinem Verhältnis zu dem der Urgemeinde in Sitzungsberichte der Preussischen Akademie der Wissenschaften*, vol. 53, 1921, pp. 937 ff.: see criticism in R. N. Flew, *Jesus and His Church*, 1938, *ad loc.*

and rend you.' The sentence is omitted in Luke. How is it to be understood in Matthew? There are three possibilities. It may be merely a bit of cautionary *gemara*, i.e., it urges discriminatory caution following on the prohibition of judging in 7:1–5, or again an 'ecclesiastical' addition directed against Gentiles (this would explain Luke's omission of the verse, if he knew it; it might prove distasteful to the readers at which he aimed—the Gentiles),[16] or again it might be merely ironical. This last is unlikely: the deliberateness of the verse is against it. As we shall attempt to prove elsewhere, there is a strong element of *gemara* in Matthew and this verse is undoubtedly such. But what is its purpose? It is probably directed not against the Gentiles or heretics as such but against 'those without' whoever they might be. A parallel emerges in DSD ix:17. Among the other duties enjoined by the wise men upon the community are: 'Further, not to admonish or dispute with the men of the Pit, but to conceal the counsel of the Torah in the midst of men of perversity'—just as Christians in Matt. 6:7 are forbidden to cast the Torah of Jesus before 'swine'. Again in DSD ix:22: 'Let there be eternal hatred toward the men of the Pit in the spirit of secrecy.' The conception of things hidden appears also in DSD viii:12: 'And every matter which was hidden from Israel and is found by a man who seeks, let him not hide it from these out of fear of an apostate spirit.' Here we are almost certainly, to take Israel, as often, if not always, elsewhere in DSD, to refer to the community of the New Covenant which is the true Israel.[17] On the other hand it is possible to take Israel here in its

---

[16] See A. H. McNeile, *op. cit.*, p. 91.

[17] In DSD i:22 f. the meaning of Israel may be doubtful, but in ii:22 it refers to the community, as probably also in iii:24. In v:6 the community is a 'house of truth' in Israel, but in v:5 the community itself is Israel, as in v:22 (so also W. H, Brownlee, *op. cit.*, p. 22 n. 52), v:14 and probably in viii:4, 5, 10a, 12, ix:3; in ix:6 those who walk in perfection are called Israelites (see W. H. Brownlee, *op. cit.*. *ad loc.*), ix:11. In DSH ii:8 the members of the community, if we are to follow W. H. Brownlee, are the children of Israel: but in DSH viii:10 Israel stands for the people as a whole. It is noteworthy that in DSD viii:12 the phrase *beisrā'el* has a superlinear reading *leyaḥad*. W. H. Brownlee translates: 'Now when these things come to pass in Israel to the community' as if *leyaḥad* followed *beisrā'el*. Probably however *leyaḥad* is an interpretative note to explain that Israel here refers to the community as such and not to the whole of the people of Israel, a suggestion made to me by W. H. Brownlee. It should be noted that I. Rabbinowitz in a series of papers read to the Society of Biblical Literature and Exegesis takes 'Israel' throughout to refer to the people as a whole: he does not regard the DSS as emerging from a sect.

usual sense as referring to the people of Israel as a totality, in which case viii:12 means that there are things hidden from Israel, i.e., the whole of the people, which the seekers in the community may discover: their discoveries are to be transmitted to the council of the community. In any case there is an 'esoteric' knowledge in the possession of the community. The spirit of truth enables the members of the community to walk humbly 'in the prudence of all that is discreet according to the truth of the mysteries of knowledge' (DSD vi:6).[18]

Taken separately not one of the above three factors can be deemed to carry much weight: it is only cumulatively and especially in conjunction with the many other parallels to New Testament documents, which the DSS have been shown to offer,[19] that they gain significance and justify the expectation that perhaps passages dealing with 'knowledge' in the DSS can illumine our understanding of Matt. 11:25-30.

II

The emphasis on 'knowledge' in the DSS was pointed out by Dupont-Sommer;[20] and, indeed, it is quite unmistakable. The following is an attempt to classify those passages which deal with knowledge in the DSS:

[18] See below.

[19] K. G. Kuhn, 'Die in Palästina gefundenen hebräischen Texte und das Neue Testament' in Zeitschrift für Theologie und Kirche, 1950, pp. 192–211; W. Grossouw, 'The Dead Sea Scrolls and the New Testament' in Studia Catholica, December, 1951, pp. 289–299, and 1952, p. 1 ff. Some scholars have claimed a Jewish Christian origin for the texts, e.g., J. L. Teicher, Journal of Jewish Studies, II, No. 2, 1951, 91 ff., No. 3, 1951, pp. 115 ff.: the members of the sect were Ebionites, see DSH xii:2 ff.: the teacher of righteousness was Jesus and the Prophet of Untruth none other than Paul. But see W. Baumgartner, Theologische Rundschau, N. F. XIX, 1951, p. 142. R. Eisler identified the Teacher with John the Baptist. The literature on this need not, for our purposes, be recapitulated; see H. H. Rowley, op. cit.; also S. E. Johnson, 'The Jerusalem Church of the Book of Acts and the Community of the Dead Sea Manual of Discipline' in The Scrolls and the New Testament, New York, 1957, pp. 129–142; and K. G. Kuhn, 'Πειρασμός, ἁμαρτία, σάρξ im Neuen Testament und die damit zusammenhangenden Vorstellungen' in Zeitschrift für Theologie und Kirche, 1952, pp. 200 ff.

[20] The Dead Sea Scrolls, Eng. Trans., 1952, pp. 42, 65, n. 1; also, M. Burrows, in Oudtestamentische Studien, VIII, 1950, pp. 168 f.

1. *Passages where da'ath or its cognates simply mean intelligent discernment.*

DSD iii:2

Nor shall his mind [21] (*da'athô*) nor his strength nor his property be brought into the council of the community.

Milik [22] translates *da'athô* as *scientia*. Bo Reicke [23] favours 'inclination', or 'interest', a sense which is preserved in Brownlee's rendering. The meaning is not so much knowledge as capacity or inclination to know or reason. (See Jastrow, *op. cit., ad loc.*: he gives instances where *da'ath* means reason and mind.) G. Lambert gives '*Son savoir*'.

At least in the second occurrence of *da'ath* in the following from DSD ix:17 f. it means 'discernment' or something similar:

But to admonish with true knowledge (*da'ath 'emeth*) and righteous law those who choose the way: each according to his spirit, according to the proper reckoning of the time, guiding them with knowledge (*b°da'ath*) and so instructing them in the mysteries of marvel and of truth.

Milik renders the *b°da'ath* by *sapienter*. Doubtless the *da'ath 'emeth* refers to the peculiar knowledge which the sect possessed. Here Milik renders by *scientia*: it may however be that in both instances *da'ath* stands for the special 'knowledge' of the sect.

In addition to the above might be added DSD vi:9:

And in that order they shall be asked with regard to judgment and any counsel or matter which concerns the Many each presenting on request his knowledge at the Council of the Community.

[21] W. H. Brownlee also introduces the term 'mind' into his translation of DSD iii:3

And defilement is in his restitution
He cannot be justified while he conceals his stubbornness of heart
And with darkened mind (*w°hôshec*) looks upon ways of light.

Following W. F. Stinespring, W. H. Brownlee interprets *w°hôshec* as an adverbial accusative, and thus imports the term 'mind' into his translation as above. But this is hardly necessary. J. van der Ploeg, *Bibliotheca Orientalis*, Mai-Juli, 1952, p. 128b, prefers 'et il regarde vers les ténèbres au lieu de (vers) des chemins de lumière'; J. T. Milik gives 'et tenebras intueatur pro viis lucis'. In *Manuale Disciplinae*, Romae, Pontificium Institutum Biblicum, 1951 *ad loc*. H. E. Del Medico, *op. cit.*, p. 38, gives 'c'est l'obscurité qu'il apercevra à la place des chemins de lumière'.

[22] *Op. cit., ad loc.*

[23] Handskrifterna Från Qumran, Uppsala, 1952, *ad loc.*

Milik here renders *opinionem suam*. Nevertheless in view of a passage such as viii:12 this too may refer to the knowledge which each has discovered: he is to contribute this to the common store of secret knowledge. Brownlee's translation of v:19 favours this: he notes the possibility also that the meaning may be 'each answering his intimate'.[24]

In DSD v:12, vii:3, 4, x:9, viii:18, and DST A 1.18, Col. 11, *da'ath* simply means 'discernment' of some kind or other.

2. Passages where knowledge is closely associated with the Law.

DSD i:12

To clarify their mind (*da'athâm*) by the truth of God's ordinances.

Milik renders *Scientia*; according to Bo Reicke, *Interesse* is the meaning of *da'ath* though he translates *hâg*-knowledge.

DSD iii:1

For his soul has refused instruction
And knowledge (*da'ath*) of righteous laws.[25]

DSD viii:9

A most holy abode belongs to Aaron with eternal knowledge to enact laws.

To get this translation Brownlee emends *b*da'ath côlâm* in the text to *b*da'ath 'ôlâm*. This differs from that of J. T. Milik who translates *scientiam omnium eorum*. So J. van der Ploeg and G. Lambert.

DSD ix:17

See above under (1) and below under (3).

DSD x:25a

And by the subtlety of knowledge ('*ormath da'ath*) I will hedge the [congregation].

---

[24] He follows H. L. Ginsberg here. See W. H. Brownlee, *op. cit.*, p. 25 n. 20.

[25] Note that J. van der Ploeg, *op. cit.*, p. 128a, doubts whether there is a poetic section here: in sapiental literature it is always difficult to state where poetry turns into prose and *vice versa*. J. T. Milik does not print the section as poetry. To achieve this translation W. H. Brownlee emends the text from *bîswrê da'ath* to *bîswrê w*da'ath*. He renders *misph*te* by 'laws'. J. T. Milik gives: 'instructiones scientiae, leges iustitiae'. G. Lambert does not connect *mishp*te tzedeq* with *da'ath* at all; he gives: 'car son âme a pris en dégoût les instructions de la connaissance. Il n'a pas accepté pour la conversion de sa vie les jugements de la justice . . .' *op. cit.*, p. 959. But even if we reject W. H. Brownlee's rendering here, the connection of knowledge with *mishpâṭ* is clear.

Here possibly the 'subtlety of knowledge' is meant to refer to knowledge of the Torah (see DSD ix:17 below) which was a hedge around Israel and which was itself hedged by the oral law.

It will be noted that in almost all the above passages the meaning of *da'ath* is somewhat like 'discernment' such as we traced in (1) above except that the discernment here centres in the Law.

3. *Passages which express or imply a secret knowledge.*

DSD ix:17

Further not to admonish or dispute with the men of the Pit but to conceal the counsel of the Torah in the midst of men of perversity.

The sect claimed a hidden or secret understanding of the Law.

DSD ix:22

Let there be eternal hatred toward the men of the Pit in the spirit of secrecy.

This may rightly be taken to imply a secret knowledge and one of the baser motives for secrecy.

DSD viii:18

He who wilfully removes a word from all that He commanded he shall not touch the Purity of the holy men; nor shall he have any knowledge of any of their counsel, until his deeds are purified from every kind of perversity that he may walk in perfection of way.

This implies that when occasion demands there is secrecy even within the community itself: a certain degree of 'perfection' or achievement is the *sine qua non* of being allowed to enjoy 'knowledge'.

Perhaps in this connection it is relevant to note that the community is often designated as that which is dedicated to the truth,[26] i.e., a special truth known to them (see DSD i:5, 11; ii:26; v:3, 10): its members have received instruction (DSD iii:1, 6, 13, iv:5). Moreover if we accept Brownlee's rendering at DSD x:25 then the congregation of the community is hedged 'by the subtlety of knowledge'; he gives:

'And by the subtlety of knowledge I will hedge [the congregation].'

[26] Cf. A. Dupont-Sommer, 'Observations sur le Manuel de Discipline découvert près de la mer Morte', a paper read to the Académie des Inscriptions et Belles-Lettres, 8 June 1951, *ad loc.*

The Hebrew is *wbᵉormat daᶜath 'eshôc* [   ]*h*. Brownlee fills the lacuna as *hᵃᶜêdâh* there being no room for the word *hatôrâh*. Bo Reicke refers to Job 1:10 and reads *baᶜᵃdâh*;[27] so also J. T. Milik. Whichever of these readings be the original the metaphor of a hedge suggests some kind of peculiar knowledge even if not secret knowledge, and this last in the light of other passages is more probable.[28]

Finally, we have to refer to Brownlee's rendering in DSD v:11 f:

> For these are not reckoned in His covenant, for they have not sought or inquired after Him in His ordinances to know the unconscious sins (*lᵉdaᶜath hanistârôth*).

Brownlee's note (*op. cit., ad loc.*) on this runs: 'Literally, hidden things as in Ps. 19:12. CDC iii:14 f. (v:1 f.) interprets these as errors in the observance of the Sabbath and other holy seasons.' Lambert and Milik retain the literal meaning, however; so too Bo Reicke. In a later article Brownlee has also accepted the literal meaning.[29]

4. *Passages where knowledge is concerned with the interpretation of events or has an eschatological significance.*[30]

DSD iv:2

The way of the Spirit of truth is to enlighten the heart of man, and to make

---

[27] Where the idiom *sûk baᶜad* emerges.

[28] As to the previous line, which W. H. Brownlee renders 'In the Counsel or Council of Wisdom I will relate knowledge', which is the better translation of *bᵃᶜtzath twshiiâh 'saᵖtêr* here? If we read *bᵉᶜtzath* in the following line the correct interpretation would seem to be: 'In the Counsel of wisdom I will hide knowledge' which was 'corrected' by a scribe who misunderstood *bᵃᶜtzath* to mean 'in the council'. The non-corrected reading finds a natural parallel in the next line, as W. H. Brownlee suggested to me.

[29] This is the implicit correction of *The Biblical Archaeologist*, Sept. 1951, p. 58. It is important to note that the hidden things refer to the peculiar interpretation of the Torah which the Sect cherished, not to cosmological and other mysteries. The covenantal context makes this explicit.

[30] In DSD ii:3 the phrase 'eternal knowledge', literally 'knowledge of "ages"', has no eschatological significance perhaps. Its parallel is 'life-giving wisdom', and the knowledge referred to here may merely be 'knowledge' in the sense of discernment, without any eschatological nuance: this last, however, must not be ruled out. On *daᶜath ᶜôlâmîm* see M. Delcor, 'L'eschatologie des documents de Khirbet Qumran', in *Revue des Sciences Religieuses*, October 1952, p. 370, who takes it eschatologically: the 'eternal knowledge' is a possession in this world and also in the world to come. In the same way, he emphasizes that the members have a *gnosis* while they sojourn on earth but that the *daᶜath ᶜôlâmîm* is also related to the future, when it will be superior to any knowledge possible on earth. See DSD xi:3 which speaks of a mystery to come; see below.

straight before him all the ways of true righteousness, and to make his heart tremble with the judgments of God, and a spirit of humility and slowness to anger, and great compassion and eternal goodness, and understanding and insight and mighty wisdom which believes in all God's works, and leans upon His abundant mercy, and a spirit of knowledge in every purposeful work.

Brownlee rightly compares John 6:28 f.; 9:3. The member of the community needs to understand the significance of events: his 'knowledge' has to do with God's *works* and *ways* and *judgments*.

DSD iv:18 ff.

Now God through the *mysteries of His understanding and through His glorious wisdom has appointed a period for the existence of wrong doing*; but at the season of visitation [31] He will destroy it for ever. For it has been defiled by [or, has wallowed in] the way of wickedness under the dominion of wrong doing until the season of the decreed judgment. And then God will purge by His truth all the deeds of man, refining for himself some of mankind in order to abolish every evil spirit from the midst of his flesh, and to cleanse him through a Holy Spirit from all wicked practices, sprinkling upon him a Spirit of truth as purifying water to cleanse from all untrue abominations and from wallowing in [or, being defiled by] the spirit of impurity—so as *to give the upright insight into the knowledge of the Most High and into the wisdom of the Sons of Heaven, to give the perfect of way understanding*.

Here God possesses knowledge of the future—the period of wrongdoing is set by Him and the season of visitation. This knowledge of the *eschaton* which God possesses, He imparts to the upright of way, so that the knowledge they possess enables them also to have understanding of the events of the *eschaton*.

[31] In DSH viii:11 W. H. Brownlee translated 'for all His summer fruits God will bring into their storehouse, just as He decreed for them through the mysteries of His wisdom'. A Dupont-Sommer renders 'for all the times of God arrive in their due season in accordance with what He has decreed about them in the Mysteries of His prudence'. H. E. Del Medico's translation, *op. cit.*, agrees with that of A. Dupont-Sommer, and W. H. Brownlee has subsequently abandoned the translation he first proposed and now gives a rendering *BASOR*, September 1951, substantially like that of A. Dupont-Sommer. The parallels between the language of this passage and much in the New Testament will be obvious: Luke 19:44; 1 Pet. 2:22; Acts 17:26; Gal. 4:2. The term *râz* occurs frequently in the DSS. For a lexicographical note on it see M. Delcor, *op. cit., ad loc.*

There seems to be an eschatological reference in DSD xi:3:

> For from the fountain of His knowledge (*da⁺ath*)
> He has opened my light,
> And mine eye has beheld the wonders He has done
> And my heart is illumined with the Mystery to come.[32]

Also in DSH:

> For there is yet a vision for the fixed time; it speaks of the end and it does not deceive (Hab. 2:3a).
> The explanation of this is that the final time will be of long duration and it will exceed all that the prophets have said for the mysteries of God will be marvellous.
> If it delays, wait for it; for it will surely come and it will not be late. (See on Hab. 2:3b cited before.)

A. Dupont-Sommer points out that 'the final time' here is the ultimate period of history, known only to God. It will be marked by an overwhelming revelation of knowledge:

> For the earth will be filled with the knowledge of the glory of Yahweh as the waters cover the sea (Hab. 2:14). . . . and then knowledge shall be revealed unto them in abundance, like the waters of the sea.[33]

The comment on Hab. 1:5—DSH ii:5—makes it clear that a mark of the men of the community is that they 'know' the nature of the work which God will perform at the end, while unbelievers do not.[34]

---

[32] For his justification of this translation see W. H. Brownlee, *BASOR, Supplementary Studies*, Nos. 10–12, 1951, pp. 54 ff., Appendix H. Difficulty arises in the translation of the last line: Brownlee argues for interpreting *niheieh* as a Niphal participle with reference to the future, hence his translation. H. E. Del Medico reads: 'Car de la source de Sa connaissance, il a ouvert Sa lumière et, par Ses miracles, mon oeil est devenu capable de percevoir et mon coeur s'est éclairé dans la jubilation.' He reads *berôn niheieh*. J. van der Ploeg rejects W. H. Brownlee's translation, *op. cit.*, p. 130a: G. Lambert, *op. cit.*, p. 974, renders the last line as: 'et mon coeur a été illuminé par le mystère de ce qui est accompli.' This last translation it is claimed by J. van der Ploeg and G. Lambert is supported by a fragment of an unknown work found in the cave, see *Revue Biblique*, October 1949, pp. 605 ff., where R. de Vaux rendered *lô'yad⁺w râz niheie[h w]* by 'Ils n'ont pas connu le mystère passé.' Since then, however, I am informed by W. H. Brownlee that R. de Vaux in a private communication to him has retracted and accepted the future reference, as have also I. Rabbinowitz and J. T. Milik, *op. cit.*, p. 156.
[33] A. Dupont-Sommer's translation, *op. cit.*, p. 42.
[34] W. H. Brownlee, *BASOR*, 'The Jerusalem Habakkuk Scroll', No. 112, December 1948, p. 10.

The *gnosis* which will mark the final time will be the understanding of all the things which will happen, i.e., it is an eschatological knowledge not only in the sense that it belongs to the final
time, but in the sense that it gives insight into the meaning of the
events of that time.[35] This kind of knowledge is always the mark
of the true members of the community. They are not to take a
single step outside any of the works of God, (but to accomplish
them) in their time.[36]

Again in DST, Psalm D, the connection between the works of
God and the knowledge which He gives breaks through in the lines:[37]

> For Thou hast caused me to know Thy marvellous mysteries
> And in Thy marvellous Assembly Thou hast exalted my place;
> And Thou hast worked wonders in the presence of many [38] because
>   of Thy Glory.
> And *to make known to all living Thy mighty works.*

5. Passages which suggest knowledge of a personal or intimate kind.

It is not impossible that such knowledge is to be understood in
DSD ii:3 and DSD xi:3 which we have already cited in other
connections. But more certain are the following:

DSD xi:6

My eye has beheld that wisdom which was hidden from men of knowledge
And that prudent purpose which was hidden from the sons of men.[39]

So too in Psalm E, DST in the lines [40]

> Yes I am only dust and ashes
> What could I meditate unless Thou didst will it
> And what thought could I have without Thy good pleasure?
> How could I display my powers, if Thou didst not keep me alive
> And how could I be intelligent if Thou dost not form my thoughts?

[35] M. Delcor, *op. cit.*, pp. 385, 379 n. 1, would make 'eternal life' with which he
equates the *gôrâl* of DSD xi:8 a kind of '*gnosis*'; and he thinks of this 'eternal life'
as supra-terrestrial, although he also insists that O. Cullmann is right in refusing to
recognize a temporal distinction between time and eternity in Jewish thought as in
early Christian.

[36] Cf. DSD viii:4.

[37] A. Dupont-Sommer, *The Dead Sea Scrolls*, p. 76.

[38] On *rabbîm* see S. Lieberman, *op. cit.*, and the note by J. van der Ploeg, *op. cit.*,
p. 131b.

[39] Bo Reicke objects to this translation; he prefers 'which was hidden from men,
providence and that prudent purpose. . . .' So too J. T. Milik.

[40] A. Dupont-Sommer, *op. cit.*, p. 77.

The intimate dependence upon God for knowledge is here clear, as also in the line,

'Nothing has understanding without Thy good pleasure.'

It has been suggested that it is not unlikely, that DST is, in part at least, the work of the Teacher of Righteousness himself [41] and we have here something like a doctrine of grace, all is of God.

6. Passages which conceive of knowledge as mediated.

In DSD ix:10 f. the full interpretation of Torah awaits the coming of a future prophet [the Teacher of Righteousness revived?]: this Teacher of Righteousness who, according to some, was a Messianic figure is to be the mediator of a new understanding.[42]

And they shall not depart from the whole counsel of the Torah to walk in all their hardness of heart; but they shall be ruled by the first laws with which the men of the community began to be disciplined until the coming of a Prophet and the anointed ones (m'shîḥê) of Aaron and Israel.

Note that the Mediator when He comes will have his company[43] —according to Brownlee's rendering.[44]

In a passage in the Jerusalem Habakkuk Scroll on Hab. 2:7 f. the coming teacher will not only give new interpretations of the Torah

[41] A. Dupont-Sommer, op. cit., pp. 69 f.

[42] See W. D. Davies, Torah in the Messianic Age and/or the Age to Come, 1952, for the setting of such an expectation in Judaism. The relation of the Teacher of Righteousness to the Messiah has been much disputed. H. H. Rowley, op. cit., p. 143, rejects the identification. The evidence of CDC, however, may be regarded at least as ambiguous, although there seems to be nothing in the DSS that demands the identification of the Teacher and the Messiah. For bibliographical details see H. H. Rowley, op. cit.

[43] In this the Prophet resembles the Messiah of Judaism: See references to the Messianic Community which accompanies the Messiah in R. N. Flew, Jesus and His Church, 1938, ad loc., and references there given and especially A. Schweitzer, The Mysticism of Paul the Apostle, Eng. Trans., 1931, ad loc.

[44] The plural m'shîḥê is accepted by W. H. Brownlee, op. cit., Appendix D, p. 50. He alludes to CDC ii:12 f. If the Teacher is to be identified with the Messiah, this fits in with the expectation of a messianic community which should accompany the Messiah. It is, however, rejected by M. Delcor, op. cit., p. 366. J. T. Milik translates without explanation 'the prophet and the two Messiahs of Aaron and Israel'. Lambert and J. van der Ploeg find the text strange. M. Delcor thinks we should read m'shiah not m'shîḥê. H. E. del Medico, op. cit., p. 33, translates 'jusqu'à ce qu'arrive le prophète et messie d'Aaron et d'Israel'. He supplies a lost h before nabi'. For other treatments, see H. H. Rowley, op. cit. See also M. Black, The Scottish Journal of Theology, 1953. Most scholars now consider that the Sect expected two Messiahs; see above pp. 114 f.

but will also reveal the secrets of the prophets; his teaching will, in short, be eschatological:

> The last generation (will hear) from the mouth of the priest whom He has given unto the children of Israel for a teacher to give the meaning of all the words of His servants the prophets . . . by whom God *has related all that is to come upon His people* . . .

The same eschatological reference appears in DSH vii:3 f. where we read:

> And when it says 'That he may run who reads therefrom' its meaning concerns The Teacher of Righteousness to whom God has made known all the mysteries of His servants the prophets.

Note that the prophet Habakkuk is denied knowledge of the 'final phase of the end', whereas the Teacher of Righteousness is given this, i.e., all the mysteries; see before on Hab. 2:27 f. As such he inspires faith, a faith which, along with labour, saves: see DSH, viii:1. The idea of mediation appears again in DSH ii:2 where the Teacher of Righteousness (has spoken) from the mouth of God— he had mediated that which is worthy of belief. The whole verse runs:

> for (they do) not believe in all that the Teacher of Righteousness (has spoken) from the mouth of God.

As already stated, the authorship of DST is unknown: it is not certain whether they are a community product or that of the Teacher himself. In any case either the community or the Teacher, probably the latter, appears there as the mediator.

DSD x:23

> With thankful praises I will open my mouth
> And the righteous acts of God shall my tongue continually relate.

In DST, Psalms D, E the members of the community are taught by the Teacher just as the Teacher himself in turn has been taught by God. Note the following, already cited in another connection.

> And through me Thou hast illumined the face of many
> For Thou hast caused me to know Thy marvellous mysteries
> And in Thy marvellous Assembly Thou hast exalted my place;

> And Thou hast worked wonders in the presence of many because
>   of Thy glory
> And to make known to all living Thy mighty works.
> . . . how could I speak if Thou didst not open my mouth
> And how could I answer if Thou didst not instruct me?

DST, Psalm A, reveals the same consciousness of mediation on the part of the author of the Psalm.

> For from Thee proceed my steps,
> And if they attack my soul, this also comes from Thee
> That thou mayest be glorified when the wicked are
> judged *and thou mayest be strengthened in me in the*
> *presence of the sons of men.*[45]

In his work of mediation the author of the Psalms suffers scorn, ill-usage and rejection, see Psalm D; and Dupont-Sommer goes so far as to suggest that we have in the figure of the suffering Teacher of Righteousness an anticipation of the concept of a suffering Messiah which emerges in the New Testament.[46]

III

The above catalogue and classification of the chief passages dealing with knowledge in the DSS invites certain conclusions. But first we must reject the temptation of connecting the references to knowledge in these documents with a second-century milieu when gnostic movements were a menace to Judaism,[47] as to the Church. And at this point the meaning of terms like 'gnostic' and 'gnosticism' as applied to certain phenomena in the second century must be carefully noted. Casey has pointed out that 'there is no trace in early Christianity of "gnosticism" as a broad historical category and the modern usage of "gnostic" and "gnosticism" to describe a large but ill-defined religious movement, having a special scope and character, is wholly unknown in the early Christian period.' Accordingly, like F. C. Burkitt,[48] who also regarded 'gnosticism' as referring to

---

[45] Translations from A. Dupont-Sommer, *op. cit.*

[46] *Op. cit.*, p. 99. On the debate on this problem see H. H. Rowley, *Oudtestamentische Studien*, VIII, 1950, pp. 100 ff.

[47] See e.g. A. Marmorstein, *Studies in Jewish Theology*, ed. J. Rabbinowitz and M. S. Lew, 1950, pp. 1 ff.

[48] *The Church and Gnosis*, 1932, pp. 4 ff.

aberrant movements within Christianity, Casey treats gnosticism as a Christian phenomenon. He confines the term 'to a group of theologians and sects in the second century characterized (a) by their obligations to Christianity, (b) by the autonomous quality of their systems which made them rivals of orthodox Christianity rather than modifiers of it in point of detail, and (c) by a demand for theological novelty which their frequent appeals to a remote antiquity have obscured but not concealed'.[49] As will have emerged almost without examination, the knowledge revealed in the DSS at no point coincides with gnosticism in this sense.

So too we must reject the view of I. Sonne.[50] He makes the following points. (1) That the use of Scripture by the authors of the non-Biblical DSS [51] reflects the exegetical methods of the *Doreshe Reshumot* who belonged to the second century A.D. (2) That the documents show a strong tendency toward gnostic modes of thinking, e.g., the passage in lines 24 f. of the hymn is directed against the view that Jesus came in the flesh and looks to the doctrine expounded in Col. 1:22 which was rejected by most of the gnostic sects in the second and third centuries. (3) There are other traces of polemic against the Christian use of the Old Testament. Thus Mark 15:36 and John 19:28 recall Psalm 69:22. The Church Fathers seized on Psalm 69:22 and referred it to Jesus. Sonne does not support his contention here with evidence, but he writes: 'The allegorical interpretation of the verse [52] by our author and in other Jewish circles contains in all probability a subtly polemic touch. They would not object to the contention that the verse refers to Jesus. They would, however, construe the verse as branding the doctrine of Jesus with the stigma of heresy.[53] This would support a conjecture we expounded elsewhere that the *Doreshe Reshumot*, to whose school our author seems to belong, used their symbolical method of

---

[49] *The Journal of Theological Studies*, vol. XXXVI, 1935, pp. 45 ff.

[50] *Hebrew Union College Annual*, vol. XXIII, pp. 275 ff.

[51] I. Sonne deals with only one 'hymn' but we can assume that the author of the hymn belongs to the same milieu as the author of the DSS; the Psalm concerned is printed by I. Sonne on pp. 287 f. of his article.

[52] He refers to line 7 which he renders . . . 'And they withhold the drink of knowledge from those who are thirsty, and give them vinegar to drink in their thirst, so that they may direct their eye to their false doctrine.'

[53] I. Sonne takes *ḥômêtz* to be a symbol of heresy.

interpretation mostly in refuting the Old Testament "witnesses" of Jesus' mission.'[54] On all these grounds Sonne connects the DSS with a Jewish gnostic sect of the second century A.D. Let us examine his arguments in inverse order. It is hardly credible that the figure of vinegar has the polemic intention against Christians he finds therein; and certainly, in view of DSH which deals with a part of Scripture which was not markedly used by the Early Church,[55] and of the traces of other commentaries found,[56] it is erroneous to claim that the sect was chiefly concerned with refuting Old Testament 'witnesses' to Jesus' mission. Nor is it necessary to refer to the *Doreshe Reshumot*, about whose exegesis we know little, to elucidate the sect's use of Scripture. This last reflects midrashic usage of a type well known elsewhere.[57] Moreover to find polemic against Col. 1:22 in lines 24 f. is clearly an over-refinement of scholarship. The doctrine of the flesh in the DSS is highly significant for the New Testament[58] but the reference to which Sonne appeals is too tenuous to claim that it signifies anti-Christian polemic.

But the term gnosticism has also a wider connotation than that with which we have dealt: it is often used in a more generalized way to refer in the second century and previously to 'movements' or groups which emphasized *gnosis*, both in the higher paganism and in the Hellenistic mysteries and elsewhere.[59] Do the DSS reveal a *gnosis* similar to this, whether Jewish or otherwise? Bo Reicke has rightly warned us against such a view in footnotes to his monograph *Handskrifterna Från Qumrân*, Uppsala, 1952.[60] And we must agree with Bo Reicke.

[54] I. Sonne, *op. cit.*, p. 298. On the *Doreshe Reshumot* see the *Jewish Encyclopedia*, *ad loc*.

[55] See C. H. Dodd, *According to the Scriptures*, London, 1952.

[56] Thus it is possible that the Sect had 'commentaries' on many Old Testament books if not all. Discoveries have already yielded such on Micah and possibly Psalm 107.

[57] See W. H. Brownlee, *BASOR*, September 1951, and his subsequent article on DSH and the Targum of Jonathan.

[58] See K. G. Kuhn, *Zeitschrift für Theologie und Kirche*, 1952, Heft 2, pp. 200 ff.

[59] See R. Bultmann in *Theologisches Wörterbuch*, ed. G. Kittel, Band I, pp. 588 ff. For a convenient statement see E. C. Blackman, *Marcion and His Influence*, 1949, pp. 82 ff.

[60] pp. 61 n. 11, 64 n. 23, 67 n. 38. Cf. M. Burrows, *Oudtestamentische Studien*, VIII, 1950, pp. 169 f. K. G. Kuhn, *Zeitschrift für Theologie und Kirche*, 47, 1950, pp. 192–211 finds 'gnosticism' in the DSS, see pp. 203 ff.

If we examine the *gnosis* which characterized Hellenistic mysteries, it becomes almost immediately apparent that the knowledge of which the DSS speaks has little in common with it. At two points there might appear to be, at first glance, a similarity between them. A recent succinct presentation entitled *Cadre de la mystique Hellénistique* by Festugière [61] recalls us to the fact that two concepts which are central in DSS are also central in Hellenistic mysticism, namely those of 'revelation' and of 'chosenness'. *Gnosis* can only come to man if God chooses to reveal Himself and the acceptance of this revelation constitutes those who accept it into a 'chosen people' in whose custody lies the *mustêrion* which is hidden from the masses and cannot be divulged to them. We saw that the initiates of the 'Dead Sea Sect', which regarded itself as the true Israel and was therefore 'chosen', also had a secret knowledge which was closely related to a revelation—the Law and the Prophets. In this general way the *da'ath* of the DSS and the *gnosis* of Hellenistic mysticism are not unlike. But here the similarity ceases. When we turn to the strict content of the Hellenistic '*gnosis*' we find that it differs radically from the *da'ath* of the DSS. Festugière summarizes the content of salvation in Hellenistic mysticism in the following terms: 'Le contenu de la gnose peut se résumer en trois points. C'est une connaissance:

(1) de Dieu, particulièrement sous son aspect de Sauveur ($\gamma\nu.\ \theta\epsilon o\hat{v}$);

(2) de soi, en tant qu'issu de Dieu et susceptible de retourner à Dieu ($\gamma\nu.\ \dot{\epsilon}av\tau o\hat{v}$);

(3) des moyens de remontrer à Dieu et du mode de cette remontée[62] ($\gamma\nu.\ \dot{o}\delta o\hat{v}$)'.

At none of these three points does the knowledge referred to in the DSS coincide with Hellenistic *gnosis*. We saw that the DSS do speak of an intimate knowledge of God and of God's grace in giving such knowledge, but its very intimacy possesses a quality which removes it from the *gnosis theou* of Hellenistic 'mysticism'. This, to use the words of Festugière, 'implique essentiellement la connaissance du Dieu suprême en tant que transcendant et des Puissances ou Hypostases divines qui jouent le rôle d'intermédiaires (à la fois séparant et reliant) entre ce Premier d'une part et, d'autre part, le monde et l'homme.'[63] Knowledge of God and His intermediaries

[61] See *Aux Sources de la Tradition Chrétienne, Mélanges offerts à M. Maurice Goguel*, Paris, 1950, pp. 74 ff.

[62] *Op. cit.*, p. 78.   [63] *Ibid.*

in this sense is not what we find in the DSS; nor is there any indication in them of a knowledge issuing in deification—which is the end of Hellenistic *gnosis*.[64] On the contrary the knowledge of which the DSS speak coexists with an acute awareness of sin and frailty.[65] And when we turn to points (1) and (2) in Festugière's analysis we find no parallels at all in the DSS. There we read nothing of *Gnôthi seauton* in the sense of knowing one's origin and destiny nor of the way of ascent from this world to God. In short, the three questions with which gnostics were usually preoccupied, i.e., 'Whence evil and by what means? Whence man and how? Whence God?'[66] are not relevant to the understanding of *da'ath* in the DSS.

But although the DSS do not present us with what Hellenistic circles termed *gnosis* they nevertheless do emphasize their own kind of knowledge. And we shall now seek to describe further its connections and nature. There is one point, as section III (4) above shows where the knowledge of the DSS differs sharply from Hellenistic *gnosis*. Although there are passages which suggest that the sect was possibly, and even probably, concerned with cosmological speculations such as were native to the *Ma'aseh Bereshith*,[67] specu-

---

[64] See, e.g., *Corpus Hermeticum*, ed. W. Scott, 1. 26, *et alia*; A. D. Nock in *Essays on the Trinity and the Incarnation*, ed. A. E. J. Rawlinson, p. 105 n. 1.

[65] See, e.g., DSD x:11, xi:3 f., 9 ff., 12 ff., 21 f.; DST, Psalm C. A. Dupont-Sommer, *op. cit.*, p. 72.

[66] Tertullian, *de Praescriptione*, VII. DSD iv–v present quasi-Iranian doctrine not Hellenistic *gnosis*.

[67] See DSD x:1 ff. and W. H. Brownlee's note *BASOR, Supplementary Studies*, Nos. 10–12, 1951, pp. 38 n. 3; 50 f. Is it possible that there is also a reference to this kind of speculation in CDC xvi:1 which according to R. H. Charles asserts that the censor of the camp is 'to instruct the many in the works of God', and is to make them 'understand His wondrous mighty acts', and 'to narrate before them the things of the world since its creation'. It is unlikely that there is here any cosmological reference. The Hebrew as given by S. Schechter, *op. cit.*, p. 13, reads: *wi'sapêr liph'nêhem nih'iôth 'ôlâm bprtiâh* and is rendered by him as 'and shall narrate before them the happenings of eternity in the Law of God'. This would give an eschatological meaning to the sentence, and it must be conceded that this fits the context which speaks of the works and acts of God. Notice that S. Schechter reads *b'tôrâh yâh* for *bprtiâh*. The latter word, he suggests, may be a corruption of *bprtiâh*, 'in details'. This would give a good sense, but M. Jastrow, *Dictionary of the Talmud*, gives no form *prtiâh* under *p'rat*. R. H. Charles emends *bprtiâh* to *mib'rîithô*, but such a conjectural reading cannot be solid ground for finding a cosmological interest in CDC. Moreover the term *'ôlâm* which R. H. Charles renders 'world' referring it to the physical universe can only be doubtfully so translated; Hebrew does not have a term for the universe as such; see W. H. Bennett, *The Post-Exilic Prophets*, 1907, pp. 171 f. All this makes it impossible to use CDC xvi:1 to support a cosmological interest in CDC. Note that while in this article we have used chiefly DSD, the evidence of CDC on

lations which Bentwich has traced to Hellenistic sources,[68] the DSS are mainly concerned with the interpretation of the works of God in history, and especially with events conceived as belonging to the period of the End, that is, with the 'mysteries' of the prophecies of the Old Testament. This it is that explains the nature of the so-called commentary on Habakkuk; attempts to describe this as a pure midrash have led to justifiable protests; what it presents rather is a sustained effort to interpret a Biblical prophecy in the light of current events which are regarded as the final events.[69] In short, one of the best ways in which we are to understand the treatment of Habakkuk by our sect is to see in it a parallel activity to that in which early Christians engaged when they exploited the Old Testament in trying to interpret Jesus as the *eschaton*.[70] The exegesis of Habakkuk in

[68] See N. Bentwich, *Hellenism*, 1919, *ad loc.*

[69] See H. H. Rowley's summary of the literature, *op. cit.*, p. 112 n. 3. He writes 'actually DSH is neither like an ordinary midrash nor like the usual commentaries on Scripture books. It is rather an application of the Scripture text to contemporary events and an often forced interpretation of the text in terms of those events.'

[70] See on this G. Vermès, 'Le Commentaire d'Habacuc et le Nouveau Testament', in *Cahiers Sioniens*, No. 4, 1951, where also the relevant literature on the Jerusalem Habakkuk Scroll is cited. Cf. I. Sonne, *op. cit.*, p. 277. In the *Journal of Jewish Studies*, vol. III, No. 2, 1952, pp. 53 ff., 'Jesus in the Habakkuk Scroll', J. L. Teicher has sought to prove that 'nothing' confirms better the identity of *môreh hatzedeq* with Jesus than the arguments used by Vermès himself to the contrary', p. 53. We are not concerned in this article to enter into this controversy but merely to point out the similarity of much in Matt. 11:25-30 with the DSS. It should be noted that the parallelism between the early Christian use of Scripture and the 'commentaries' of the Dead Sea Sect cannot be carried too far. C. H. Dodd, *According to the Scriptures*, London, 1952 shows that the early Church did not apparently comment on particular Old Testament documents as a whole or use testimony books as Rendal Harris had urged. They used instead certain well-defined blocks of Scripture for their purpose.

---

knowledge is similar to that found in DSD. In CDC also the members of the sect have understanding in the works of God (i:1); God has knowledge 'of the periods for all the years of eternity' (ii:8). The emphasis on knowledge also appears in ii:2 where God 'loveth knowledge, wisdom. . . . Prudence and knowledge minister unto Him'. In ii:10 the Messiah is to mediate knowledge of the Holy Spirit; the community is an instructed one vi:5, cf. vii:18; to them are revealed hidden things (v:1), which are however defined as referring to 'His holy Sabbaths and His glorious festivals, the testimony of His righteousness and the ways of His truth and the desires of His will', here 'the hidden things' do not refer to esoteric doctrines but as elsewhere to God's commands and ways. The term *nistârôth* in DSS and CDC would seem to include (1) knowledge of the proper way to observe the holy days, etc., but this in turn meant (2) the capacity to interpret the Torah and its mysteries properly and (3) in one passage as we saw the reference is to esoteric cosmological speculation. But such speculation too would be rooted in the Scripture and is not to be confused with the redemptive cosmological *gnosis* of Hellenism, e.g., as in the Hermetica.

DSH is eschatological exegesis in this sense. The sect from which it arose thus has affinities far more with apocalyptic than with 'gnostic circles'.[71] This in turn amply accounts for the esoteric character of the da'ath of the sect, because apocalyptic is in its nature esoteric.[72]

Furthermore not only does the eschatological character of da'ath in the DSS set it apart from Hellenistic gnosis but its connection with the Law is significant of another fact. As Bo Reicke has remarked, the knowledge of the DSS is often not so much intellectual as practical:[73] it is not so much understanding as obedience (it can also mean faith, the fear of God). This accounts for the frequency of its occurrence in covenantal contexts, and its close connection with that perfection of way with which we have previously dealt. In short, there is an unmistakably ethical nuance to da'ath in the DSS which is not always a mark of Hellenistic gnosis, but links the da'ath of which the DSS speak with that of the New Testament—where knowledge is never far removed from obedience and is a mark of the ideal future.[74]

Nevertheless, one thing is observable when we seek to understand the circles in which the DSS emerged. They seem to have placed a greater emphasis upon the concept of knowledge, whatever its exact connotation, than the more strictly Jewish circles, whose literature across the centuries is preserved in the Old Testament. This

[71] Contrast A. Dupont-Sommer, op. cit., p. 46, who thinks that the sect recalls the thiasoi of the Hellenistic mysteries. Again A. Dupont-Sommer, Observations sur le Manuel Discipline, 1951, has referred to the use of gâlâh, râz, as indicating a gnosis; see p. 21. But M. Delcor, op. cit., points to the significance of the fragments of Daniel in the cave which proved that the sect knew and used that book. Moreover he finds a positive literary influence from Daniel. Thus the term rabbîm to designate the community derives, he thinks, improbably, from Dan. 11:33, cf. 12:3, etc. It is worth noting here that F. C. Burkitt regarded the rejection of eschatology as a distinctive mark of second century gnosticism, op. cit., ad loc.

[72] Cf. L. Ginsberg, The Journal of Biblical Literature, xi:1. See Ezra 14:6, 12:37 f., 14:15 ff.

[73] Op. cit., pp. 61 n. 11, 64, n. 23.

[74] On this see R. Bultmann, Theologisches Wörterbuch, ibid. It would be erroneous to deny all ethical concern to the mysteries; see on this A. D. Nock, 'Early Gentile Christianity and its Hellenistic Background' in Essays on the Trinity and Incarnation, ed. A. E. J. Rawlinson. But their strength did not lie in that direction, whereas the Dead Sea Sect reveals ethical passion. Along with this goes the strong communal awareness of the DSS. Here is no 'flight of the alone to the alone' as so often in Hellenistic gnosticism but the recognition of belonging to the true Israel. See on this aspect of the Mysteries, Paul and Rabbinic Judaism, p. 90. Usually the societary emphasis of the DSS is largely absent in Hellenistic gnosis.

may well be due to the influence of Hellenistic factors. We have argued elsewhere that such Jewish and Hellenistic factors cannot be sharply distinguished in the first and preceding centuries even in Palestine itself.[75] It is probably safe to infer that where the DSS emerged Hellenistic influences were sufficiently strong to colour the *terminology* of the sect without radically affecting its thought. There is a parallel in the use which the Fourth Gospel makes of Hellenistic terms while often retaining for them a Hebraic connotation.[76]

IV

This reference to the Fourth Gospel brings us back to Matthew 11:25–30 which has often been wrongly regarded as a kind of Johannine outcrop in the Synoptics. Here again it is best to see the use of a terminology which despite its Hellenistic undertones retains an Hebraic connotation. We cannot doubt that the Christian tradition as reflected in this passage was formulated in circles which in many ways were similar to those reflected in the DSS. And in particular

[75] See W. L. Knox, *Some Hellenistic Elements in Primitive Christianity*, 1944, pp. 30 f.; *Paul and Rabbinic Judaism*[2], 1955, pp. 1–16; Saul Lieberman, *Greek in Jewish Palestine*, 1942. According to S. Lieberman, and D. Daube in *Hebrew Union College Annual*, vol. XXII, pp. 239 ff., even the Rabbinic methods of exegesis have been influenced by Hellenistic modes. See also G. D. Kilpatrick, *The Gospel according to St. Matthew*, 1946, pp. 105 ff. who warns us in the study of Matthew against 'identifying the linguistic frontier between the Greek and Semitic worlds with the cultural frontier between Hellenism and Judaism', and R. M. Grant, *The Journal of Religion*, XXXI, 1951, p. 213. E. R. Goodenough, in *Jewish Symbols in the Greco-Roman Period*, Bollingen Series, New York, 1953, shows that the sharp dichotomy between Palestinian and Diaspora Judaism is untenable. See also W. F. Albright, *From Stone Age to Christianity*, 1946, pp. 274, 337 n. 26. A. Altmann, 'Gnostic Themes in Rabbinic Cosmology', in *Essays in Honour of J. H. Hertz*, 1942, pp. 19 ff.

[76] See K. G. Kuhn, *Zeitschrift für Theologie und Kirche*, 47, 1950, pp. 192–211; W. Grossouw, *op. cit.*, pp. 285 ff.; does this bear on the question of the date of the Gospel? See W. F. Albright, in *BASOR, Supplementary Studies* Nos. 10–12, Appendix. On the presence of mystical groups in first-century and earlier Judaism which had a 'gnosis', see references in *Paul and Rabbinic Judaism*, pp. 14 f., and in I. Sonne, *op. cit.* Whether Judaism knew a Hellenistic 'mystery', see E. R. Goodenough, *By Light, Light*, 1935, and a *gnosis* of the same kind cannot here be discussed. If it did, it is not revealed in the DSS. Dom Jacques Dupont, *La connaissance religieuse dans les Epîtres de Saint Paul*, Louvain, 1949, thinks that it is probable that even in Hellenistic mysticism the conception of *gnosis* derives ultimately by way of Alexandria from Judaism, pp. 357–65, and that the Pauline *gnosis* is in no way influenced by the Hellenistic. See the review by R. Bultmann, *The Journal of Theological Studies*, vol. III, April 1952, pp. 10 ff. J. Daniélou, *Études*, 1950, p. 181, *Les Découvertes de Manuscrits en Egypte et en Palestine*, finds confirmation for J. Dupont's thesis in the DSS.

at one point, in the concept of knowledge, we now suggest that the DSS illumines Matt. 11:25–30.

This passage can be understood in two ways: first, as integrally related to its context. The immediate context, it has been held, is unsuitable for the passage; the partial parallel in Luke 10:21 f. appears in a far more fitting setting. This is so because the pronoun *tauta* in Luke 10:21 refers to the glowing report of their success brought back by the Seventy and more immediately to the fact that the names of these are written in heaven. But it is easily possible to exaggerate the difference in the context supplied by Matthew and Luke respectively: only the *immediate* context differs. The total context, if we may so express it, is much the same. Especially does the context in both Matthew and Luke deal with events which are eschatological in their significance. The Lukan address in which the Seventy are sent forth closes with the woes on Chorazin, Bethsaida and Capernaum (10:3 f.); these are followed by the report of the Seventy that they have seen Satan fall (10:19), this, which is an eschatological datum (10:24), leads to the command to rejoice because the names of the Seventy are written in heaven. The Lukan context is thus throughout eschatological; and, indeed, it is probable that we are to take the *tauta* in Luke 10:21 to refer not only to the fall of Satan and the writing of the names in heaven, but also to the woes on the cities, as well as to all those things which 'prophets and kings have desired to see and have not'. Similarly, taken strictly in the light of its context the *tauta* in Matt. 11:27 refers to the woes on the cities of Chorazin and Bethsaida; what has been revealed is the eschatological significance of events of which the judgment upon Chorazin and Bethsaida are a part. In view of the similarity between the total context of Matt. 11:25–30 and Luke 10:21 f. the claim of those scholars, who have urged that the Lukan context is far superior to the Matthaean, and that Jesus would hardly rejoice after pronouncing the woes on Chorazin and Bethsaida, wears thin. In both Matthew and Luke what has been revealed (the *tauta*) has to do with events of eschatological significance. We need not therefore pay too much attention to the claim that Luke has preserved the context more truly than Matthew.

Accepting then the fact that *tauta* in Matt. 11:27 as in Luke 10:21

refers to the awareness of the eschatological nature of certain events, we next note that this 'eschatological' awareness is coupled with the 'knowledge' which the Father has transmitted (*paredothê*) to the Son and the 'knowledge' which the Son has of the Father, a knowledge which can only be mediated to others by the Son. We thus have the juxtaposition here of insight into the eschatological nature of events—a revealed insight—and an intimate 'knowledge' between Father and Son. But we have already shown that in the DSS we have precisely this same kind of juxtaposition—insight into the *eschaton* and intimate 'knowledge' of God are conjoined.

But, in the second place, it is to be recognized that this understanding of Matt. 11:25–30 in the light of its context can be questioned. Thus it is suggested by Professor Nock to the author that the passage, like other sayings of Jesus, is a statement preserved without any special setting, so that we are to treat it in isolation, and the comparison we have drawn above between it and the DSS consequently falls to the ground. We hesitate, however, to accept this view of the passage. There are certain documents where the various pericopae which constitute them can be treated in isolation but the Gospel according to St. Matthew in particular is hardly such: it presents us with a well-knit architectonic structure in which the parts fit into the whole and are to be understood in the light of that whole.

Nevertheless, even if we treat Matt. 11:25–30 as a passage unrelated to its setting, there is still much in the DSS to recall it. Thus the idea of mediation is also present in the DSS as we saw, as it is in our passage. Nor are we wrong in finding a spiritual climate comparable to that of Matt. 11:25–30 in DSD x:20 f., where we read the following:

> [I am to accept] [God's] ordinance as the measure of times,
> And to practise truth and righteous [purpose]
> And loving devotion toward the humble
> And to strengthen the hands of the timid of heart
> And to teach the straying of spirit understanding
> And to make murmurers wise through instruction
> And to respond humbly before the naughty of Spirit
> And with broken spirit to men of injustice.

Although we find here no strict parallel, nevertheless, the way in which the mission of the Teacher of Righteousness is conceived does recall the invitation of Christ in Matt. 11:27–30. Indeed the whole sequence in DSD x:23–xi:2 is strangely reminiscent of Matt. 11:25–30.

In conclusion, we repeat that the use of knowledge in the DSS suggests that it is unnecessary to find the context of 11:25–30 in Matthew a difficulty: the *tauta* can well refer to 11:20 ff., and it is unnecessary to go outside a Jewish milieu to account for our passage. Indeed, the DSS reveal a remarkable parallel to what we find there. They probably emerge from a milieu in which Judaism had been invaded by Hellenistic terminology which had not, however, modified its essential nature. It is probable that a similar background is reflected in Matt. 11:25–30.[77]

[77] As stated previously we cannot here discuss the relation of the DSS to Christianity or to other movements. The strongest tendency perhaps has been to regard them as Essene, but note S. Lieberman's caution against such identifications in the article already cited. That the problem of *gnosis* in the DSS, as will have appeared, is largely a matter of terminological inexactitude is paralleled by the fact, for example, that while most scholars have treated the Pseudo-Clementines as containing 'gnostic' material, H. J. Schoeps has found in the Preaching of Peter, which is incorporated therein, an anti-gnostic motif; see his *Theologie und Geschichte des Judenchristentums, ad loc.* For the whole question discussed above, see K. Schubert, *Theologische Literaturzeitung,* 1953, pp. 502 ff.; Bo Reicke, *New Testament Studies,* 1954–5, pp. 137 ff.; M. Burrows, *The Dead Sea Scrolls,* New York, 1955, pp. 253 ff.; F. Nötscher, *Zur theologischen Terminologie der Qumran-Texte,* Bonn, 1956, *ad rem*; R. McL. Wilson, *The Gnostic Problem,* London, 1958, pp. 73 ff., 225 ff.; H. J. Schoeps, *Urgemeinde, Judenchristentum, Gnosis,* Tübingen, 1956

VII

PAUL AND THE DEAD SEA SCROLLS:
FLESH AND SPIRIT

Modern scholarship has sought to approach Paul along certain well-marked avenues, those of the Old Testament, of Hellenism, of Hellenistic Judaism, Apocalyptic, and more recently, Rabbinic Judaism.[1] In varying degrees each avenue has contributed to the understanding of the Apostle. Nevertheless, because of signs which could not easily be ignored, each has also pointed beyond itself. The recognition has grown that the first-century milieu against which we are to place Paul was variegated and, above all, complex. In particular has it become clear that the traditional convenient dichotomy between Judaism and Hellenism was largely false. In the fusions of the first century the boundaries between these are now seen to have been very fluid. This has emerged as much from the work of those who set Paul primarily over against the Hellenistic world, as from that of those who have emphasized his affinities with Judaism;[2] and it has been indubitably confirmed by archaeologists.[3] Thus the discovery of the Dead Sea Scrolls has occurred at a time when the multiple intricacy of the background of Paul is becoming increasingly evident. Have they merely added to this intricacy, as they inevitably must, by adding another item to the sectarian scene in the first century, or do they also open a new

---

[1] See A. Schweitzer, *Paul and his Interpreters* (Eng. Trans., 1912); J. Klausner, *From Jesus to Paul* (Eng. Trans., 1942); W. D. Davies, *Paul and Rabbinic Judaism* (1948, 2nd ed., 1955).

[2] E.g., W. L. Knox, *St. Paul and the Church of the Gentiles* (1939); W. D. Davies, *op. cit.*

[3] See, especially, E. R. Goodenough, *Jewish Symbols in the Greco-Roman Period* (1953 etc.); S. Lieberman, *Greek in Jewish Palestine* (1942); and, for other bibliographical notes, W. D. Davies, *op. cit.*, p. 354 and also p. 16.

avenue, and perhaps a more excellent one, than those that have previously been available, for the approach to Paul?

Before we begin the examination of the Scrolls from this point of view, it is well to recall that they have also appeared when what we may call the foreground of Paulinism has come to be far better recognized and understood. The old view of Paul as a solitary colossus who dominated the early Church, even while he was not understood by it, has given place to the awareness that the Apostle was rooted in the life of the early Church with which he shared a common faith. Paulinism is no longer regarded as 'an isolated entity without connection with the past or influence in the future'.[4] It is no longer studied as a watertight compartment but far more in relation to the rest of primitive Christianity. And this same primitive Christianity, to judge from the many points of contact that have been discovered between it and the Scrolls, now appears, even before the advent of Paul, to have been deeply open to sectarian influences such as we can study in the Scrolls.[5] Thus there are those who claim that John the Baptist, who can hardly have failed to have been aware of the Qumrân sect, was profoundly influenced by it, so that the stream of Christian tradition would from the first be coloured by its ideas.[6] Some have urged that the priests who joined the Church, as recorded in Acts 6:7 are to be connected with Qumrân,[7] some that this was true of the Hellenists of Acts 6[8] while others hold the same of the Hebrew Christians.[9] Each of these views implies that Paulinism, if it was rooted in the early Church, could not but have been indirectly, to some extent at least, influenced by the sectarians. But it has further been suggested that Paul would have been quite directly under sectarian influences at Damascus (a city always hos-

[4] A. Schweitzer, op. cit.

[5] The literature on this is already large. For a convenient summary, J. Schmitt in Rev. des Sciences Rel., 29 (1955), pp. 381 ff.; 30 (1956), pp. 55 ff.

[6] See The Scrolls and the New Testament (chap. 3 by W. H. Brownlee), New York, and London, 1958.

[7] See The Scrolls and the New Testament (chap. 2 by O. Cullmann, p. 29), New York and London, 1958.

[8] Ibid., pp. 25 ff. But it is difficult to accept Cullmann's view that Christian universalism owes much to the sectarians or that the term 'Hellenists' is likely to point to representatives of anything like what we have at Qumrân.

[9] H. J. Schoeps, Urgemeinde, Judenchristentum, Gnosis (1956), pp. 69 ff. But see J. A. Fitzmyer's essay in The Scrolls and the New Testament.

pitable to dissentients), because at one stage the sect had actually
been stationed there and because it is not unlikely that there were
sectarians living in the city at the time of Paul's conversion.[10] But
just as we cannot stay with Dr. Teicher's thesis,[11] that Paul is
actually represented by the wicked priest in the scrolls, so we cannot
examine these different views. It will not be our concern to pin
down any one point through which the influence of the sectarians
reached Paul. This could at best produce only conjectural results.
Rather, it will be our aim to begin by inquiring whether the Apostle
shares a common reservoir of terminology with the sect. Even
though the scholarly sifting of the Scrolls is still incomplete, this
can be assessed fairly accurately on the comparatively solid ground
offered by a comparison of the Pauline epistles and the pertinent
literary remains of the sect. But particular words and phrases do
not in themselves prove very much (as so often in the political
sphere, East and West have recently painfully discovered when
they use the same terms, for example, 'freedom', 'democracy' and
'liberty'). We, therefore, have to go on further to ask whether the
conceptual world of the sect or, as Schweitzer would put it,[12]
whether the 'sets of ideas' in the scrolls are allied to, and illumine,
those of Paul.

Apart from a number of words and phrases [13] which recall similar
ones in the Pauline epistles, at several specific points the Scrolls

[10] See Cullmann, op. cit., p. 25, and references in note 20. The meaning of the
term 'Damascus' is in dispute, however; R. North holds it to refer not to the city
of Damascus but to almost all the area around the Dead Sea, including Damascus,
Pal. Expl. Quart. 87 (1955), pp. 34–38. Rabbinowitz has rejected the geographic
interpretation of Damascus, Journ. of Bibl. Lit. 73 (1954), pp. 11 ff. See also Charles
T. Fritsch, The Qumran Community (1956), pp. 21 ff., on Damascus as a place of refuge.

[11] For this, see his various articles in Journ. of Jewish St., since the treatment in
these articles is always greatly rewarding even though we may not accept the main
positions advanced.

[12] Op. cit., p. 219. For the ease with which terminology can mislead, I may refer
to a dissertation by my former student, G. R. Edwards, The Qumran Sect and the New
Testament, Duke University, 1955 (unpublished). He rejects the view that yahad and
koinonia are identical.

[13] For these and other parallels, see especially W. Grossouw, 'The Dead Sea
Scrolls and the New Testament', Studia Catholica 27 (1952), pp. 1–8; the notes in
W. H. Brownlee's translation of DSD are invaluable; S. E. Johnson, 'Paul and the
Manual of Discipline', Harv. Theol. Rev. 48 (1955), pp. 157 ff. Also the relevant pages
in F. M. Braun, 'L'arrière-fond judaïque du quatrième évangile et la Communauté
de l'Alliance', Rev. Bibl. 62 (1955), pp. 5–44.

have been thought to have a bearing upon Paulinism. Anticipations of the doctrine of justification by faith have been discovered in them,[14] and much light on the Pauline terminology about 'mysteries' and 'wisdom' and 'knowledge' of God now revealed in Christ.[15] The exegetical methods of Paul have been claimed to recall those of the sect.[16] Space forbids the examination of all these points here. We shall, therefore, confine ourselves to one field where sectarian affinities or influences have been detected in Paul—his understanding of the 'flesh' and of the 'Spirit'.

I

In many traditional Pauline studies the point which has been most emphasized as suggesting Hellenistic influences is Paul's concept of the flesh. In an examination of this, published in 1948, I pointed out that there is no need to turn to Hellenistic sources for its elucidation, but that the Pauline idea of the flesh seemed to be 'adequately explained as an accentuation of the ethical connotation that the term already had in certain late documents in the Old Testament'.[17] One thing appeared clear, that Rabbinic Judaism offered no parallel to this accentuation nor had we a parallel in any other Judaistic milieu then known to us. Perhaps I then dismissed the rabbinic sources too categorically.

There is a passage in Mishnah Aboth 2:7 where the term 'flesh' (*basar*) may have an ethical nuance. It reads: '[Hillel] used to say: the more flesh the more worms; the more possessions the more care; the more women the more witchcrafts; the more bondwomen the more lewdness; the more bondmen the more thieving; the more study of the Law the more life; the more schooling the more wisdom; the

---

[14] W. Grossouw, *op. cit.*, p. 1; S. E. Johnson, *op. cit.*, pp. 160 ff.

[15] For a rich treatment, see the three articles by S. Lyonnet, 'L'étude du milieu littéraire et l'éxegèse du Nouveau Testament', *Biblica* 35 (1954), pp. 480–502; 36 (1955), pp. 202–12; 37 (1956), pp. 1–38. For the Synoptics, see L. Cerfaux, in *New Testament St.* 2 (1955/6), pp. 238 ff.

[16] See, e.g., E. Earle Ellis, 'A Note on Pauline Hermeneutics', *New Testament St.* 2 (1955/6), pp. 127 ff.; E. Dinkler, *Journ. of Rel.* 36 (1956), pp. 121 ff., finds possible Essene influence on Paul's conception of predestination and individual responsibility in Rom. 9–11; see M. Burrows, *The Dead Sea Scrolls* (1955), p. 336.

[17] *Op. cit.*, pp. 19 ff.

more counsel the more understanding; the more righteousness the more peace. . . .' Israelstam's comment on the term 'flesh' here is too trite.[18] He takes it quite literally to refer to obesity. But the context gives to 'flesh' here a possibly ethical connotation. The collocation of 'flesh' and 'worms' re-emerges in T. B. Sotah 5a: 'R. Johanan said: The word for man indicates dust, blood and gall; the word for flesh indicates shame, stench and worm. Some declare that [instead of "stench" we should have the word] Sheol, since its initial letter corresponds.'

A passage in the Targum of Jerusalem on Gen. 40:3 might also perhaps be taken to imply that the flesh is prone to sin: 'Joseph left the mercy above, and the mercy beneath, and the mercy which accompanied him from his father's house, and put his confidence in the chief butler: he trusted in the flesh and the flesh he tasted of, even the cup of death. Neither did he remember the scripture where it is written expressly, Cursed shall be the man who trusteth in the flesh, and setteth the flesh as his confidence. Blessed shall be the man who trusteth in the Name of the Word of the Lord and whose confidence is the Word of the Lord. Therefore the chief butler did not remember Joseph, but forgot him, until the time of the end came that he should be released.'[19] Jastrow,[20] it should be noted, takes 'flesh' here to refer to 'a mortal'. But at least it has the connotation of untrustworthiness. In view of the above, therefore, an accentuation on the ethical connotation of 'flesh' should not, perhaps, altogether be denied to Rabbinic Judaism.

Nevertheless, the examples we have quoted are not numerous or entirely unambiguous. Certainly they do not compare in cogency to what we find in the Scrolls from Qumrân, where the term 'flesh' appears in several contexts which suggest a close parallel to Pauline usage, i.e., where the ethical connotation of the term is as evident as in Paul.[21]

[18] Our translation is that of Danby, *The Mishnah* (1933). Israelstam's comment is found in the Soncino Talmud. Contrast R. T. Herford, *Pirqe Aboth* (1945), pp. 48–49.

[19] Translation by J. W. Etheridge, *The Targums of Onkelos and Jonathan ben Uzziel* (1862).

[20] *The Dictionary of the Talmud, ad loc.*

[21] See *The Scrolls and the New Testament*, New York and London, 1958; the basic treatment is by K. G. Kuhn in chap. 6, pp. 101 ff.

In the Qumrân texts there are passages where the term 'flesh' signifies merely a physical entity without moral connotation, as in DSD ix, 4, 'The flesh of whole burnt offerings'; CDC vii, 1 ('The kin of his flesh'); viii, 6.[22] Other passages point to the 'flesh' as designating the frailty and mortality of man: 'What flesh is like this . . . And what is a vessel of clay to exalt thy wondrous deeds?' DSH iv, 29.)[23]

There are other sections where the meaning of 'flesh' is ambiguous. What, for example, is its meaning in the following passage from DSD iii, 6 ff., the most pertinent words of which are in italics. 'But in a spirit of true counsel for the ways of a man all his iniquities will be atoned, so that he will look at the light of life, and in a holy spirit he will be united in his truth; and he will be cleansed from all iniquities; and in an upright and humble spirit his sin will be atoned, *and in the submission of his soul to all the statutes of God his flesh will be cleansed*, that he may be sprinkled with water for impurity and sanctify himself with water of cleanness?' (Burrows' translation.)

Kuhn takes 'flesh' here to have a merely physical meaning. But in the preceding verses (iii, 4, 5), the person who has refused to enter God's covenant (ii, 26) is regarded not only as having refused instruction (iii, 1) and practised dishonesty (iii, 2), so that acceptance of him into the community is defiling (iii, 3), and not only as having a darkened mind, but also as being so corrupted that no atonement or baptismal rite can cleanse him. In iii, 6 ff., it is only the spirit that can avail to make him clean. Before any water rite can cleanse his 'flesh', that flesh must previously have been 'cleansed' by submission to the statutes of God. Is there not here the thought that the flesh has been involved in rebellion? The implication is that the flesh is polluted in such a way that it requires moral purification: the same verb is used for cleansing iniquities, which are here parallel to 'flesh', as for cleansing the flesh. The verb is thus used in Ps. 51:4, 9, which is often echoed in the Scrolls.[24]

Similarly in DSD iv, 20, Kuhn finds a purely physical meaning for 'flesh'. The passage reads: 'And then God will refine in his truth all

---

[22] Compare on all this J. A. T. Robinson, *The Body* (1952), for the 'flesh' in Paul.

[23] Cf. Gen. 63. For other references in the Scrolls, see Ph. Hyatt, 'The View of Man in the Qumran Hodayot', *New Testament St.* 2 (1955/6), pp. 276 ff.

[24] E.G., DSD x, 11; cf. Ps. 51:3 f.

the deeds of a man and will purify for himself the frame of man, consuming every Spirit or error in his flesh, and cleansing him with a holy spirit from all wicked deeds' (Burrows). The peculiar problems presented by the Hebrew of this passage do not concern us.[25] The significant point is that the flesh is the seat of evil spirits and can be purged only by God's truth. The term is at least ambiguous in this context.

In other passages, however, as Kuhn has so persuasively indicated, the association of the flesh with evil becomes so close that it seems to denote the morally lower nature of man. Thus in DSD xi, 12, we read: 'As for me, if I slip, the steadfast love of God is my salvation forever; and if I stumble in the iniquity of the flesh my vindication in the righteousness of God will stand to eternity' (Burrows). 'Flesh' is here used somewhat absolutely; the reference is not to what we normally understand by 'sins of the flesh'. Nor is it clear whether 'flesh' has reference here to mankind which is, as a whole, in iniquity or to the psalmist's own flesh as such, in which case we should, however, expect 'my flesh'. In DSD xi, 7, the phrase 'the company of flesh' (Burrows) seems to be used simply of 'mankind', because it is parallel to 'the sons of man' in line 6. But even here the implication is that mankind, the company of flesh, outside the Covenant is in ignorance and unrighteousness. In DSD xi, 9, the 'company of erring flesh' is parallel to 'wicked humanity'. In 1 QM 'erring flesh' denotes the 'sons of darkness'. The phrase 'The Hundred of God, a hand of war against all erring flesh' is placed on one of the standards of the sons of light.[26] The point might be made that if the term 'flesh' bore in itself the connotation of evil it would not be necessary, as here, to qualify it by the addition 'of error' or 'of wickedness'. The same phenomenon, however, of a term being qualified by that which it already designates is met with elsewhere.[27]

[25] See W. H. Brownlee, 'The Servant of the Lord in the Qumran Scrolls', *Bull. of the Amer. Sch. of Oriental Res.* 135 (1954), pp. 36–38; Y. Yadin in *Journ. of Bibl. Lit.* 74 (1955), pp. 40–43; G. Vermès in *Cahiers Sioniens* 9 (1955), pp. 56 ff.

[26] M. Burrows, *The Dead Sea Scrolls*, p. 393. The interpretation of 1 QM has a bearing on the meaning of the struggles in which Christians are engaged. This may confirm the views on the forces fought by the early Church suggested by A. N. Wilder, 'Kerygma, Eschatology and Social Ethics'; Davies and Daube (ed.), *The Background of the New Testament and its Eschatology* (1956), pp. 527 ff.

[27] See G. Friedrich in *Theol. Wörterb. z. N.T.* (ed. Kittel), vol. II, p. 705, on 'good "good news" '.

Moreover, this difficulty is here offset by the simple fact that 'the company of flesh' is equivalent to 'the company of erring flesh', and probably to 'the company of flesh and those who walk in darkness' (see DSD xi, 6–10). It seems clear that to belong to the flesh is to belong to that sphere where the spirit of perversion, and angel of darkness, rules. Kuhn asserts that '["flesh"] becomes almost synonymous with evil'.[28]

Nevertheless, as Kuhn rightly insists,[29] it is not a Hellenistic view of the 'flesh' that we encounter here. The author of the psalm in DSD xi can, here and now, while physically he is in the flesh, yet belong to the 'chosen of God', the 'sons of heaven', to the 'lot of the holy ones'. If, as is likely, we are to understand by these terms in lines 6 ff. angelic or celestial beings with whom the sect shares its worship,[30] so that, while still on earth, its members participate in a heavenly community, it is clear that existence in the flesh does not in itself, as in Hellenistic thought, suggest or signify perversion. Similarly, as we have seen, the flesh can be 'cleansed' and 'purified' (DSD iii, 6 ff.; iv, 20). In Hellenistic thought it is not the purification of the flesh that is desired but escape from it, because the 'flesh' is conceived there not only as the sphere where evil dwells but as itself constituting evil.[31]

When we turn to Paul we find that the term 'flesh' is used in two broad ways as in the Scrolls—with and without a moral connotation. Where the moral connotation is present we find the Pauline use of the word very similar to that in the Scrolls. The evidence for this has been given by Kuhn and need not be repeated here; a glance at the passages listed in the second group below would confirm his conclusions. Let it suffice here to compare the sentence quoted above from Kuhn with some definitions made by J. A. T. Robinson: 'Flesh represents mere man, man in contrast with God—hence man

---

[28] *Op. cit.*, p. 101.

[29] *Ibid.*, p. 104.

[30] So W. H. Brownlee's translation, *ad loc.* S. E. Johnson rejects this apparently, *op. cit.*, p. 159, where he writes that 'the newly discovered literature does not mention angels'. This position can hardly be maintained in the light of the sources now available, apart from DSD xi, 6 ff. Angelology is very marked in 1 QM especially. The angelology of the sect illuminates much in the New Testament. See Barthélemy and Milik, *Qumran Cave I*, p. 117, comments to 1 QSa ii, 8.

[31] See, e.g., *Encycl. of Rel. and Ethics*, vol. II, p. 66b.

in his weakness and mortality' . . . 'Flesh stands for man, in the solidarity of creation, in his distance from God' . . . 'One could describe the situation by saying that flesh as neutral is man living in the world, flesh as sinful is man living for the world.'[32]

But identity of terminology, we wrote above, does not mean very much. It is more important to ask whether the sets of ideas within which the term 'flesh' is used are identical or similar. At this point it will be well to tabulate the incidence of the term 'flesh' (*sarx*) in its various broad meanings in the Pauline epistles:

> (1) *With a physical connotation*: Rom. 1:3; 2:28; 3:20; 4:1; 9:3, 5, 8; 1 Cor. 1:26, 29; 5:5; 6:16; 7:28; 10:18; 15:39, 50; 2 Cor. 4:11; 7:5; 12:7; Gal. 1:16; 2:16, 20; 3:3; 4:13, 14, 23, 29; 6:12, 13; Eph. 2:11, 14; 5:29, 31; 6:5, 12; Phil. 1:22, 24; 3:3, 4; Col. 1:22, 24; 2:1, 5, 23; 3:22; Philem. 16.
> (2) *With a moral connotation*: Rom. 6:19; 7:5, 18, 25; 8:3, 4, 5, 6, 7, 8, 9, 12, 13; 2 Cor. 1:17; 5:16; 7:1; 10:2, 3; 11:18; Gal. 5:13, 16, 17, 19, 24; 6:8; Eph. 2:3; Col. 2:11, 13, 18.

These listings prompt two comments. First, it is noteworthy that the term 'flesh' with a moral connotation occurs far less frequently in the Pauline epistles than discussions of Pauline theology would lead us to expect. Secondly, almost all the instances where Paul uses 'flesh' with that connotation occur in three types of material: (a) in Rom. 7 and 8, where Paul is concerned with the individual experience of sin; (b) in the polemic portions of Colossians; and (c) in the paraenetic section in Galatians. Let us look more closely at these.

In Rom. 7 and 8 Paul deals with the problem of sin not metaphysically or theologically but experientially: he uses the term 'flesh' in describing his personal struggle with his lower nature, as it were. Where Paul is concerned to speculate on the origin of sin on a large scale in Rom. 1, 2, and 5, and not to enlarge upon its working in his own life, the term 'flesh' does not occur with a moral connotation. He there deals with sin in terms of idolatry and of the Fall, without having recourse to the nature of the 'flesh' at all.[33] The mere fact that in Rom. 1, 2, and 5 Paul is concerned with the universal and corporate aspects of sin and in Rom. 7 with its more

[32] *Op. cit.*, pp. 19, 25, and 31.
[33] W. D. Davies, *op. cit.*, pp. 22 ff.

personal aspects does not in itself sufficiently account for the emphasis on 'flesh' in the latter section and its neglect in the former, if his understanding of 'flesh' was an *essential* element in his approach to the problem of evil. It seems that his concept of the flesh has perhaps *not* been integrated into the main structure of his thought: is there a kind of hiatus between his experiential awareness of the flesh as his lower nature and his theoretical understanding of sin?

But the same phenomenon confronts us in the Scrolls. Those passages in which *basar* (flesh) has a moral connotation occur mainly (and, if we follow Kuhn, exclusively) in those sections where the personal experience of sin is being described, namely, in the psalms.[34] Where the Scrolls present a system of belief the term is notably absent. Thus in DSD iii, 13–iv, 26, there is only one reference to 'flesh' which, as we saw, Kuhn treats as having no moral connotation. Elsewhere in the Scrolls the term is not particularly significant for our purpose. Thus, as in Paul, so in the Scrolls the concept of the 'flesh', as having moral connotation, seems to stand outside the fundamental theology of the sect, and emerges fully only where the more directly experiential aspects of life are described. When we encounter the theology of the sect as such, we find not a treatment of 'flesh' in its relation to sin but a dualism, derived, according to Dupont-Sommer[35] and Kuhn,[36] from Iranian sources. While, therefore, the use of the term 'flesh' in Paul recalls its use by the sect, it does not necessarily follow that there is any fundamental similarity between Paul's thought on sin and that of the sect. In itself it merely proves that Paul's conceptual milieu coincides at this one point with that of the sect. The 'sets of ideas' with which Paul associates the term are not the same as those with which the sect seems to associate it.

If what we have written above be valid, we find the term 'flesh' used by Paul in connection with the Fall and idolatry, ideas which belong to the main stream of Judaism: the sectarian term 'flesh' coexists with what would seem to be ultimately Iranian concepts

[34] On the problem of whether the 'I' of the Psalms is to be taken individually or corporately, see K. G. Kuhn, *op. cit.*, pp. 102 f. We take them individually at least in DSD x and xi. The fact that they could be used publicly does not militate against this, cf. Ph. Hyatt, *op. cit.*, p. 276.

[35] *The Jewish Sect of Qumran and the Essenes* (Eng. Trans., 1954), pp. 118 ff.

[36] K. G. Kuhn, 'Die Sektenschrift und die iranische Religion', *Zeitschr. f. Theol. u. Kirche* 49 (1952), pp. 296–316.

which have been yoked to Jewish monotheism. It is tempting to suggest that it is the Hellenization both of Judaism and of Zoroastrian currents in Palestine that accounts for this phenomenon. I have elsewhere [37] pointed out that in Rom. 7 what we have is a description of Paul's struggles with his Evil Impulse. Throughout he uses rabbinic concepts, *except* where he locates the Evil Impulse in the flesh. A lengthy quotation may be permitted: 'We saw that the Evil Impulse was located generally in the heart, whereas Paul clearly regards the "flesh" as the base of operations for sin. The question is inevitable whether, had Paul been describing the conflict with his Evil Impulse, he too would not have spoken of "the heart" rather than "the flesh"? It has been suggested that the Apostle regarded the "flesh" as the seat of sin because he was thinking more particularly of sins in the "flesh" in a restricted sense; but that the sins of the flesh included for Paul not merely sexual sins but also such things as pride is clear from Gal. 5. The probable explanation, however, of why Paul used "flesh" is not far to seek. There was no scientific fixity or accuracy about the use of psychological and anthropological terms in his day, and the Old Testament use of "flesh" would naturally and suitably suggest itself to him. In addition to this the location of the Impulse in the heart, while dominant in Rabbinic thought, must not be too hard pressed. The Evil Impulse had a long start over the Good Impulse in man, and some passages suggest that it has gained dominion over the whole 248 members of the human body: it would not be difficult then for Paul to envisage sin as invading all his members and having its base in all his flesh.'

In the light of the Scrolls, however, we now see that Paul had predecessors; there was much precedence for the accentuation of the moral connotation of the Old Testament term 'flesh'; and we may recognize that it may have been Hellenistic influences in Palestine that supplied the impetus for this. And this same impetus may have affected the 'Zoroastrianism' of the sect. The source criticism of DSD and the other sectarian documents, has not been much attempted as yet, but it may well be that the section iii, 13 ff., reflects

---

[37] W. D. Davies, *op. cit.*, p. 27. On the Evil Impulse in the Scrolls, see Ph. Hyatt, *op. cit.*; also E. Schweizer, 'Gegenwart des Geistes und eschatologische Hoffnung', *The Background of the New Testament and its Eschatology*, pp. 489 ff.

an earlier 'uncontaminated' stage in the history of the sect before
Hellenistic influences had deeply coloured its thought, while the
Psalms reflect a later stage when this had taken place. It is tempting
to see in the Pauline and the sectarian 'flesh' a common term which
emerged into significance in a Hellenized Rabbinic Judaism and a
Hellenized Zoroastrian Judaism, respectively. This common term
does not necessarily point to identity of thought but merely to a
common background where Hellenistic forces were at work, nor
is it inconsistent to claim this while at the same time holding that
neither in Paul nor in the Scrolls is 'flesh' a totally Hellenistic concept.

Do the other passages where Paul uses 'flesh' with an ethical connotation justify us in going further than this? Let us next look at
Col. 2:11–23:

> In him also you were circumcised with a circumcision made without hands,
> by putting off the body of flesh in the circumcision of Christ; and you were
> buried with him in baptism, in which you were also raised with him through
> faith in the working of God, who raised him from the dead. And you, who
> were dead in trespasses, and the uncircumcision of your flesh, God made alive
> together with him, having forgiven us all our trespasses, having cancelled the
> bond which stood against us with its legal demands; this he set aside, nailing
> it to the cross. He disarmed the principalities and powers and made a public
> example of them, triumphing over them in him.
>
> Therefore let no one pass judgment on you in questions of food and drink
> or with regard to a festival or a new moon or a sabbath. These are only a
> shadow of what is to come; but the substance belongs to Christ. Let no one
> disqualify you, insisting on self-abasement and worship of angels, taking his
> stand on visions, puffed up without reason by his sensuous mind, and not
> holding fast to the Head, from whom the whole body, nourished and knit
> together through its joints and ligaments, grows with a growth that is from
> God.
>
> If with Christ you died to the elemental spirits of the universe, why do
> you live as if you still belonged to the world? Why do you submit to regu-
> lations, 'Do not handle, Do not taste, Do not touch' (referring to things which
> all perish as they are used), according to human precepts and doctrines? These
> have indeed an appearance of wisdom in promoting rigour of devotion and
> self-abasement and severity to the body, but they are of no value in checking
> the indulgence of the flesh (RSV).

Recently this whole section has been understood to reflect the
presence of Qumrân sectarian influences. The 'heresy' confronting

Paul at Colossae may have had Stoic undertones.[38] Nevertheless, its predominantly Jewish character is indicated clearly by the references to 'principalities and powers' and to 'the rudiments of the world' (RSV: 'elemental spirits of the universe'); to the observance of rules on meat and drink, holy days, the new moon and Sabbath days, the worshipping of angels. But it has always been difficult to gauge the exact nature of the forces at work, and scholars have hitherto had to be contented with vague references to Jewish Gnosticism.[39]

The Scrolls, however, present what seem to be specific points of contact with the Colossian heresy. The exact phrase 'the body of the flesh', a highly puzzling one, has appeared in the Habakkuk Commentary on 2:7, 8: '(7) *Will they not suddenly arise, those who torment you; will they not awake, those who torture you? Then you will be booty for them. (8) Because you have plundered many nations, all the remainder of peoples will plunder you.* This means the priest who rebelled . . . his scourge with judgments of wickedness; and horrors of sore diseases they wrought in him, and vengeance in his body of flesh.' Here the phrase 'body of flesh' means the physical body and there is an exact parallel in Col. 1:22, while in Col. 2:11 the phrase is made to refer to man's lower nature which the Christian has put off in Christian 'circumcision'.[40] But more important are

---

[38] See the commentaries on Colossians.

[39] For bibliographical details, consult the studies in *Biblica* by S. Lyonnett; see pp. 148 n. 15 above; P. Benoit, 'Corps, tête et plérôme dans les Epîtres de la Captivité', *Rev. Bibl.* 63 (1956), pp. 5 ff.

[40] The term 'body of flesh' occurs also in Greek in Sir. 23:17, I Enoch 102:4-5. In DSH it apparently merely means the physical body or flesh. We are not to understand here a rigid distinction between 'flesh' and 'body.' So too in Paul 'body' (*soma*) and 'flesh' (*sarx*) are often synonymous (Gal. 6:17, 1 Cor. 9:27, etc.). The anthropology of the Scrolls has not been sufficiently examined. Hyatt has dealt in a broad way with the view of man in DST, *op. cit.*, but does not think a strict anthropology possible because the Hymns are 'not a theological work' (p. 278). But we may ask the question whether the scrolls throw any light on the Pauline doctrine of the 'body'. The term *gewiyyah* may mean in Mishnah Mikwaoth 10:7 'the inner part of the body' (so Jastrow); in the Jerusalem Targum on Gen. 7:23, it seems identical with 'flesh'. In the Old Testament the term occurs mostly in the sense of corpse, but is also used of the form taken by visionary creatures (Dan. 10:6). In Gen. 47:18, Neh. 9:37, K. Grobel (in *Neutest. St. für Rudolf Bultmann*, 1954, p. 56), takes it to stand for the 'self'. (See *Hastings' Dictionary of the Bible*, p. 156.) The evidence is too meagre to connect the fully developed Pauline concept of the 'body' with *gewiyyah*, however. There are passages which suggest that, in part, what Paul calls the 'body' is in the Scrolls designated by 'spirit'—if we take 'body' as a designation of the 'self'. (See

the echoes of the scrolls in other matters. There is the same emphasis on calendrical niceties, although it must be noted that this would not be a peculiarity of our sect. Passages such as CDC iii, 13–16; DSD i, 14; x, 1–9, point to a calendar different from that of official Judaism, a solar one. (The phrase which appears in Gal. 4:10 recalls exactly DSD i, 14.) The specific reference in Col. 2:16 to the Sabbath comports with the many regulations of the Sabbath in CDC x, 14–xi, 18; so too the distinctions between meats and drinks find an echo in CDC vi, 18. Thus the asceticism condemned in Col. 2:20 ff. could well be illustrated by the life of the sectarians. But, finally, behind all these particular points, stand the references to wisdom and knowledge in the Epistle and the warning in Col. 2:8 'Beware lest any man spoil you through philosophy and vain deceit, after the tradition of men, after the rudiments of the world and not after Christ.' The claim of the sect to a special wisdom or knowledge needs no emphasis; it is writ large over the Scrolls.[41] Moreover, this 'knowledge' is bound up not only with the observance of Sabbaths, Festivals, etc., but also with an understanding of the world which recalls much in Colossians. In DSD iii, 13 ff., we read of the spirit of truth and the spirit of error: the former is the prince of lights, the latter the angel of darkness, and there are destroying angels under his dominion. The spirit of truth is also called the angel of truth. The angelology of the Scrolls may indeed illumine for us the reference to the worship of angels in Col. 2:18, and the 'intruding into those things which he hath not seen' may be aimed at the kind of thing referred to in 1 QM x, 10 f., where the people of the Covenant are said to be those who hear the voice of the venerated One and see the holy angels and who hear ineffable things. The most frequent term for the supreme force of evil in the scrolls is Belial, who is the

---

[41] See W. D. Davies, above, pp. 119 ff.; Bo Reicke, 'Traces of Gnosticism in the Dead Sea Scrolls', *New Testament St.* 1 (1954/5), pp. 137 ff.

---

references in J. A. T. Robinson, *op. cit.*, pp. 26 ff.) This is another instance of the distance that separates the sectarian conceptual milieu from Paul. See, further, Marc Philonenko, 'Sur l'expression "corps du chair" dans le Commentaire d'Habacuc,' *Semitica* 5 (1955), pp. 39–40. He concludes: 'It is of interest to observe that this expression . . . which is rather rare, is found both in one of the Qumrân Scrolls, in the Book of Enoch, fragments of which are found in the Qumrân caves, in Ecclesiasticus and also in the New Testament.'

angel of darkness.[42] In Colossians the terms used of the forces of evil ranged against Christians (and the Law itself is included among these forces, Col. 2:14) are 'the power of darkness' (1:13), 'principalities', 'powers' (2:15), 'thrones' (1:16), 'the rudiments of the world' (2:20), and, in a more individual vein, 'the old man'. The correspondence in terminology, it must be conceded, is not here very exact and, by itself, could not be taken to point to influences of the Qumrân type as certainly as some have so unhesitatingly held. Nevertheless, along with the other factors mentioned above, it would seem that the forces of evil in Colossians may be the same as those referred to in the scrolls. This is particularly reinforced when we turn to Ephesians, which is at least deutero-Pauline, and where the correspondence with the scrolls is perhaps more close. There too we meet principalities and powers, might and dominion, 'and every name that is named'; 'the prince of the power of the air'; 'the spirit that now worketh in the children of disobedience'—this last especially being reminiscent of the scrolls (DSD iii, 13 ff.).[43]

Assuming then that Paul confronts belief in the kind of 'evil forces' which emerge in the scrolls, are we to conclude from Colossians (and Ephesians) that he himself accepts their reality? Does he take them seriously? Do they constitute an important element in his thought or is Paul merely using his 'opponents'' terms without really giving credence to them? To judge from Colossians and Ephesians alone it might be argued that he is merely using the terms. This was the view, for example, of Lightfoot,[44] and C. H. Dodd [45] urges the same. On the other hand, Paul refers to these same powers in Galatians, Romans and 1 Corinthians, where the argument seems to demand the belief in their reality.[46] The question, perhaps, cannot be fully decided. Nevertheless, it may be said that it was the necessity to fight against the significance attached to such powers

[42] See note by C. Rabin, *The Zadokite Documents* (1954), p. 16.

[43] On this see further C. G. Howie, 'The Cosmic Struggle', *Interpretation* 8 (1954), pp. 206 ff. It is not irrelevant to note the marked affinities between the 'Ephesian Gospel' and 'Qumrân' tendencies at this point. Those influences may have been strong in Asia Minor. See, e.g., W. F. Albright in *The Background of the New Testament and its Eschatology*, pp. 164 ff.

[44] *Commentary, ad loc.*

[45] *Abingdon Commentary, ad loc.*

[46] 1 Cor. 2:8; Rom. 8:38 f.; Gal. 4:3, 9.

among Christians not untouched by the conceptual climate of the sectarians that led Paul to deal with them, and thereby to formulate some of his most profound assertions on the all-sufficiency and supremacy of Christ. For our present purpose, which is the examination of the term 'flesh' in the scrolls and in Paul, what is noteworthy is that it is precisely where Paul has most clearly to combat what seem to be influences of the Qumrân type of idea that there emerges in his epistles the use of the term 'flesh' with a moral connotation. Polemic against sectarian ideology seems to call forth his use of the term: he comes to speak the language of his opponents (Col. 2:11, 13, 18). He can express himself otherwise, as, for example, in Col. 3:5, we read: 'Mortify, therefore, your members which are upon the earth', where we should expect him perhaps to say simply, 'Mortify therefore your flesh'. The obvious fluidity, however, with which Paul can use language, a fluidity which is the despair of his expositors, makes the particular incidence of the term 'flesh' in his epistles even more significant. It is sectarian contexts that seem to be evocative of it. The occurrence of 'flesh' in 2 Corinthians, in which there are traces of what can be claimed to be Qumrân terminology, confirms this [47] (See especially 2 Cor. 6:14 f.: 'Be ye not unequally yoked together with unbelievers: for what fellowship hath righteousness with unrighteousness? and what communion hath light with darkness? And what concord hath Christ with Belial? or what part hath he that believeth with an infidel?')

There remains to consider in connection with the term 'flesh' the paraenetic section in Gal. 5:13-21, which reads:

> For you were called to freedom, brethren; only do not use your freedom as an opportunity for the flesh, but through love be servants of one another. For the whole law is fulfilled in one word, 'You shall love your neighbour as yourself.' But if you bite and devour one another take heed that you are not consumed by one another.
>
> But I say, walk by the Spirit, and do not gratify the desires of the flesh. For the desires of the flesh are against the Spirit, and the desires of the Spirit are against the flesh; for these are opposed to each other, to prevent you from doing what you would. But if you are led by the Spirit you are not under the law. Now the works of the flesh are plain: immorality, impurity, licentiousness, idolatry, sorcery, enmity, strife, jealousy, anger, selfishness, dissension,

[47] See W. Grossouw, *op. cit.*, p. 3.

party spirit, envy, drunkenness, carousing and the like. I warn you, as I warned you before, that those who do such things shall not inherit the kingdom of God (RSV).

This list recalls other similar ones in the New Testament such as that in Mark 7:20 ff., which runs: 'And he said, That which cometh out of the man, that defileth the man. For from within, out of the heart of men, proceed evil thoughts, adulteries, fornications, murders, thefts, covetousness, wickedness, deceit, lasciviousness, an evil eye, blasphemy, pride, foolishness: All these evil things come from within, and defile the man' (AV). The items that are the same in both passages are adultery, fornication, lasciviousness, murders. The Galatian list is more directed, however, at those evils which create disunity—hatred, variance, emulations, wrath, strife, seditions, heresies, envying; it also slightly emphasizes more the specifically religious ills, idolatry, witchcraft, although the Marcan list also includes the 'evil eye' and 'blasphemy'. Moreover, we are equally reminded of lists of vices found in the Qumrân material: 'but to the spirit of error belong greediness, slackness of hands in the service of righteousness, wickedness and falsehood, pride and haughtiness, lying and deceit, cruelty and great impiety, quickness to anger, and abundance of folly and proud jealousy, abominable works in a spirit of fornication and ways of defilement in the service of uncleanness and a blasphemous tongue, blindness of eyes and dullness of ears, stiffness of neck and hardness of heart, walking in all the ways of darkness and evil cunning' (DSD iv, 9–11). The list in Galatians, despite its points of similarity—anger, folly, jealousy, fornication, uncleanness, blasphemy—is more directed against 'heretical' tendencies to disunity. The Qumrân list concentrates on the immoral tendencies within the community.

Lists drawn from Hellenic sources [48] have rightly been compared with those in Galatians and Mark, and any direct relation between the Pauline and the Qumrân material cannot be assumed. But it should be recalled that the paraenetic sections of the Pauline epistles have previously been connected with Jewish sources. D. Daube in particular traced the imperatival participle which often appears in

[48] See the commentaries. The scrolls do not present us strictly with *Haustafeln*, but we do find something not dissimilar in 1 QSa i, 6–18.

these sections to Rabbinic usage. There is, therefore, considerable justification for a readiness to see the same paraenetic tradition behind Paul and the sect, especially since the imperatival participle is emerging in the scrolls.[49] Moreover, the combination of 'doctrine' and 'paraenesis' which emerges in the Pauline epistles is precisely what we find in the Qumrân tradition: the 'form' of the paraenesis and its setting would appear to be much the same in Paul and the scrolls.[50] In addition, we have previously indicated the possibility that influences similar to those found in the scrolls appear among the Galatian 'judaizers'.[51] At least we can claim in the light of all this that it is not impossible that Paul was drawing upon a didactic tradition within Judaism which is represented for us in one of its forms in the scrolls.

But at this point we must again halt. The vices in Mark are described as coming 'from within, out of the heart of man', there being no specific reference to the flesh. In the scrolls the vices are those of the 'spirit of error'. The term for error is used elsewhere in the scrolls in connection with the 'flesh', but it should be noted that the ethical dualism of the sect is expressed in terms of two spirits whereas in Paul it is expressed in terms of the antithesis of flesh and spirit. Nowhere is the 'flesh' in the scrolls equated with the spirit of error, rather is it the sphere where this works. The parallelism between Paul and the scrolls at this point, therefore, is loose. The terms used by the sect and its literary conventions reappear in Paul but the fact that Paul thinks of a dualism of flesh and spirit still further confirms what we have previously noted, that the influence of the sect on Paul cannot be regarded as in any way determinative: Paul shares its terminology at certain points but not its doctrinal formulations. This will further appear as we turn to the doctrine of the Spirit. Does Paul's understanding of the Spirit reveal points of contact with that of the scrolls?

[49] See D. Daube, *The New Testament and Rabbinic Judaism* (1956), pp. 90 ff., especially p. 101.
[50] The structure of CDC is instructive here, as is the combination in DSD of 'Theology' and 'Ethics'.
[51] See p. 161.

II

Fortunately the scrolls are fairly rich in their use of the term 'spirit'. The fundamental treatment of it occurs in a section which is remarkably well constructed and apparently a self-contained unit.[52] The section is DSD iii, 13–iv, 26, and its substance may be set forth in the following tabulated form:

THE GOD OF KNOWLEDGE
(Sources of all that is or will be)

The designs [53] of all things
(These and all things are unchangeable)

Man created for dominion over all

SPIRIT OF TRUTH	SPIRIT OF ERROR
(from abode of light	(from source of darkness
= Prince of Lights	= Angel of darkness)
= Angel of Truth)	

Both shine in the heart of man

Counsels of Spirit of Truth	Counsels of Spirit of Error
Spirit of humility	Greediness
Slowness to anger	Slackness of hands in service of
Great compassion	righteousness
Eternal goodness	Wickedness
Understanding	Falsehood
Insight	Pride
Mighty wisdom	Haughtiness
Leaning on works and love of God	Lying
Spirit of knowledge in acts	Deceit
Zeal for right judgments	Cruelty
Holy thought	Impiety
Sustained purpose	Quickness to anger
Love for sons of truth	Abundance of folly
Purity	Proud jealousy

[52] Cf. Dupont-Sommer, op. cit., p. 120.

[53] On 'their designs', cf. DSD xi, 11. Burrows translates 'and before they came into being he established all their designing'. Erich Dinkler, op. cit., p. 125, n. 23, finds here a parallel to the 'purpose of God' in Rom. 8:28; 9:11. He refers, among others, to J. Dupont, Gnosis (1949), pp. 88 ff., where other New Testament parallels are given. See also Strack-Billerbeck, vol. II, pp. 335 ff. Ph. Hyatt, op. cit., p. 280, n. 1, sees a parallel idea in a familiar passage on the Torah as the plan of the world in Gen. Rabbah 1:1.

Counsels of Spirit of Truth	Counsels of Spirit of Error
Abhorrence of idols	Fornication
Walking with humility	Uncleanness
Prudence	Stiffness of neck
Concealing the truth of the the mysteries	Blasphemous tongue
	Hardness of heart
	Blindness of eye
	Walking in darkness
	Deafness of ears
	Walking in cunning

Rewards for Sons of Truth	Punishment for Sons of Error
Healing	Afflictions by destroying angels
Peace	Eternal perdition in fury of God's vengeance
Length of Days	Eternal trembling
Seed	Destroying Disgrace in dark places
Eternal Blessings	Sorrowful mourning
Everlasting Joy	Bitter calamity
Crown of Glory	Dark disasters
Raiment of Majesty in Eternal Light	No Remnant
	No Escape

All men share in both: both spirits are at enmity

But

A PERIOD OF RUIN FOR ERROR IS SET BY GOD

Truth of the world will emerge
Man purified of evil spirit: sprinkled with spirit of truth
Given wisdom and knowledge of God and Sons of Heaven
The new comes.

In the above table there is described a sharp dualism between two spirits. These spirits are both the creation of God, but (and it is important to notice this) they are regarded as a kind of permanent element in every man, since creation, until the 'End' decreed by God. On the other hand, that they are not merely inherent properties of man, as such, emerges clearly from the use of the term 'angel' to describe the two spirits: this preserves the 'otherness' of the two spirits even when they appear to be merely immanent.[54] Neverthe-less, the emphasis in the scrolls is not on the invasive, transcendent

[54] Cf. E. Schweizer, *op. cit.*, p. 491.

character of the two spirits, but on their enduring presence and persistence until the End: they suggest not an *inrush* of specially given energy but, if we may so express it, two constant *currents* of good and evil forces in conflict.

But, it will be asked, is not the coming of the Spirit a mark of the End in the scrolls? There is one passage where it is declared that at the End '*the truth of the world*' will emerge victorious. But the meaning of the phrase 'the truth of the world' is difficult to assess. Some have found here a personification of the Messiah as truth,[55] but in view of the sect's expectation of two Messiahs this is hardly tenable. Probably it is best to take the phrase here to be a kind of synonym for the spirit of truth. At the End, this will appear and will be 'sprinkled upon man'. The whole passage reads:

> But God in the mysteries of his understanding and in his glorious wisdom has ordained a period for the ruin of error, and in the appointed time of punishment he will destroy it forever. And then shall come out forever the truth of the world, for it has wallowed in the ways of wickedness in the dominion of error until the appointed time of judgment which has been decreed. And then God will refine in his truth all the deeds of a man, and will purify for himself the frame of man, consuming every spirit of error hidden in his flesh, and cleansing him with a holy spirit from all wicked deeds. And he will sprinkle upon him a spirit of truth, like water for impurity, to make the upright perceive the knowledge of the Most High and the wisdom of the sons of heaven, to instruct those whose conduct is blameless . . . (DSD iv, 18 ff.; Burrows).

Here the Spirit's function at the end of time is not merely a negative one, one of purification. It is positive: 'to make the upright perceive the knowledge of the Most High, etc. . . .' Nevertheless, the reference to the Spirit here somehow lacks that connotation of empowering energy which we associate with the eschatological gift of the Spirit in both the Old Testament and the New. Moreover, it must be doubly emphasized that it is only here that the Spirit is ascribed a strictly eschatological significance at all in the scrolls. This is particularly noteworthy in the literary remains of a sect which was steeped in the interpretation of Scriptures that made the Spirit a sign of the End, and which apparently regarded itself as living in the period preceding the End. Nor does the 'charismatic' character

[55] See references in n. 25 above.

of the sect make the absence of a markedly eschatological interpretation of the Spirit more understandable; on the contrary, it is
precisely such *charismatic* groups that we should expect to emphasize
the eschatological role of the Spirit.[56]

So far, then, the scrolls reveal two spirits who are constantly
opposed to each other, until the good spirit prevails at the End. But
this same spirit, which can be regarded, along with its rival evil
spirit, as a kind of permanent possession of man since his creation,
is also deemed to have expressed itself in certain particular persons.
There were special manifestations of it through Aaron and Moses,
just as, on the other hand, there were special manifestations of the
spirit of perversity. Thus the two spirits, which are from one point
of view abiding elements in man's constitution, as it were, are also
conceived as occasionally invasive. The pertinent passage is CDC v,
16 ff.: 'For also in ancient times God visited their deeds and his
anger was kindled against their practices, "for it is a people of no
understanding." "They are a nation void of counsel, inasmuch as
there is no understanding in them." For in ancient times Moses and
Aaron arose by the hand of the Prince of Lights and Belial raised
Jannes and his brother by his evil device, when Israel was delivered
for the first time . . .' (Rabin's translation).

The Prince of Lights, it will be recalled, is the spirit of truth, and
Belial the most frequent term employed for the spirit of error. The
spirits here are deemed to have been especially given at particular
times. The same concept appears in CDC iv, 13 ff., perhaps: 'And
during all those years shall Belial be let loose upon Israel as He spoke
by the hand of the prophet Isaiah son of Amoz, saying: "Fear, and
the pit, and the snare are upon thee, O inhabitant of the land."
Its explanation: the three nets of Belial, about which Levi son of

---

[56] We can think of the spirit of truth in the scrolls as eschatological, in the sense
that it forwarded the victory of the Good and thus hastened the 'End'. We should
not, however, too certainly assume that the 'End' was expected soon, as Matthew
Black pointed out to me. The phrase 'When these things come to pass . . .' is
vague. On the other hand, the interim ethic which seems to mark the sect (e.g., DSD
ix. 21 ff.) would suggest the nearness of the 'End'. It is difficult to agree with Cullmann, *op. cit.*, p. 32, that the sect did not know the Spirit. The warmth of its piety is
inexplicable otherwise. Cullmann writes: 'Instead of the Spirit, the Qumrân
movement had an organization.' This is to introduce a false antithesis. Daniélou's
view that we have both 'order' and 'ardour' at Qumrân is to be preferred. See
Rev. d'Hist. et de Phil. Rel. 35 (1955), pp. 104–15.

Jacob said that he "catches in them the heart (or 'the house') of Israel" and has made them appear to them as three kinds of un-righteousness . . .' (Rabin). The term 'Belial' is virtually defined in what follows it: what is meant is that the spirit of error would express itself in three ways—whoredom, wealth, conveying unclean-ness to the sanctuary; and it could express itself, at a particular point, in such a way that it could be said to be 'let loose'. In a similar way the same spirit of error, which we repeat, could be understood from one point of view as being a permanent ingredient of man's constitution, can be deemed to depart from a man, although we should not think of this departure probably as complete, because the spirit of error is in man till the End. This appears from CDC xvi, 4: 'And on the day that a man imposes upon himself by oath to return to the Law of Moses, the angel Mastema will depart from behind him, if he carries out his words. For this reason Abraham "was saved" on the day when he acquired knowledge' (Rabin).

Further, just as Moses was regarded as having been given the spirit, so too the spirit was the source of prophecy, as it is elsewhere in Judaism.[57] Thus in DSD viii, 14 ff., we read: 'When these things came to pass for the community in Israel, by these regulations, they shall be separated from the midst of the session of the men of error to go to the wilderness to prepare there the way of the Lord; "upon the wilderness prepare the way of the Lord, make straight in the desert a highway for our God". This is the study of the law, as he commanded through Moses, to do according to all that has been revealed from time to time, and as the prophets revealed by his Holy Spirit' (Burrows). The awareness of the spirit of truth as a specially given energy emerges again in a much-discussed passage in CDC ii, 9 ff.: 'And He knows (or: knew) the years of their existence and the number (or: set times) and exact epochs of all them that come into being in eternity (or: in the worlds) "and past events", even unto that which will befall in the epochs of all the years of eternity (or: the world). And in all of them He raised for Himself "men called by name", in order to leave (?) a remnant for the land and to fill the face of the universe of their seed, and to make (or: be made) known to them by the hand of His anointed ones His

[57] See Moore, *Judaism,* vol. I, p. 237.

C.O.–G

holy Spirit and shew them (or:demonstration of) truth . . .' (Rabin).
Thus Rabin takes the Hebrew word for 'His anointed one(s)' to
be a plural (with a defective writing in the text, a feature which is
found elsewhere: MSHYHW instead of MSHYHYW) and interprets
it as referring to 'the prophets'.[58] Burrows [59] reads it as a singular
and simply translates 'And through his anointed one he shall make
them know his Holy Spirit and a revelation of truth', and interprets
it as referring to Zadok. Teicher claims this to be a reference
to Christ, since in his view the scrolls are Jewish-Christian
documents.[60]

This last reference to Teicher's thesis reopens the question of the
relation of the Messiah to the spirit in the scrolls. If we reject the
strictly messianic reference in DSD iv, 20, and in CDC ii, 9 ff., then
in no case in the scrolls is the spirit specifically connected with
the Messiah(s), although in DSD iv, 20 f., it is connected with the
End. The problem of the relation of the spirit to the Messianic
Age emerges with peculiar force in DSD ix, 3 ff., which Burrows
renders thus: 'When these things come to pass in Israel according
to all these regulations, *for a foundation of a holy spirit*, for eternal
truth, for a ransom for the guilt of transgression and sinful faithless-
ness . . . at that time the men of the community shall be set apart,
a house of holiness for Aaron, to be united as a holy of holies and a
house of community for Israel, those who conduct themselves blame-
lessly. . . . They shall not depart from any counsel of the law, walking in all the stubbornness of their hearts; *but they shall judge by
the first judgments by which the men of the community began to be*

---

[58] *Op. cit.*, p. 8, n. 4. Cf. above on DSD viii, 14 ff.

[59] *Op. cit.*, p. 264.

[60] In *Journ. of Jewish St.* 5 (1954), pp. 139–40. Teicher translates 'and He has
imparted to them knowledge through His Christ His Holy Spirit, who is the truth',
which he asserts contains 'the germ of the doctrine of the Trinity'. His translation
demands a reading which, according to Rabin, it is impossible to substantiate in the
manuscript. Rabin then claims that, on the ground of 1 QM xi. 7–8 ('. . . by thy
anointed ones, seers of testimonies . . .'), there can be no doubt that *mashiah* can
mean 'prophet' and need not refer to a messianic figure in CDC ii, 12. On Kuhn's
solution, in the context of the Two Messiahs, see *The Scrolls and the New Testament*,
p. 59. The interpretation of MSHYHW must remain doubtful and so too much
cannot be built upon it. The discussion is summarized by P. Wernberg-Møller in
Journ. of Semitic St. 1 (1956), pp. 116 ff. He deals with previous translations and suggests his own: '. . . and He made known to them, through those who were
anointed with the holy spirit of His true community . . .'

disciplined, until there shall come a prophet and the Messiahs of Aaron and Israel.'

Brownlee renders the first of the phrases we have put in italics by 'for an institution of a holy spirit', but tentatively suggests also 'for an institution of spiritual holiness'. One thing alone is clear. The period 'when these things happen' is to be distinguished from the Messianic Age: when the two Messiahs have come, they shall presumably bring new judgments with them, which are to be sharply distinguished from the judgments, i.e., the laws, prevailing in the pre-Messianic Age. There are two possibilities. *Either* the community in the days immediately preceding the End is to be in possession of the Holy Spirit, on the grounds of its fulfilment of the Law in the right way *or* the strict discipline of the sect becomes a foundation on which, when the Messianic Age has come, the Holy Spirit will be given. The first possibility goes with the translation 'institution' and means that the 'holy spirit' is preparatory to the End and not strictly necessarily a mark of it. The second possibility goes with the translation 'foundation' and conceives the Spirit as a future sign of the End. This last, it must be conceded, involves a somewhat tortuous understanding of the text.[61] Moreover, the context suggests that the life of the sect before the Messianic Age is throughout in view as in DSD viii, 5 ff., and it is possible that all that is meant by 'holy spirit' here is 'a spirit of holiness', the emphasis being on 'holiness', not on 'spirit'—i.e., 'spirit' here refers primarily to disposition or character, as it often does in the scrolls (see DSD iv, 3; viii, 3; ix, 14 ff.; ix, 22; xi, 2).

It would in any case be too precarious to see in DSD ix, 3 ff., anything that would seriously cause us to modify what we wrote above, that the scrolls do not *emphasize* the spirit as a sign of the End.[62]

Before we turn to Paul himself there is one further possibility to be noted, namely, that the term 'spirit' in the scrolls came to mean

[61] See Brownlee's translation, p. 35.

[62] Perhaps we have underestimated the possible messianic significance of the term 'man' in DSD iv, 20. See the discussion in W. H. Brownlee, 'The Servant of the Lord in the Qumrân Scrolls,' *Bull. of the Amer. Sch. of Oriental Res.* 135 (1954), pp. 23–38. G. Vermès, *Cahiers Sioniens* 9 (1955), pp. 57 ff., finds in the term a messianic significance which had not in the sect been synthesized with other elements of the messianic expectation. But even if the Spirit is to be more closely related to the messianic hope than we have allowed above, its role is still not emphasized.

what we would refer to as 'the self', this under the influence of Persian ideas about the *daēna*. This is suggested by Schweizer.[63] Not all his evidence for this is equally convincing.

Thus in DSD vii, 18: 'If a man's spirit wavers from the institution of the community, so that he becomes a traitor to the truth and walks in the stubbornness of his heart . . .'—as in DSD vii, 23: 'If any man is in the Council of the community for ten full years and his spirit turns back so that he becomes a traitor to the Community . . .' (Burrows)—'spirit' may refer merely to 'disposition', although Schweizer's claim that it refers to 'man's total existence, particularly that of man facing God, i.e., man as religious being' is probable.

More doubtful is the use of DSD viii, 12, in this connection. The whole passage reads: 'When these men have been prepared in the foundations of the community for two years with blameless conduct, they shall be separated in holiness in the midst of the Council of the men of the community; and when anything which has been hidden from Israel is found by the man who is searching, it shall not be hidden from these men out of fear of an apostate spirit' (Burrows). The phrase 'out of fear of an apostate spirit' may merely anticipate a situation where a member of the community might be led not to communicate new truths (of Scripture) to them—truths revealed particularly to him—when he was afraid that, by his words, he would appear heretical. It is not difficult to imagine how stifling and prohibitive could be the inquisitorial atmosphere of the sect.[64]

More convincing is Schweizer's reference to DST viii, 5: 'Thou hast cast for man an eternal lot/With the spirits of knowledge/to praise Thy name together in joyful song/And to recount thy wonders in the presence of all thy works . . .' Here the 'spirits of knowledge' are the members of the community.

At obvious points the use of the term *ruaḥ* in the scrolls will have recalled that of *pneuma* in the Pauline epistles. In both the terms

---

[63] *Op cit.*, p. 493.

[64] Should we understand the Pauline emphasis on 'liberty' in Galatians partly in the light of this, if, as was suggested above, there were possibly sectarian influences at work in the Galatian churches? A particularly bad instance of inquisitorial methods occurs in DSD i, 11, where the wife is to bear witness against her husband.

are found respectively to express disposition or temperament;[65] to denote the self;[66] to indicate the origins of prophecy.[67] Moreover, the marked communal emphasis of the Spirit in Paul finds its counterpart in the scrolls.[68] The limitation of the use of the term *ruaḥ* to human and moral realities, without reference to the created order, is largely the case with Paul and the scrolls.[69] The longstanding discussion as to whether Paul was the first to 'ethicize' the Spirit can now be regarded, in the light of the scrolls, as closed.[70] Over a large area, therefore, the sectarian documents and the Pauline epistles reflect a common understanding of the concept of 'Spirit' (*ruaḥ/ pneuma*).

Furthermore, before we seek to assess the degree to which they shared a common milieu, it is fair to observe that Paul, who lived in a community which believed that the Messiah had come, could not but differ radically in his understanding of the 'Spirit', in emphasis, at least, from the sectarians who still awaited their Messiahs. Complete identity in this, as in other things, it would be unreasonable to expect for this reason. Perhaps the real relation between Paul and the sectarian influences that may have been upon him can be clarified by asking a simple question: Had Paul been much influenced by the kind of thought on the spirit revealed to us in the scrolls, would he have developed his 'doctrine' of the Spirit as he did? To ask this question is at once to be made aware of the points at which Paul differs from the sectarians.

Here again the incidence of Paul's use of the term *pneuma* is instructive. The frequency with which it occurs in various senses is as follows:[71] of the spirit of man (22 instances); of the spirit as opposed to flesh (6); *of the spirit of God (Holy Spirit: 72)*; of the spirit as opposed to the Law and the letter (4); of the spirit denoting

---

[65] Rom. 1:4; 8:15; 1 Cor. 4:21; 2 Cor. 4:13; Gal. 6:1; Eph. 1:17.

[66] See R. Bultmann, *Theology of the New Testament*, vol. I (Eng. Trans., 1951), pp. 205 ff.

[67] We cannot doubt that Paul regarded Old Testament prophecy, like prophecy in the Church, as the gift of the Spirit: 1 Cor. 12:8, *et al.*

[68] See W. D. Davies, *Paul and Rabbinic Judaism*, pp. 200 ff.

[69] *Ibid.*, pp. 188 ff. Contrast E. Schweizer, *op. cit.*, p. 485, n. 1.

[70] See *Paul and Rabbinic Judaism*, pp. 217 ff. The scrolls add force to our contention there that Paul was not the first to 'ethicize' the Spirit. Cf. G. R. Edwards, *op. cit.*

[71] No account is here taken of the phrase *diakriseis pneumaton*, 1 Cor. 12:10; 14:14–32.

a quality or disposition (13); of the spirit of Christ (8); of the spirit of evil or of the world (2).

There would, perhaps, be differences in the interpretation of some of the passages in the categories submitted above, but the lists are at least sufficiently accurate to supply a broad picture of the Pauline emphasis.

The predominance of references to the Spirit of God, or the Holy Spirit as the Spirit of God, and the paucity of references to the spirit of evil is clear. There are only two examples of the use of *pneuma* specifically as an evil force:[72] 1 Cor. 2:12 and Eph. 2:2. As for 1 Cor. 2:12, the whole passage concerned is 1 Cor. 2:6–16. The Jewish affinities of the opponents of Paul in the Corinthian Church have been recently urged particularly by Dupont.[73] They are made more than ever probable by the parallelisms which the above passage, as others also, offer to the scrolls. The 'mystery' revealed to Christians (2:10), which is hidden from this world and was not recognized by the powers of this world (2:6),[74] recalls the 'mysteries' revealed to the sect and hidden from the 'men of the pit' (DSD ix, 17, 22), and also recalls the expectations of a fullness of knowledge at the End anticipated by the sect. Paul virtually claims that this is already his 'in Christ'. The 'wisdom' spoken by Paul among the 'perfect' echoes the wisdom cherished by the sectarians who regarded themselves as 'perfect'. In the light of all this, perhaps we should expect the Pauline use of *pneuma* to suggest further the conceptual milieu of the scrolls.

But here caution is right. The term 'holy spirit', as we have seen, occurs frequently in the scrolls, but there is no direct parallel in them either to the term 'the spirit of God' or 'the spirit from God', or to the phrase 'the spirit of the world'. Is it, then, the same opposition between two spirits that we find in DSD iii, 13 ff., and in Paul in 1 Cor. 2? The meaning of the phrase, 'the spirit of the world', which might be taken, at first glance, to correspond to 'the spirit of perversity' in the scrolls, is difficult to assess. Does it refer to 'a system of organized evil, with its own principles and its own

---

[72] It does denote evil dispositions elsewhere, as was above noted.
[73] *Op. cit.*, pp. 247–61.
[74] See pp. 127 ff. above.

laws' (cf. Eph. 2:2, 6:11, which, we have already suggested, recall the scrolls), or is it a somewhat colourless phrase meaning merely 'the spirit of human wisdom', with no suprasensible undertones such as we find in Eph. 2:2?[75] But even if we connect 'the spirit of the world' with Eph. 2:2, we still have no exact terminological parallel with the 'spirit of error' in the scrolls. Moreover, difficult as it is to define 'the spirit of the world' in 1 Cor. 2:12, it is equally clear what Paul means by the Spirit of God, because he himself defines it for us as 'the Spirit (which comes) from God'; its divine origin is emphasized. It will at once be recalled that, although God is the creator of both the spirit of truth and of error in the scrolls, in DSD iii, 19 ff., the source of the spirit of truth is defined as being 'in the abode of light'. It is not said to be 'from God', although made by God. So too the spirit of error is derived from 'a source of darkness'.[76] The parallelisms between the two spirits mentioned by Paul and those opposed in the scrolls cannot, therefore, be too closely pressed in 1 Cor. 2.

There is a more likely parallel in Eph. 2:1–2. As we previously suggested, it is not difficult to see here, as elsewhere in Ephesians, the reflection of a conceptual climate like that revealed in the scrolls. The spirit 'that is now at work in the sons of disobedience' is reminiscent of the 'spirit of error' in DSD iii, 13 ff., by whom is 'the straying of all the sons of unrighteousness'. It is noteworthy that in DSD iii the 'spirit of error' is not called 'a prince' or 'a power', but 'an angel'. The term 'prince' is reserved for the 'spirit of truth' who is called both 'angel' and 'prince of lights'. However, too much should not be made of this because the 'spirit of error' has a dominion over its minions, the evil spirits, so that by implication it too is a prince.[77] The author of Ephesians, it seems not unlikely, combated ideas such as emerge in the scrolls and used these very ideas in the service of the gospel.

But apart from these two passages—and the one in Ephesians

[75] See Robertson and Plummer, *Intern. Critic. Com., I Cor.* (1911), pp. 45 f.

[76] Brownlee: 'From the spring of light (issue) the generations of truth . . . but from a fountain of darkness (issue) the generations of perverseness'. His reading requires an emendation which Burrows avoids in translating: 'In the abode of light. . . .'

[77] See E. Schweizer, *op. cit.*

alone offers anything like a close parallel—Paul does not mention the spirit of evil. He is primarily concerned with another spirit—the Spirit from God; indeed he is almost exclusively so concerned. The evidence need not here be repeated that Paul is aware of himself as living in the community of the Spirit, in the New Israel, the people of the End, called into being by Christ.[78]

Whereas in the scrolls the eschatological significance of the Spirit is not emphasized, for Paul the Spirit is the sign of the End *par excellence*. The difference can perhaps best be expressed by saying that, whereas in the scrolls the 'spirit of truth', already and constantly at work in men, would again find expression in a renewed 'sprinkling' at the End, in Paul we find a dynamic sense of the 'newness' of the gift of the Spirit. This is not to deny that Paul would regard the Spirit, which had been poured forth in Christ, as the same Spirit that was previously at work in prophecy and in other ways in the Old Testament. But his emphasis is not on the continuity of the Spirit in the Old and New Dispensations, real as this was for him, but on the new creation which the coming of the Spirit in Christ had inaugurated.[79]

This is illustrated in two ways. First, in the relation which the Spirit in Paul bears to the Law. One of the most striking aspects of the scrolls is the coincidence in them of a 'legalistic' and a 'charismatic' piety.[80] The obedience to the Law demanded in the sectarian sources is even sharper than in Rabbinic Judaism.[81] But at the same time there is found, especially in the Hymns, an awareness of the need of God's justifying help which surpasses anything known to us in pre-Christian Judaism. The community is aware of itself as under 'the Law' and yet as a 'household of the spirit'; it reveals no sense of an *essential* incompatibility or *essential* tension between life under 'the Law' and life under 'the Spirit'. On the other hand, Paul sets 'the Law', as we are often reminded, in radical opposition to 'the Spirit'. To judge from the table given on pp. 171 f. this opposition occurs far less

[78] *Paul and Rabbinic Judaism*, pp. 177 ff.

[79] In this Paul is in line with the whole of the New Testament: the Christian Dispensation is regarded as a new creation.

[80] See J. Daniélou, *op. cit.*, pp. 104–16.

[81] It is instructive to note how often the term 'all' occurs, for example, in DSD. I counted 73 instances. See, further, H. Braun, 'Beobachtungen zur Tora-Verschärfung im häretischen Spätjudentum', *Theol. Lit. Zeit.* 79 (1954), cols. 347 ff.

frequently in Paul than treatments of his theology would lead us to suppose. Nevertheless, that Paul did set life under 'the Law' over against life 'in the Spirit' is clear. To this there is no parallel in the scrolls. The chief pertinent passage is 2 Cor. 3:4–9. Paul here asserts that a New Covenant has come into being of which he is a minister. The terms of this New Covenant are written not on tablets of stone or in letters of ink; terms written in and on such media 'kill'. Sectarian influences, such as we are here concerned with, as we saw, may well have been active in the Corinthian Church, and it is not impossible that Paul in 2 Cor. 3 is casting a side glance at our sectarians or at Jerusalem Christians;[82] the true New Covenant, Paul may be implying, has no *written* code. Nevertheless, the contrast drawn by Paul is with the Covenant at the Exodus and it is to the Israelites, in a general way, that he explicitly refers.[83] It is, therefore, precarious to find polemic against the Covenanters here. What is noteworthy is that, whereas the concept of the Spirit in the scrolls has been domiciled within a 'legalistic' community, it refuses to be so neatly domiciled in Paul. There are, indeed, passages in Paul where the Law itself seems to be regarded as one of the hostile forces, which belongs to the 'spirit of error' (see p. 159).

But secondly, the difference between Paul and the scrolls emerges in a point related to the first one made. We claimed that Spirit and Law are antithetical in Paul. But, as we have written elsewhere, this antithesis is transcended in Paul through the Christifying of the Spirit, so that the Spirit itself becomes both gift and demand: Paul almost equates the Spirit with the Christ and so, in part at least, resolves the tension between Law and Gospel.[84] On the other hand, as we saw above, there is no very close relation in the scrolls between the Messiahs expected and the Spirit. This is not to be pressed, because on the basis of Scripture, the sect would naturally expect the Messianic Age to be an age of the Spirit. Nevertheless, in the scrolls the connection between the Messiahs and the Spirit is not explicitly made, whereas for Paul the Lord, if not identified with, is at least equivalent to the Spirit.[85]

[82] So S. E. Johnson, *op. cit.*, p. 159.
[83] 2 Cor. 3:7,13.
[84] W. D. Davies, *op. cit.*, p. 225.
[85] See our caveat to this in note 62.

Are we to conclude from all the above, therefore, that Paul, while he used the term 'spirit' much as did the sectarians, nevertheless, shows no marked parallelism and, certainly, no dependence on them in the essentials of his 'doctrine' of the Spirit? This would seem to be the case. The Spirit in Paul is far more understandable in terms of the Old Testament expectation than in those of the scrolls.[86]

[86] There is, however, a caveat to be issued here. We stated above that 'Law' and 'Spirit' coexist in the scrolls. Is their juxtaposition easy or are they uneasily yoked? Explicitly there is no reference to any tension between them; but if we look closer perhaps we can discern such. Is it possible that the scrolls reveal the kind of tension within Paul's experience and within Judaism which issued in or rather found its resolution in the Gospel? There are passages which imply that 'the Law' under which the sect is living is not completely adequate. The prevailing view in Judaism was that the Law given on Sinai was perfect and eternal. Passages referring to a New Law are late and difficult to assess. In the scrolls we do find, however, along with an unmistakable and intense awareness that the days of the Messiahs would introduce changes, one explicit description of these as the coming of the New. In DSD iv, 25, we read: 'For in equal measure God has established the two spirits until the period which has been decreed and the making new' (Burrows' translation). Brownlee renders: '. . . and the making of the New'. When this new epoch dawns, there will be a change in the laws governing the community. The pertinent passage reads: 'When these things come to pass in Israel (DSD ix, 3) . . . They shall not depart from any counsel of the Law, walking in all the stubbornness of their hearts; but they shall judge by the first judgments by which the men of the community began to be disciplined, until there shall come a prophet and the Messiahs of Aaron and Israel' (9–11). There can be little doubt that the term 'first judgments' refers to the law of Moses, as understood by the sectarians; this is mentioned in DSD viii, 15, 22. Does the passage contemplate changes in the Law or merely in the application of the Law in the ideal future? Is the 'making of the New' to include the *mishpatim* ('judgments') themselves? On this term, see *Qumrân Cave I*, p. 113, on line 11 (IQSa i,ii).

Whatever the answer to this question, we are justified in finding here perhaps a sign of tension under the Law. The concentration, relentless and rigid, on obedience to the Law in the sect we have already noticed. The awareness of sin which accompanied this concentration shines equally clear. In no other sources is failure to achieve the righteousness of the Law more recognized and at the same time its demands pressed with greater ruthlessness. May it be that this condition may have led to the hope that the Age of the Messiahs would bring relief? (See, further, W. D. Davies, *Torah in the Messianic Age* [1952].) This possibility we can perhaps further discern in the yearning of the sect for the 'fullness' of knowledge in the Messianic Age. The passage in DSD iv, 18 ff., is pertinent here. In iv, 22 ff., the outcome of the sprinkling of the spirit of truth is 'to make the upright perceive the knowledge of the Most High and the wisdom of the sons of heaven, to instruct those whose conduct is blameless. For God has chosen them for an eternal covenant, and theirs is all the glory of man; and there shall be no error, to the shame of all works of deceit' (Burrows' translation).

The chief end of man, if we so term the matter, is here defined in terms of knowledge of God; it is to share in the wisdom of the angelic hosts. Note that there is no suggestion of absorption in God as in Hellenistic sources. Contrast, for example, the frequently quoted words from the *Corpus Hermeticum* 1, 26: 'This is the good end (*telos*) of those who have knowledge: To be deified.' Knowledge of God, which is the aim and end (*telos*) of the perfect of way, implies that the distinction between

Thus our discussion of 'flesh' and 'spirit' in Paul has led to the same conclusion. The scrolls and the Pauline epistles share these terms, but it is not their sectarian connotation that is determinative of Pauline usage. As the epistles themselves [87] would lead us to expect, Paul stands in the essentials of his thought on these matters more in the main stream of Old Testament and Rabbinic Judaism than in that of the sect. There is no reason to suppose that in other aspects of his thought the case would be different. But this does not mean that the scrolls have no significance for the understanding of Paul, because, as we have seen, they do supply an added clue to the connotation of terms that he used. [88]

[87] Gal. 1:14; Phil. 3:4 ff.

[88] See G. Johnston, ' "Spirit" and Holy Spirit in the Qumran Literature', in *New Testament Side Lights*, Hartford, Conn., 1960, pp. 33–60. Professor R. C. Zaehner informs me in a private communication that in Iranian sources the idea of the 'flesh' as having moral connotations does not occur; see above pp. 154 f.

---

creature and creator is preserved; it has a parallel in 1 Cor. 13:12 and John 17:3. How is this knowledge to be understood? Is it more knowledge in and through the Law, or is it knowledge beyond the Law? I have cited evidence elsewhere that the 'knowledge' about which the scrolls speak as marking the final time is eschatological not only in the sense that 'it belongs to the final time, but in the sense that it gives insight into the meaning of the events of that time' (see above, pp. 119 ff.). Should we go further and find among the sectarians a yearning for a knowledge which itself constitutes 'life eternal', which transcends the knowledge supplied by the 'Law' as known in this present age? Of this we cannot be sure, because the Law itself for people such as the sectarians would be the sum of all wisdom and knowledge. But it does seem that in the yearning for 'knowledge' which we find here, we see Judaism straining at the leash of the Law. Is it too much to say that the scrolls reveal Judaism at 'boiling point'? Much that we have written will recall Paul's cry in Rom. 7:24. The life under the Law which Paul describes echoes much in the scrolls, so that these must be taken into consideration in any future discussion of Paul's experience, which it is now customary to treat without much reference to his struggles under the Law in his pre-Christian days.

VIII

A NEW VIEW OF PAUL—J. MUNCK: 'PAULUS UND DIE HEILSGESCHICHTE'

The broad outlines of Professor Munck's understanding of Paul and the early Church were published in Bulletin form [1] and in the *Journal of Theological Studies*.[2] But it is in a volume entitled *Paulus und die Heilsgeschichte*,[3] that he has first set forth the detailed arguments upon which that understanding is founded, so that it is only now that this can be justly assessed. Since it demands a radical change in much of the traditional interpretation of Paul and his relation to the early Church, it deserves the closest scrutiny.

Professor Munck begins with Paul's conversion. Explanations of it in terms of a release from psychological tensions arising from Paul's pre-Christian experience within Judaism or Hellenism he rejects, because these rest not on evidence but conjecture. He also criticizes Lake's attempt to explain the inconsistencies in the accounts of the conversion in terms of source criticism.[4] All these accounts show

[1] *Bulletin of Studiorum Novi Testamenti Societas* (1950), pp. 26 ff.

[2] New series, vol. II (1951), pp. 3–16.

[3] *Acta Jutlandica,* Publications of the University of Aarhus, XXXVI, 1, Teologisk Serie 6, Copenhagen, 1954.

[4] Lake's assumption that the accounts in Acts cannot be reconciled with that in Galatians arises from a too literal exegesis, because there need be no fundamental inconsistency between Paul's insistence on the purely divine origin of his call and the existence of a human intermediary at that call in the form of Ananias. The accounts of the conversion prevalent at Jerusalem or elsewhere did not conflict with that of Paul himself in Galatians. Nor was the latter aimed at the former. Thus it is unthinkable that the story of Ananias should not have been known at Galatia; and if the account in Galatians was aimed, as Lake held, at refuting the tradition at Jerusalem, it is strange that the mediation of Ananias, which was part of the Jerusalem tradition, should find no echo in Galatians. It is equally strange that, if the three accounts in Acts are from different localized traditions, with peculiar emphases, there should be no greater variation among them in essentials. Moreover, two of the three accounts in Acts occur in speeches and would, therefore, naturally be coloured by the character

assimilation to the records of the calling of major Old Testament prophets (Jeremiah, Isaiah, The Servant of the Lord, Moses) and also of Enoch. This is the significant fact about them all. Paul's call is understood by him (for the accounts must have originated with him) and by the early Church as having a prophetic and eschatological meaning, it reveals him to himself as belonging to the noble army of prophets, as a figure in the *Heilsgeschichte* [5] revealed in the Scriptures, a person who had a quite peculiar part to play in those eschatological events which, now that the Christ had appeared, awaited their fulfilment. In fact, Paul became convinced that it was on the effectiveness of his work as an, or rather *the*, apostle to the Gentiles that the consummation of all things depended.

To support this view Professor Munck appeals chiefly to three passages of a non-polemical and, therefore, especially cogent character. First, in 2 Thess. 2:6–7 τὸ κατέχον and ὁ κατέχων refer not to the Roman state and Emperor or to the powers of evil associated with the End in apocalyptic but to the preaching of the Gospel to the Gentiles and to Paul himself as the one to whom this preaching was committed. [6] Thus Paul, as apostle, is the pivot which determines the very incidence of the End, because this awaits the fulfilment of his mission to the Gentiles. [7] Hence the extraordinary eschatological significance that belongs to Paul's work. Secondly, in Rom. 9–11 Paul not only knows the eschatological plans of God but is the

[5] The points at which Paul differs from the Old Testament figures are two. First, Paul's call came to him not merely when he was unprepared for it, as was Amos, for example, for his, but when he was in fierce opposition to the people of God. Secondly, Paul is of greater eschatological significance than they, because his lot was cast in the New Age and his call directed not only to Israel but to the nations. 'Für Paulus ist seine eigene Zeit und daher auch seine eigene Aufgabe von grösserer Bedeutung als diese Gestalten des alten Bundes. Er hat sie nämlich als "den alten Bund" im Lichte von Christus und seiner Kirche gesehen, weil es jetzt die Zeit der Erfüllung ist' (p. 50).

[6] Here Munck follows O. Cullmann in *Revue d'histoire et de philosophie religieuses* (1936), pp. 210–45.

[7] The significance here ascribed to the preaching of the Gospel is consonant, so Munck urges, with the eschatological traditions of Judaism and with what appears elsewhere in the New Testament.

of the audiences to which they were addressed. (Thus, for example, Munck would explain the Jewish tone of Acts 22 as due to the fact that the audience addressed was Jewish.) On all these grounds Munck refuses to regard the accounts as variously derived.

peculiar instrument in bringing these to fulfilment.[8] Thirdly, Rom.
15:14 ff. makes it clear to the Roman Church that Paul is authorized
to speak to them because he is the apostle to the Gentiles. He had
not done so previously because it was only now that his work in
the East ('by representative salvation') was completed, and he was
free to turn to the West.[9] It was not missionary strategy, concentrating on crucial cities, that led Paul to turn to Rome but an
eschatological dogma that he was the chosen instrument to bring in
the fullness of the Gentiles.[10]

But, if the case for thus regarding Paul is so clear, what has
hindered scholars from recognizing it? Professor Munck insists that
it is the Tübingen School, and he devotes the second chapter to the
Hegelian distortion which that school introduced into Pauline as
into other studies. Unfortunately Pauline research, while it has
necessarily rejected the Tübingen *dating* of the New Testament
documents, has retained the Tübingen *interpretation* of them: it has
merely transferred to the first century conflicts that Baur and his
followers placed in the second. Thus Paul is still pictured as a solitary
colossus destined to spend himself in founding churches, the life of
which was constantly jeopardized by emissaries from Jerusalem, which
was the centre of that Jewish Christianity to which Paul was opposed
and which opposed him. Lietzmann, Goguel, Nock, Knox, Dibelius-
Kümmel have all in various ways succumbed to the Hegelianism

---

[8] While there have been others engaged in preaching to the Gentiles, it is Paul
who is their true priest destined to bring in the fullness of the Gentiles. But this
ministry to the Gentiles is also directly related to the fate of Israel. The fact that the
Gentiles through Paul's work have come to inherit the promises made to Israel
provokes the old Israel to jealousy and thus all—both Jews and Gentiles—through
Paul's work at last enter into salvation.

[9] His work in the East was now complete, not in the sense that every individual
in the East had been converted, nor that the great cities of the East had become centres
of evangelism for surrounding areas, but in the sense that *all* peoples of the East
through some of their number had been confronted with the Gospel and had accepted
it. Thus through 'representative salvation' the whole of the East from Jerusalem to
Illyria had been 'saved', and hence Paul is free to turn West.

[10] But there are other polemic passages which point to the same thing. In 2 Cor.
3:7–18 the implication is that Paul is a figure of greater significance than Moses.
'Der Grösste in Israels Geschichte ist unter den herumreisenden Zeltmacher gestellt'
(p. 53). In the Christian Dispensation, in Gal. 2:7–8, he compares himself to the great
Peter. Peter is a pillar not the Rock of the Church, and Paul finds his apostleship to the
Jews comparable with—not greater than—his own to the Gentiles. In addition
Munck refers to Acts 11:3–13; 20:17–38; 1 Tim.; 2 Tim.; the understanding of Paul
which we find in the later Church goes back to Paul himself.

of the Tübingen School. In addition to endorsing Sundkler's criticisms [11] of this school, Professor Munck points out essential weaknesses of Tübingen origins in Pauline scholarship. While he does not go so far as John Knox,[12] Professor Munck insists that, though avowed in principle, the recognition of the priority of the epistles for the understanding of Paul has been more honoured in the breach than the observance: the Tübingen picture of the first century based on Acts is still the dominant one. Another vicious Tübingen legacy has been the tendency to treat all Paul's opponents, who differed according to localities and were not always to be connected with Jerusalem, as one group.[13] All this leads Professor Munck to state three methodological canons: first, the epistles must be taken seriously as our primary sources for Paul; secondly, each epistle must be given its full individual significance; in particular, there should be no blurring of the differences between the various opponents of Paul on the facile assumption that they were all Judaizers; thirdly, not all historical situations can be fitted into a clear systematic theological pattern.

Having thus stated his methodology Professor Munck proceeds to examine some of the greatest of the Pauline epistles. In a chapter entitled 'Die judaistischen Heidenchristen' he claims that the 'Judaizers' of Galatians are not Jews but Gentiles recently circumcised and that the Judaizing movement in 'Galatia' was quite independent of the Jerusalem Church between which and Paul there was no gulf. The phrase οἱ περιτεμνόμενοι in Gal. 6:13 refers to

[11] Namely: (1) That the antithesis between particularism and universalism is a modern one which should not be read back into the first century (the antithesis itself Munck claims is a product of Tübingen). Neither Paul nor Jesus was a universalist in the modern sense. (2) That it was incredible, as Baur held, that the disciples almost completely forgot the message of their Lord. (3) That the Tübingen position leaves inexplicable the mildness with which Jewish Christianity recognized Paul's Gentile mission.

[12] Because his criticisms of Acts are too rigid and do not sufficiently recognize that Acts does provide secondary material which re-endorses that of the Pauline epistles. See John Knox, *Chapters in a Life of Paul* (1950).

[13] The seriousness of this is that Baur had made the presence of polemic one of the tests of the genuineness of the epistles and under his influence the opponents of Paul, as stated, were lumped together as Judaizers related to the Jerusalem Church. Non-polemic sections of the epistles were reduced to insignificance—but this, together with the primacy given to Acts, meant that secondary sources and polemics determined the interpretation of Paul.

Christians who were being circumcised.[14] They were not Jewish but
Gentile Christians who were now insisting on circumcision for other
Gentiles, because they had three misconceptions: first, of Paul whom
they claimed to be dependent on Jerusalem for his commission to
preach and for the nature of his preaching, except that Paul had
adulterated this by his desire to please men; secondly, of the Jerusalem
Church (and of Jerusalem itself): that Church, they held, demanded
the circumcision of Gentiles; thirdly, of the nature of Christianity.
Attention to these three factors sufficiently illuminates the epistle.
Paul's aim in Galatians is to show how 'Der Judaismus der Heidenchristen schwebt in der Luft und ihr Sichberufen auf ein ursprünglich
umfassenderes paulinisches Evangelium mit Jerusalems Autorisation
ist eine freie Erfindung' (p. 86). The Jerusalem Church had not sought
to impose its own point of view on Paul at all: it recognized from
the start the validity of his mission to the Gentiles. Galatians itself
is made to prove 'dass der Judaismus nicht wie die Tübinger Schule
es meinte, die ursprüngliche Christentumsauffassung der Kirche in
der Zeit von Jesus bis Paulus darstellt, sondern *dass er eine heiden-
christliche Ketzerei ist*, nur möglich in den paulinischen Gemeinden'
(p. 126).[15] (Our italics.)

[14] See C. F. D. Moule, *An Idiom Book of New Testament Greek*, Cambridge, 1953,
p. 107, who takes Gal. 6:13 to mean '*for not even the very ones who get circumcised keep
the law*'.

[15] From the point of view indicated Munck holds the following interpretations
of passages in Galatians: (1) Gal. 2:1 f. is usually interpreted in the light of Acts 15:
behind the visit lies Paul's attempt to seek an agreement on circumcision with the
Jerusalem Church. But this, Munck urges, cannot be the case: for Paul to admit even
by implication, in referring to his Jerusalem visits, that he had sought an agreement
with the Church there would be to stultify his own position. The need to show
independence of Jerusalem also lies behind the necessity of showing how Peter bent
before Paul. To attempt to interpret Gal. 2:1 f. in terms of Acts 15 is merely perverse.
Gal. 2:1 f. is not an objective historical statement but a polemic. (2) 2:4-5, the case of
Titus, refers to the fact that Titus was not circumcised, but this has no reference to the
presence of Judaizers in the Council of Jerusalem, but to Judaizers whom Paul
confronted in his Churches. 2:4-5 do not clarify 2:3 (so Lietzmann) but are a kind of
aside—a side-glance by Paul towards the Churches. (3) The phrase ὁποῖοί ποτε ἦσαν
is usually taken to refer to the fact that the apostles concerned had once been com-
panions of Christ and were, therefore, superior to Paul who had not been such:
Paul's reference to them is polemic, he insists that his ministry is equal to theirs. This
polemic intention Munck denies. He refers the ποτε to lapses in the lives of the
'pillars'—such as they had in common with Paul, the arch-persecutor! (4) These
apostles had added nothing to Paul: this refers not—as is usually held—to rules such
as those mentioned in Acts 15 as those claim who argue that Acts 15, Gal. 2:1 f. do
not refer to the same events: it refers to the fact that the Jerusalem Church had made

But if so, what becomes of those parties of Christians which have been discovered in 1 Corinthians? To this Professor Munck devotes his fifth chapter entitled 'Die Gemeinde ohne Parteien'. The term αἵρεσις in 1 Corinthians has an eschatological significance: it is a

---

no demands such as Paul's opponents thought they must have made. They claimed that Paul, in reliance on Jerusalem, had at first preached a gospel which demanded circumcision and the Law but that later in order to please men Paul had left these demands out of his preaching. (5) The conflict between Peter and Paul at Antioch did *not* occur after the agreement reached between Paul and the Jerusalem Church. This would imply that the agreement between Paul and Jerusalem was short-lived and would play into the hands of Paul's opponents who claimed that he was only in superficial agreement with Jerusalem. Instead, by insisting on the significance of the change of sequence from ὅτε in 1:15 to ἔπειτα in 1:18, 1:20 and back again to ὅτε in 2:1 Munck urges that 2:11 f. does not indicate a chronological sequence but merely a most striking proof of Paul's independence of Jerusalem. The question as to *when* 2:11 f. happened remains open. (6) The phrase τινὰς ἀπὸ 'Ιακώβου Munck explains to refer to Jewish Christians from Jerusalem who had no specific connection with James at all. (7) The phrase μὴ πως εἰς κενὸν τρέχω ἢ ἔδραμον (2:2) does not mean that Paul (*a*) had to go up to Jerusalem to have his Gospel recognized, or (*b*) that Paul could not afford to allow emissaries from Jerusalem to enter his churches to ravage them—these are the customary views. The concept of emissaries sent out from Jerusalem is unhistorical: the idea first emerges in Acts where Jerusalem is given a central place. There is nothing really corresponding to these emissaries in history and even in Acts it is only Peter, John, Barnabas, Silas, Judas who are official emissaries. As a matter of history the Jerusalem Church, Munck urges, did not exercise control over the Gentile Churches. There are no emissaries mentioned in 1 and 2 Corinthians and Romans. The conflict between Peter and Paul in Antioch occurred before Acts 15 and there is nothing in Acts to suggest that Peter at Antioch was on an inspection. And those from James are not a party of inspection. Again the phrase φοβούμενος τοὺς ἐκ περιτομῆς does not refer to Jewish Christians but to Jews. The phrase μὴ πως εἰς κενὸν τρέχω then has reference to eschatology. Paul had to know what position the Jerusalem Church took on the Gentile mission. It regarded this as secondary: it was not concerned to interfere with Paul's work. But Paul could not well continue his *Heidenmission* without being sure that the mission to Israel was also being adequately taken care of. (8) What was the nature of the agreement between Paul and the pillars? Paul speaks of them in a friendly fashion: the expression in 1 Thess. 2:14 that the *Jews* were hindering the preaching of the Gospel to all creatures would be very strange if Jewish *Christians* were doing the same thing; Paul speaks of the attitude of the Jewish-Christian pillars as friendly to his work. 1 Thess. 2:14 seems to suggest good relations between Paul and the Jewish-Christian Churches of Palestine. This is also suggested by the collection for the Jerusalem Church and by the friendly relations between Paul and Peter everywhere in 1 Cor. 15:5; 1:12; 3:22. 1 Cor. 9:5 is not polemic against Jewish leaders of the Church. (9) The character of James as a rabid Jewish-Christian—such as Pauline research usually gives us—is unhistorical. Josephus does not support this picture: it is wholly derived from Hegesippus, who has been accepted because his picture of James coincides with what the Tübingen School desired. The missionary position of James is clear. The Gentiles are not to be regarded as outside the pale, but their conversion is to *follow* that of Israel. Nor is it correct to regard Peter as the compromising figure we usually think of: he is on the same side as Paul in essentials. The point at which Peter and Paul differed is clear. Peter took the

sign of the End.[16] The σχίσματα refer not to enduring parties but to quarrelling groups.[17] The themes dealt with in the rest of the epistle cannot be related to the kind of parties that scholars have usually isolated.[18] It is odd, if these parties ever existed, that they have left no trace, because in 1 Corinthians there is no evidence for a Paul and Peter party, and the existence of an Apollos party only became credible because 1 Corinthians was read in the light of Acts 18, it being assumed, quite gratuitously, that because he came from Alexandria Apollos had to be a kind of Alexandrian philosopher. But Paul does not attack the 'wisdom' of Apollos. 1 Cor. 1:17 ff. is not a polemic against specific persons or parties but against the Corinthian Church as such, because, through its *Sophialehre* it was confusing the Gospel with the philosophy and sophistry of its Hellenistic milieu and had thus come to misunderstand the nature of the Gospel, of its own Christian leaders and of its own character. Thus not the parties in the Church but the whole Church itself was Paul's object of attack: indeed there were no parties there and no Judaizers.

Similarly in his treatment of 2 Corinthians in chapter six ('Der wahre und der falsche Apostel') Professor Munck claims that the two passages in 2 Cor. 3:6 ff. and 11:22 ff. which are usually claimed

---

[16] Behind 1 Cor. 11:19 lies according to Munck a *Jesuswort* such as is cited by Resch, *Agrapha* (1906), from Justin, Dialogue 35, 3, with which compare Matt. 24:10, Acts 20:30, 2 Pet. 2:1 (in Gal. 5:19–21 αἵρεσις is a work of the flesh), i.e., in 1 Cor. 11:19 the reference is eschatological as is shown in the phrase ἵνα οἱ δόκιμοι φανεροὶ γένωνται ἐν ὑμῖν. The αἱρέσεις in the Corinthian Church are part of the pangs of the Messiah, which Paul already finds to be breaking out.

[17] In 1 Cor. 11:18 this is the case, so Munck; and in 1 Cor. 12:25 the reference is too general to be applied in detail to 'parties', and this is true of 1 Cor. 1:10.

[18] The claim that there is a Christ-party referred to in 1 Cor. 10:7 is rejected by Munck.

---

standpoint of the Jerusalem Church—when Israel were won, the Gentiles would be won. So for Peter the conversion and baptism of the Gentile Cornelius was an exception. Paul on the other hand held the view that the conversion of the Gentiles would lead to the conversion of Israel. So the visit of Paul to Jerusalem in Gal. 2:1 f. was concerned not with the Gentile problem at all but with the problem of Israel. As stated above, Paul could not lightly turn to the Gentiles unless he was certain that someone was caring for the Jews. The problem at Antioch between Paul and Peter, as at Jerusalem, was not over Law and Circumcision but over meals. It was Gentile Christians who introduced these problems. These, however, were not only opposed to Paul but also to Jewish Christianity and to the oldest apostles at Jerusalem. Paul and Jerusalem are at one. There was no school at Jerusalem behind the Judaizers. At many points in Munck's work we are reminded of J. H. Ropes, *The Singular Problem of the Epistle to the Galatians* (1929).

to point to the presence of Judaizers are not to be so understood. The first contrasts Christianity and Judaism, not Paulinism and Judaizing, and the second proves only that the false apostles concerned were Jews but not that they were Judaizers. Throughout 2 Corinthians, which, contrary to many, Professor Munck holds to be a unity, Paul is concerned not with his own opponents but with the Church as a whole which had so tragically misunderstood the nature of the Christian apostolate that it could forsake Paul in favour of false apostles who had visited it. All we can know about these is: (1) that they boasted of their apostolate; (2) that they claimed the right to be maintained by the Church; (3) that they were Jews. But the fact that they were Jews does not mean that they were from Jerusalem. (Nor can we regard them as *Pneumatiker*.) We do know that they did not attempt to Judaize the Church at Corinth; and we can only regard them as apostles who had wandered into Corinth, whence we do not know, just at the time, on Professor Munck's view, when the recalcitrant Corinthian Christians were, at last, submitting to the authority of Paul. This constituted the seriousness of their arrival: they would perhaps undo the reconciliation wrought between Paul and the Corinthian Church: hence the bitterness with which Paul writes in 2 Cor. 10–13. As it is expressed on p. 179: 'Das Entscheidende für Paulus' Behandlung von ihnen [the Apostles] scheint in Zeitpunkt ihres Kommens zu liegen. Sie hätten keinen schlechteren Zeitpunkt wählen können. Der Streit dreht sich um den wahren und den falschen Apostel, und nach langem Kampf hatten die Korinther sich gebeugt und wollten sich über den wahren Apostel und sein wahres Evangelium unterweisen lassen. Aber gerade in dieser Situation kommen jüdische Apostel nach Korinth, die sich von Paulus und seinem Bild von wahren Apostel unterscheiden. Und der Gemeinde ist es nicht schwer gefallen, dies zu sehen. . . .'

At this point Professor Munck turns to the Roman Church, in which the Tübingen School claimed that there must have been a Jewish and a Gentile Christian group, this on the basis of the Jewish contents of Romans and the reference to the strong and the weak in Rom. 14:1–15:6, who were identified with Gentile and Jewish Christians respectively. Following T. W. Manson,[19] Professor Munck

[19] *Bulletin of the John Rylands Library*, vol. xxxi (1948), pp. 224–40.

claims that Romans was not originally directed to any particular community so that the epistle reveals nothing about the composition of the Roman Church and therefore nothing about any Jewish-Christian groups there. And this prompts the question whether Jewish-Christians ever formed a large element in Pauline churches. That this was the case has usually been held on three grounds: (1) that the Epistles and Acts point to this; (2) that the contents of the Epistles which deal with the Old Israel, the Law, the Old Testament, would largely be unintelligible and irrelevant to predominantly Gentile Churches; (3) that the Jerusalem Church was concerned with the Gentile mission field and regularly sent emissaries to his Churches to discredit Paul and 'change' the Gospel he preached. This last point (3) Professor Munck had previously dismissed (see above, p. 183 n. 15), and on the first point, (1) above, he urges that a careful study of 1 Thess. 1:9; 2:14; 2:14; 1 Cor. 12;2; Gal. 4:8, 5:2, 6:12–13; Rom. 1:5f., 13; 11:13, 15:14–16; Phil. 3:3; Col. 1:21, 24; 2:13 reveals that the Epistles only point to Gentile readers and that despite the constant references to preaching to the Jews in Acts, nevertheless, the Jews remained unbelieving and opposed to the Gospel. Only in Berea does a Jewish-Christian element in the Church unmistakably emerge. And, like the Epistles, Acts also points to purely Gentile Churches in the Pauline mission field. On the second point, (2) above, Professor Munck insists that Gentile Christians no less than Jewish would have to be concerned with the problem of the nature of the Church and so with the old and new Israel; with the problems of conduct and, therefore, with the Law; and with the Old Testament, because they had emerged from a Judaeo-Christianity. It was not till later that Gentile-Christians came to be concerned with the Hellenistic-philosophic interpretation of the Gospel. There are, therefore, no grounds for postulating the presence in Pauline Churches of a large Jewish-Christian element.

The Pauline epistles having been examined, Professor Munck next deals with Acts. Pentecost, which was a sign to Israel, did not drive the disciples to labour in fields outside Jerusalem:[20] they remained

---

[20] Pentecost was a sign to Israel as such that Jerusalem with its Temple was the centre for all Jews. That the disciples became missionaries to the Gentiles is a figment of the later Gentile Church.

there to constitute a kind of *Collegium*. But the Jerusalem Church was not merely a bit of Judaism which believed in Jesus as the Messiah. From the first it was a sharply distinguished community, its history a *Märtyrer-geschichte*.[21] Contrary to the Tübingen view it was undivided. The terms *Εβραῖοι* and *'Ελληνισταί* are names for Jews possibly differing in speech or origin: they do not refer to parties in the Church. Stephen's speech does not imply that there was a Christian group called *'Ελληνισταί* who were for making a radical break with Judaism and with the *Urgemeinde*.[22] The *'Εβραῖοί*, among whom was Peter, shared a common attitude with the *'Ελληνισταί*. The story of Cornelius makes this clear. Arising in a community which thought that the Gospel was meant only for Jews, it is no merely primitive conversion story (Dibelius) into which Luke has injected the motif of clean and unclean foods; its aim is to present the attitude of the *Urgemeinde* that the Gentile mission was to be accepted.

But who then were the Judaizers demanding of Gentiles circumcision and the Law? They emerge only in Acts 15 and 21:17-25. In Acts 15 the Judaizers are (1) Christians who came from Judaea who were, like those in Galatia, Gentiles,[23] and (2) certain Pharisees become Christian.[24] The essential fact about Acts 15 is that both Peter[25] and James recognize that the Gospel should be presented to Gentiles without the demand being made for the Law and circumcision. Israel stands first in *Gottesheilsplan* for both (cf. Rom. 1:16; 2:9; 2:10) but later the Gentiles are also to be redeemed *as Gentiles*.[26] Thus it could not be that those who demanded the Law and circumcision were sent out from the Apostles and elders of

---

[21] Persecution was widespread and confined not merely to radicals like Paul and Stephen.

[22] There is nothing that Stephen utters that cannot be traced back to Jesus Himself, and in Luke's account there is no reference to a difference between Stephen, Jesus and the primitive community. The clinging of the disciples to the Temple does not mean that they held a purely Jewish point of view, neither do the Greek names of the Seven signify that they were Greeks.

[23] Professor Munck points out that Acts 15 assumes the division of missionary labour mentioned in Gal. 2:7-9.

[24] This is peculiar because seldom does Acts refer to the Pharisees at all.

[25] Peter is not here speaking as a Paulinist: he is merely expressing the point of view of the *Urgemeinde*.

[26] Here James, the brother of the Lord, is optimistic about the reception of the Gospel by Jews. Contrast the facts as Paul gives them in Rom. 9:11.

Jerusalem.[27] Again in Acts 21:20 by an emendation of the text, which omits τῶν πεπιστευκότων,[28] Professor Munck removes any reference to Jewish-Christians opposed to Paul. He is thus able to conclude that there is no evidence in Acts that the *Urgemeinde* took a Judaizing attitude. It agrees with this that references to the Law and circumcision in Acts are surprisingly few.[29] This is due not to any penchant that Luke had for blurring differences: it arises from the history itself, for it is not probable that the demand for circumcision and the Law arose in Jerusalem, because the *Urgemeinde* there was concentrating on the conversion of Israel: though this would ultimately lead to the conversion of the Gentiles, this last as such did not interest them. Hence Professor Munck argues that Judaizers are more likely to have arisen in the Pauline mission field than in Jerusalem itself.[30]

The Synoptic Gospels, which Professor Munck regards as containing Jewish-Christian traditions little contaminated by the transition from Palestinian to Gentile soil support this view. The mere preservation of Jesus' discussions on the Law shows that the *Urgemeinde* found the Law a problem. Matt. 17:24-7 shows Jewish-Christians as aware of the essential difference between them and

[27] Luke's concentration on the significance of the city centres in the period may be responsible for leading him to connect 'Judaizers' with Jerusalem even though they actually belonged to the Pauline mission field. For example, the scenes in Gal. 2:1–10 f. may have given rise to the description of the Council in Acts 15.

[28] Professor Munck argues that we cannot ascribe the kind of duplicity which the text as it stands demands of him to James, the brother of the Lord, in which he shows one attitude to Paul and another to the *Urgemeinde*. Wendt's interpretation of ἀδελφοί in 21:17 as friends or relatives of Paul is untenable, because it is a stock term in Acts for Christians—for the community or communities. To support his emendation Munck urges: (1) that there were not in the whole of Palestine *myriads* of Jews; (2) a reference to danger from members of the *Urgemeinde* makes no sense: Jews fit the context better; (3) 21:22 is unintelligible if the reference is to Jewish-Christians whom Paul was visiting and who would therefore know of his visit; (4) the complaints made against Paul are such as Jews would make: compare the case of Stephen.

[29] They occur only in contexts where Paul and Stephen are attacked. The silence *may* be due either to the fact that they were assumed to be binding on the *Urgemeinde* or again that they were not deemed to have independent significance for the life of the Church.

[30] The silence of Acts on Judaizers is not due to its desire to defend Paul or to its calculated diminution of the contrast between Jewish and Gentile Christianity as the Tübingen School held. Luke is true to history: the *Urgemeinde* was *not* Jewish Christian. The introduction of Judaizers in Acts 15:1, 5 is due to the transference to the first-century Church of an attitude that belonged to the second.

Jewry, and the critical attitude revealed towards the Sabbath, Fasting and the Old Testament proves that the *Urgemeinde* was not conservatively Jewish. So too the attitude to the Gentiles which emerges in the Synoptics shows that the *Urgemeinde* like Jesus was not *directly* concerned to win Gentiles or to impose the Law upon them.[31] Like Jesus Himself, Jewish-Christians were anxious to preach first to the Jews, believing that the Jews in turn would lighten the Gentiles. At first this was carried on in Jerusalem and later (and Professor Munck seems to suggest that this was a deliberate act of policy) in the Diaspora.[32] But this mission to the Diaspora Jew, as to Jewry elsewhere, proved a fiasco (Rom. 10:14 ff.; Luke 5:1-11; John 21:1-14), and this Paul knew. And so, although like Jewish-Christians, Paul thought that Israel and Jerusalem were the centre of the world and that Israel's conversion therefore was of crucial significance, he came to think that his conversion was to come not by concentration on preaching to Israel but by preaching to the Gentiles, the conversion of whom would lead, through 'jealousy', to that of Israel. Thus Paul differed from the *Urgemeinde*, which said that the time for doing so was not yet, in insisting on the priority of preaching to the Gentiles, and from the later Church, which claimed that there could be no mission to Israel at all, in insisting that this would lead to the conversion of Israel.

It will be apparent that Professor Munck has removed the gulf fixed by the Tübingen School between Paul and the *Urgemeinde*, and has rooted the apostle deeply in the primitive Christian tradition. The customary view of Paul, as a missionary set on reaching Rome, but forced by the evil machinations of opponents from the *Urgemeinde* to turn again and again to Jerusalem, he rejects. This relieves us, he claims, from having to think of Paul as a kind of 'split personality', a morally ambiguous *Kirchenpolitiker* who pretended to a freedom he did not in fact possess, because, while claiming to be free from the Law, he had all the time to submit to the authority of Jerusalem. But this also enables us to look with new eyes at the place of Jerusalem in Paul's thinking (and here, as in dealing with Israel and

[31] At this point Professor Munck insists that it is erroneous to think of Judaism in the first century as showing missionary zeal. But he ignores the recent work of Braude and Bamberger in this field, and now Jeremias.
[32] See pp. 266 ff.

Jerusalem in the thought of Jesus, Professor Munck is at his best). Three things emerge: first, for Paul it was in Jerusalem that the decisive act of God was to be effected (2 Thess. 2:3–4, 8–10; Rom. 11:26–7); secondly, after every missionary journey Paul was careful to return to Jerusalem; thirdly, the collection for the poor in Jerusalem is to be understood not as a tribute (Karl Holl), nor merely as an oecumenical gesture, but as an eschatological sign: it partakes of prophetic symbolism. As stated previously, Paul saw a vital connection between the conversion of the Gentiles and that of Israel, and to this the collection is related. The purpose of the large delegation going up to Jerusalem was to confront that city with a representation of the believing Gentiles. These took with them gifts so as to fulfil Old Testament prophecies that the Gentiles should flow to Jerusalem bringing their tributes with them. Paul hoped that their presence in Jerusalem would stimulate the conversion of Israel, which would be 'life from the dead'. This novel eschatological understanding of the collection and delegation illumines Rom. 9–11, especially at 9:1 ff., 9:26, 10:10. Moreover, it supplies a sufficient motive for Paul's readiness to face suffering and even death itself in visiting Jerusalem at that time.

And to the final suffering of Paul Professor Munck turns in the last chapter, 'Paulus vor dem Kaiser'. Instead of witnessing the expected conversion of Israel, Paul was imprisoned through the instigation of Israel. How did Paul react to this and to the enforced abandonment of his preaching and to the consequent delay in the coming of the End? Two things are clear. First, Paul insists that his very trials are eschatological; they are concerned with the Hope of Israel (Acts 23:6, 24:21; 26:6; see pp. 306 ff.). Secondly, his trials in the mind of Luke and of Paul himself are to be compared with those of his Lord. These trials occupy in Acts a position roughly corresponding to that of the Passion Narrative in the Gospels, and just as in the Gospels the Passion casts its shadow over all the preceding narrative, so too in Acts there is, throughout the relevant passages, a premonition of the final suffering of Paul. Acts, so Professor Munck feels, seems to expect the imminent consummation of Paul's suffering in death. But Paul's own view of his sufferings and trials we get in Philippians. The opponents referred to in Philippians were not

Judaizers, but those who, quite naturally, thought that Paul, because he was a transgressor of the Law, a Roman prisoner, should withdraw into obscurity so that the Gospel should not suffer dishonour (it was important that the Gospel should not be closely associated with Paul in the popular mind). But Paul thought otherwise: he came to see that his suffering in Rome was for the sake of the Gospel. In and through his very trial before the Emperor, Paul would be fulfilling his destiny as the apostle to the Gentiles. Because this was the case, the active Paul learns contentment even in bonds. To illustrate his case, Professor Munck refers to contemporary *Märtyrerakten* and to Old Testament and Maccabean parallels to Paul's trials. In particular, he also refers to Matt. 10:18-20; Mark 13:9-11; 2 Tim. 4:16-18. In these passages the necessity that the Gospel should be preached to all Gentiles is connected with the certainty that its preachers should have to bear witness before the authorities. It is over against this background that Paul sees in his coming defence before the Emperor the fulfilment of his role as eschatological messenger. His witness before the Emperor would *ipso facto* be a witness to all nations; and so the End is at hand. 'Paulus war auf seinem Wege nach Jerusalem nach Rom gelangt. Er hatte vor dem Kaiser Zeugnis abgelegt, und sein Tod war nicht fern. Aber die Fülle der Heiden war Wirklichkeit geworden, und ganz Israels Errettung war zu erwarten. Und dann sollte Christus sich offenbaren, in Herrlichkeit zum Gericht und zum Heil. Deswegen kann der Apostel in gewohnter Sachlichkeit ausdrücken, was er erreicht hat; "Den guten Kampf habe ich gekämpft, den Lauf vollendet, den Glauben bewahrt" ' (p. 329).

It is impossible to deal here in detail with a volume, written very persuasively, which reopens almost every difficult issue in the life of Paul. It is always instructive even when it stirs most disagreement. If we concentrate in what follows on criticism this in no way signifies our lack of gratitude for all that we have learnt from the author: and we do so in full awareness that the range and erudition of his work is such that there will be continued disagreement and discussion on many, if not all, the points he raises.

As the above summary will have made clear, Professor Munck has taken very seriously the necessity to refute the Tübingen position.

It is at least arguable that he knocks at doors that have long been open. There must be few students of recent years who have not been warned against the excesses of the Tübingen School. Nor is it quite correct to claim that Dibelius, for example, has succumbed to Tübingen: at points such as his treatment of Acts 15 he is as cautious not to distort history in favour of Acts as is Professor Munck himself.[33] Scholars such as T. W. Manson,[34] to name only one, have paid more than lip service to the priority of the Epistles, and there have not been wanting those who have checked the impulse to interpret the 'parties' in Corinth in Tübingen terms.[35] Nevertheless, as far as the writer is aware, while the Tübingen position has tended to crumble from being nibbled at various points, it has not been subjected to a systematic frontal attack. It is the merit of Professor Munck's work that it subjects this position, as it now influences Pauline studies, to just such an attack; and in so doing he is led to a provocative, and at many points illuminating, reinter-pretation of Paul. Professor Munck rightly understands the character of the actual ministry of Jesus: it was immediately confined to Jews but ultimately concerned also with the Gentiles. In this he can claim the powerful support of Jeremias in his recent article on this theme.[36] It is also a virtue of this volume that it compels us again to recognize the large extent to which the leaders of the early Church were at one; and also delivers us from reading the New Testament too much through twentieth-century missionary eyes, especially in its under-standing of the role of Jerusalem.

But in his zeal to attack the Tübingen position Professor Munck goes too far. His work provokes two kinds of criticism that are intimately related. First, in matters of detail, in insisting that the attitude of Jesus became also that of the *Urgemeinde*, so that the latter is drawn nearer to Paul than the Tübingen School allowed, Professor Munck is led to what appears to us as forced exegesis. Here we can only indicate a few points which may be questioned. While Professor

[33] Dibelius-Kümmel, *Paul* (Eng. trans.), Philadelphia, 1953, pp. 129 ff., 9 ff.

[34] See, for example, 'St. Paul in Ephesus: The problem of the Epistle to the Galatians', in *The Bulletin of the John Rylands Library,* vol. xxiv. No. 1, April 1940.

[35] See, for example, J. H. Ropes, *The Singular Problem of the Epistle to the Galatians* (1929); W. D. Davies, *Paul and Rabbinic Judaism* (1948), p. 50.

[36] *Bulletin* III, Oxford, 1952, pp. 18 ff., 'The Gentile World in the Thought of Jesus'.

Munck's understanding of οἱ περιτεμνόμενοι in Gal. 6:13 would seem
to be right,[37] as is that of οὐδὲν προσανέθεντο in 2:6, his attempt to
carry through his theory in the interpretation of Galatians is not
convincing. It is difficult to think that Gal. 2:4, 5 refers to no specific
historical event but to the conditions which Paul was continually
facing in his churches: the phrase οἷς οὐδὲ πρὸς ὥραν εἴξαμεν τῇ ὑποταγῇ
(particularly the aorist form of the verb) is against this. So too
ὁποῖοί ποτε ἦσαν in view of the following πρόσωπον θεὸς ἀνθρώπου οὐ
λαμβάνει probably refers to something in the lives of the Apostles
which might be deemed to have given them a right to God's favour:
this, together with other passages in Paul referring to grounds on
which he was considered inferior to the other Apostles, makes the
customary interpretation preferable to the one proposed, namely, that
it alludes to the fact that the careers of the other Apostles were as
chequered as that of Paul himself. Again the attempt to place Gal.
2:11 ff. (ὅτε δὲ ἦλθε Κηφᾶς εἰς Ἀντιόχειαν) chronologically before Gal.
2:1–10 does not carry conviction.[38] The change to ὅτε in Gal. 2:11
hardly justifies this: it is sufficiently accounted for, if this has to be
justified at all, on the grounds that the subject changes from Paul to
Peter at this point. It is the necessity to insist on agreement between
Paul and the Jerusalem leaders at every point that leads Professor
Munck to this position. It is far more natural to regard Gal. 2:11 ff.
as subsequent to Gal. 2:1 ff. We cannot, further, dismiss Jerusalem
as the centre from which Judaizers sent emissaries on such general
grounds as Acts' emphasis on the significance of metropolitan
centres. The emphasis is probably true to history itself: nor does
Professor Munck, it seems to us, adequately account for τινὰς ἀπο
Ἰακώβου in Gal. 2:12. The reading of 𝔓[46] is noteworthy here: it has τινά.
It does not seem to me that the interpretation of Galatians proposed
arises naturally from the text understood against the other Epistles.
Thus, while it is unjustifiable, on the evidence available, exactly to
identify the various αἱρέσεις and σχίσματα, we are not convinced that
no Jewish-Christian influences were at work in the Corinthian
Church.[39] And to make the Pauline Churches consist almost entirely

[37] See Moule, *op. cit.*
[38] On this see T. W. Manson, *op. cit.*
[39] See J. Dupont, *Gnosis* (1949), pp. 258 ff., 266 ff.

of Gentiles seems unjustifiable both on the grounds of historical probability and of explicit references, which in part Professor Munck himself recognizes. The treatment of Pentecost on pp. 207–8 ignores the difficulties of the text not only at Acts 2:5, where Ropes suggested the omission of 'Ἰουδαῖοι on very good grounds, but all through the chapter.[40] That Pentecost is a sign not primarily to Israel, as Professor Munck holds, but signifies the 'universalism' of the Gospel is probable not only from a detailed analysis of the Pentecost narrative itself and a consideration of the motifs that have probably entered into it, but also from a fact pointed out by Goguel that Pentecost, as reported in Acts, did not impress Jewry.[41] Similarly to separate the *Urgemeinde* sharply from Judaism from the start is to minimize too much those elements that point to its adherence to it; nor can we regard as convincing the claim that Stephen represents the views of the *Urgemeinde* as a whole: it is more likely that Stephen is in critical opposition to it, as W. Manson recently insisted.[42] Nowhere is Professor Munck more stimulating and informing than in his last two chapters; but here again, to note only one point, is it likely that Paul himself explicitly interpreted his trials as the counterpart of the Passion? This question will persist despite the motif of the imitation of Christ in Paul. If anything like the *Imitatio Christi* was in the mind of Paul on his last visit to Jerusalem does not his appeal to Caesar become very difficult to understand? Although Professor Munck does recognize this, we should place greater stress than he does on the hortatory character of the last chapters in Acts, as does Dibelius.[43]

But secondly, apart from the detailed points which we are constrained to reject, there are certain broad aspects (which indeed determine the afore-mentioned details) of Professor Munck's interpretation in which we cannot follow him. We shall gather them up as follows:

(a) In his dismissal of the marked Hegelianism of the Tübingen School Professor Munck is justified, but he himself goes on to

[40] See *The Beginnings of Christianity*, ed. Foakes Jackson and Kirsopp Lake, vol. v, pp. 111 ff.

[41] *The Birth of Christianity* (Eng. trans.), New York, 1954, p. 91, n. 1.

[42] *The Epistle to the Hebrews* (1950), pp. 25 ff.; see my forthcoming, 'Law in the New Testament', in *The Interpreters' Dictionary*.

[43] *Aufsätze zur Apostelgeschichte*, Berlin, 1953, pp. 175 ff., 'Paulus in der Apostelgeschichte'.

introduce a new schema which too much simplifies the complexity of the early Church. If the *Urgemeinde* was as near to the position of Paul as Professor Munck claims, it is difficult to account for the rise of Jewish Christianity at all as we know it later,[44] and, indeed, of the Judaizing movement itself. Professor Munck gives two reasons for the emergence of the latter and that, as we have seen, on extra-Palestinian soil; first, Paul himself had given such a sympathetic picture to them of the Palestinian *Urgemeinde*, that some of his Gentile converts desired to imitate it, and secondly, the LXX which the Gentile Christians in the Pauline Churches used was easily understood to affirm that Israel after the flesh was the object of God's special favour, and, therefore, the desire to be like Israel after the flesh became natural. But we must rejoin to the first point that it is more plausible that the Judaizing movement arose from the close relation between Palestinian Christians and the Judaism from which they had recently sprung. To us looking back, especially past Paul, the distinctiveness of the Church shines clear, but it can hardly have been so to the earliest Christians. And it is easier to suppose that the earliest Jewish Christians in Palestine found it more difficult to note this distinction, as the majority of Paulinists have understood, than did extra-Palestinian Gentile Christians. However much we should allow for what H. J. Cadbury[45] calls 'over-conversion' among Gentile Christians—the zeal of converts is 'notorious'—it is still more probable that Judaizing first arose on Palestinian soil. And with regard to the second point, we will only note that Harnack's distinction between the use made by the Gentile Church of the Old Testament forms and that made by the Jewish Christians is still worth pondering.[46] Despite Professor Munck's arguments it is probable that there were Judaizers and 'liberals', like Paul and unlike him, in the *Urgemeinde*. It is as impossible not to believe this as it is extremely difficult to reach a point in the early Church when Jews and Gentiles were not involved. The traditions about James the Lord's brother

---

[44] See H. J. Schoeps, *Theologie und Geschichte des Judenchristentums*, Tübingen, 1949, who tends to go to the opposite extreme of equating 'Jewish-Christianity' with that of the *Urgemeinde*.

[45] In *The Joy of Study*, ed. S. E. Johnson, New York, 1951, 'Overconversion in Paul's Churches', pp. 43 ff.

[46] *The History of Dogma* (Eng. trans.), vol. i, pp. 290 f.

may be exaggerated, but it is a highly significant fact that, while on his last visit to Jerusalem, Paul was molested by Jewry, the Jerusalem Church as a whole was not. Professor Munck does not sufficiently allow for the compromises, complexities and ambiguities of the life of the early Church.

(b) Equally doubtful is the understanding of Paul which is offered to us. Professor Munck, in effect, does for the Apostle what Schweitzer did for his Lord: he interprets Paul in the light of an eschatological dogma. The activity of Paul was determined from first to last by his eschatological conviction that he was *the* apostle to the Gentiles. We have here to leave aside the difficult exegesis of 1 Thessalonians and other passages and content ourselves with stating certain general but crucial considerations. First, Professor Munck has dealt with the problems of Paul's life and epistles without raising questions about his thought or theology. But this concentration on the strictly eschatological determination of Paul's activity—important as this is—necessarily leads to a neglect of elements in his thinking which are perhaps of equal, if not more, significance, and this distorts the picture of Paul that emerges. For example, Professor Munck does not discuss the thesis that the Epistles of Paul reveal an increasing diminution in strictly eschatological interest.[47] 'Futurism' persists in the latest of the epistles, but there is, we think, a change of emphasis in these, or at least the Jewish Apocalyptic heritage in Paul's eschatology there coexists with a new and specifically Christian understanding of existence. This is not dealt with by Professor Munck, whose exclusive concentration on the strictly eschatological factor in Paul necessarily magnifies and distorts its significance. It thus tends, if we may so express it, to mechanize Paul. To note one detail. Was Paul so completely lacking in geographic awareness in his missionary activity—not to use the question-begging term 'strategy'—as Professor Munck implies? In Phil. 4:15 he uses the phrase ἐν ἀρχῇ τοῦ εὐαγγελίου ὅτε ἐξῆλθον ἀπὸ Μακεδονίας . . . surely, as Bornkamm,[48] among others, has pointed

---

[47] See C. H. Dodd, *The Bulletin of the John Rylands Library*, vol. xvii (1933); vol. xviii (1934).

[48] *Das Ende des Gesetzes* (1952), pp. 157 ff. For the geographic as well as theological determination of Acts, see *New Testament Studies*, vol. i, Sept. 1954, P. H. Menoud on 'Le plan des Actes des Apôtres', pp. 44 ff.

out, in full recognition of the significance of the point at which the Gospel entered Europe; and in this Acts confirms the Epistles. If we may judge from Acts further, it was not the dictates of an eschatological dogma that governed Paul's missionary work but the leading of the Spirit of God.[49] We cannot but feel that the insistence on the centrality of eschatology tends to give a picture of Paul divested of the great depths of 'Paulinism'. We may express the point roughly by saying that while all Paul's life and thought is eschatological, eschatology is not the whole of Paul. Let us illustrate this by reference to Professor Munck's very suggestive treatment of Paul's conversion. His understanding of it primarily in terms of eschatology hides the significance of the Church, the Body of Christ, in that conversion.[50] It is this that perhaps makes it difficult for Professor Munck to do justice to two apparently contradictory things; first, the extent to which Paul would be led to differ radically from certain elements in the *Urgemeinde*, and, secondly, the extent to which Paul, at the same time, was rooted in the *Urgemeinde*, as A. M. Hunter has shown in a book, *Paul and His Predecessors* (1940), which Professor Munck does not mention. We cannot believe, on the one hand, that it was primarily over the chronological point at which the Gospel should or should not be preached to the Gentiles that Paul differed with the *Urgemeinde* or, on the other, that he regarded himself primarily as having such a *peculiarly* important eschatological significance that he was set apart from all other Christians (Peter being excepted). It is not without significance that in Gal. 1:1 the ἀπόστολος is anarthrous.[51] Professor Munck might object to the above criticism that he has not attempted to deal with Paul's 'theology'; but this is the very point at issue. Can even *Paulus und Die Heilsgeschichte* be adequately dealt with in such rigid isolation from 'Paulinism' as a whole?

[49] Dibelius, *op. cit.* p. 177.

[50] See especially J. A. T. Robinson, *The Body* (1952), p. 58. Cf. Dibelius-Kümmel, *Paul*, p. 56.

[51] In no case does Paul refer to himself as ὁ ἀπόστολος (except in the phrase in 1 Cor. 15:9: ἐγὼ γάρ εἰμι ὁ ἐλάχιστος τ. ἀποστόλων). Mosbech, *Studia Theologica* (Lund, 1950), vol. ii, Fasc. ii, p. 195, on 'Apostolos in the New Testament', has claimed that it was the Judaizing controversy that made it necessary for Paul to insist on his own apostolic status. Before this controversy he merely refers to himself as Paul, 'but in all the epistles from the time of the controversies with the Judaizers (and in the Epistle to the Colossians) he has called himself . . . with small variations "Paul the Apostle of Jesus Christ".'

IX

A NORMATIVE PATTERN OF
CHURCH LIFE IN THE NEW TESTAMENT?

In his stimulating discussion, *The Gift of Ministry* (1947), D. T. Jenkins has claimed that one of our most urgent needs as Christians is 'a recovery of the conviction that Church order is divinely ordained for the true governing of the Church according to God's will in a fallen world'.[1] He assumes, I take it, that there is one order for Church life which is the expression of the Gospel, a single pattern for the Church on its institutional side which we are to discover. In this, as in other matters, Jenkins does not stand alone: he is merely a distinguished representative of a fairly general tendency to return to an assumption which, in different ways, was once accepted by our Puritan forefathers and is still accepted by Roman Catholics and many Anglicans, but which, as Jenkins is well aware,[2] still seems to many Congregationalists and others, if not positively erroneous, at least highly dubious. It is to an examination of this thorny assumption as it bears upon the New Testament that we shall apply ourselves here. We shall ask whether and in what sense, if any, the New Testament presents us with a normative pattern for Church life.

I

The problem is best understood against the background of the relevant studies of the Church in the New Testament in the period from the close of the last century to the present day. Roman Catholic studies in that period do not directly concern us, because Roman

---

[1] p. 174.
[2] *The Nature of Catholicity*, p. 542 (1942).

Catholicism has then, as always, preserved an unchangeable attitude. It has unwaveringly maintained, in the words of Batiffol, that 'as early as the Apostolic Age, Christianity presents itself as a corporate religion, a brotherhood which swarms over the earth without diminishing its cohesion, which everywhere forms itself into co-operating societies of exactly the same character. These little communities have the same faith, the same worship, the same authorities. . . .' And again: 'Built by the Apostles who knew only Jesus and Him crucified, the Church knew that only which she held from the Apostles: she was not, in the first period of her existence, in an amorphous state; history does not represent her as a mere spiritual movement whose institutions and doctrines were determined by or even borrowed from the civilization which it passed: she was a Gospel, an apostolate, a tradition, a worship, an hierarchical society, *one* Church made up of *many* Churches, a unity preserved by the unity of the *cathedra Petri*'.[3] In view of the adamant consistency of Roman Catholic studies, therefore, it is within Protestantism that the discussions of the Church which especially concern us have arisen; and, following Linton,[4] let us begin with what he calls the consensus of scholarship about the year 1880.

By that year, as we should expect, the Enlightenment had profoundly influenced New Testament scholars in the field of Christian origins, as in others. The result was that the Primitive Church had come to be regarded as made up of individual Christians who formed a religious society, which in itself, as a society, was by no means necessary for salvation, and whose organized life could be adequately understood in the light of that of similar contemporary religious groups, of which there were many in the Hellenistic as in the Jewish world. Political, sociological and other related factors in the contemporary environment sufficiently explained the organization of the primitive Christian Churches, and the application of strictly theological or dogmatic categories for their explanation was largely deemed to be superfluous: the organization of the Church was regarded as a social necessity not a divine ordinance. It was this attitude which really governed Lightfoot's approach to Christian

---

[3] *Primitive Catholicism* (1911). Eng. trans., pp. vi f.
[4] *Das Problem der Urkirche in der Neueren Forschung* (1932).

origins in his famous dissertation on *The Christian Ministry* where he wrote that: 'It must be evident that no society of men could hold together without officers, without rules, without institutions of any kind; and the Church of Christ is not exempt from this universal law'.[5] When Lightfoot speaks with precision of divine appointments in the Church, he is obviously embarrassed,[6] while Hort goes the whole hog and roundly asserts that 'there is no trace in the New Testament that any ordinances . . . were prescribed by the Lord (i.e., ordinances dealing with "offices") or that any such ordinances were set up as permanently binding by the Twelve or by St. Paul or by the Ecclesia at large'.[7]

So it had come about by the eighties of the last century that, over against the dogmatic conception of the rise of the organization of the Church which Roman Catholicism offered, Protestant scholarship generally had come to the conclusion that the Episcopate was not directly a continuation of the Apostolate, and that the constitution of the Church was not to be traced to any direct divine appointment. Broadly speaking there were postulated in the early days of Christianity a number of independent fellowships of believers, often, but not always, founded by Apostles: the leadership of these fellowships was in the hands of the elders, the presbyterate, and from the presbyterate the bishop subsequently emerged. As Lightfoot expresses it, 'the episcopate was formed not out of the apostolic order by localization but out of the presbyteral by elevation'.[8] But all this organization was conditioned sociologically not theologically. Thus, although Lightfoot is constrained awkwardly to speak of the divine appointment of the threefold ministry of Bishop, Presbyter, Deacon, his dissertation can only lead him to the conclusion that the facts do not allow him 'to unchurch Christian communities differently organized';[9] and in this he was typical of that consensus which we are seeking to describe. But more typical even than Lightfoot was Hatch whose lectures on *The Organization of the Early Christian Churches* were first published in 1881. He insisted particularly on two

---

[5] *St. Paul's Epistle to the Philippians* (1890), p. 181.
[6] *Ibid.*, p. 267.
[7] *The Christian Ecclesia* (1897), p. 230. These lectures were delivered in 1888-9.
[8] *Op. cit.*, p. 196.
[9] *Op. cit.*, p. 267.

things, (1) that the evolution of the organization of the Church was gradual, and (2) that the clue to the various elements in that organization was to be found in the contemporary societies of various kinds. Thus, for example, the Bishop in the Primitive Church achieved his prominence through his importance as the financial administrator in the society of Christians, much as in other societies, in which almsgiving was a primary duty, the *episkopoi*, financial administrators, became prominent.[10] Hatch especially reveals the sociological approach to Christian beginnings; and he, like Lightfoot, illustrates how, in the consensus of Protestant scholarship about 1881, the first century was often interpreted, and perhaps misinterpreted, in the light of the democratic idealism of late nineteenth-century Liberalism.[11]

We have now sufficiently indicated the nature of that consensus in Protestant scholarship towards the eighties of the last century. Despite protests, particularly from Anglo-Catholic writers, such as Charles Gore, who published his book *The Church and the Ministry* in 1888,[12] it had come to be generally recognized in Protestant circles that the organization of the Church was of sociological not dogmatic significance. Thus this was common ground between the two great protagonists, Harnack and Sohm, who chiefly occupied the field after Lightfoot and Hatch. Of the discussion between these two scholars we need merely remind ourselves very briefly here. To Sohm, indeed, the organized structure of the Church not merely had no dogmatic significance, but it actually involved a departure from the pristine purity of the spiritual fellowship of the saints. He wrote: 'Where two or three are gathered together in Christ's name, there is the ecclesia, the Church. . . . Where Christ is, there is the Church. The Church appears and works in *every* congregation of believers. Even where only two or three are gathered together in His name, there is Christ the Lord in the midst of them, and therefore all Christendom is gathered together with them, working with all its gifts of grace. *There is no need of any* human priesthood. There, in every congregation of believers, is the true Baptism and the true

---

[10] *Op. cit.*, pp. 32 ff.

[11] See Linton, *op. cit.*, p. 13.

[12] A significant indication of the difference between Gore and Lightfoot is that the former thinks of the bishop as 'an apostolic man' localized, not a presbyter 'elevated', as we saw above.

Lord's Supper, the full communion with Christ the High Priest and Mediator of all who believe on Him. *Still less is there need of a legal constitution. In fact every form of legal constitution is excluded.*'[13] In developing a legal constitution, a development which he connected closely with the Eucharist,[14] Sohm thinks that 'The Church has changed, not merely her constitution, but her faith. Personal communion with Christ and with God is now dependent on outward forms and conditions. This is the essence of Catholicism. Dependence on an outward organism, represented by Bishop and Presbyters, is the new law which has become binding on every Christian. . . . The Church is no longer founded on the communion of believers, as such, but upon the *office*, which is henceforth indispensable to the relations of the Church with Christ.'[15] Similar to Sohm's position was that of Sabatier.[16]

But over against it stands that of Harnack. To the latter the Church was organized from the beginning: Sohm's view that the Church at first was a soul without a body, he rejects: had that been the case Harnack insists that the Church would have been a mere idea, the object of the faith of each separate Christian in isolation from all others. He further insists that 'to associate is for those who bear the name of Christ not a secondary or unessential feature in the idea of the Church, it is a feature essentially involved in the idea itself which is only realized through the fact of the faithful thus associating themselves'. 'The divine origin of ecclesiastical right,' he holds, 'is as old as the Church itself.'[17] How the Church was organized Harnack explained in his edition of the *Didache* (1884), and later in his book *Constitution and Law of the Church in the first two centuries* (Eng. Trans. 1910). He distinguished between a charismatic ministry belonging to the whole of the Primitive Church and consisting of Apostles, Prophets, Teachers who were of direct divine appointment, and the localized, administrative ministry of Bishops and Deacons.[18]

[13] *Outlines of Church History* (1895), Eng. Trans., p. 32.
[14] *Ibid.*, p. 36.
[15] *Outlines of Church History* (1895), Eng. Trans., p. 39.
[16] See the discussion in Batiffol, *op. cit.*, pp. 143 ff.
[17] See Batiffol, *op. cit.*, p. xx.
[18] For criticisms of Harnack see J. A. Robinson in *The Early History of the Church and Ministry*, ed. H. B. Swete (1921), pp. 60 ff.; Streeter, *The Primitive Church* (1929), pp. 71 ff.

But although Harnack, unlike Sohm, speaks of a ministry by divine appointment, he is really at one with Sohm, because he, too, regards the organization of the Church as really due to 'the desire of man to externalize his religion', and by divine law Harnack merely means that man by his nature demands a law, an authority, and by demanding it has created it. As Batiffol puts it, 'the right which [Harnack] claims to call divine springs . . . only from the requirements of Christendom regarded as a visible society'. The divine appointment of the charismatic ministry in Harnack merely amounts to its human necessity.

After the discussions of Sohm and Harnack, interest in the organization of the Church in the New Testament largely waned: concentration on organization seemed destined to lead to frustrating differences. Scholars, naturally if not inevitably, tended to join one side or the other, apparently according to denominational predilections.[19] Let me refer in illustration to certain typical figures. J. A. Robinson, an Anglo-Catholic, in his work on the Primitive Ministry ignores Sohm completely, and defends Lightfoot against Harnack by insisting that all the officers of the Primitive Church were charismatic.[20] So too Karl Holl reacted against Sohm.[21] On the other hand, J. Vernon Bartlet, on the Free Church side, seems to differ little from Sohm in essentials. For him as for Sohm, as Cadoux points out, primitive Christianity, for which the possession of the Spirit was primary, is to be sharply distinguished from Catholic Christianity, in which order came to be the central pre-occupation.[22] It seems that Bartlet, perhaps quite rightly, was constantly overshadowed by the anxiety lest he should ascribe too much order to the spontaneity of the Spirit-filled life of the saints of the Early

[19] This should not be pressed; see E. Schweizer, *Gemeinde und Gemeindeordnung*, (1960), p. 1.

[20] *Op. cit.*

[21] See R. N. Flew, *Jesus and His Church* (1938), pp. 185 f. Holl's work was first published in 1921.

[22] *Church life and Church order during the first four centuries* (1943), p. lxi. (Ed. C. J. Cadoux.) Apart from Bartlet's work, as far as I am aware, there is no significant Free Church contribution to our subject in the period under consideration. Bartlet delivered his lectures in 1924. The following sentence (p. 31) gives the temper of Bartlet's treatment, though perhaps exaggeratedly: 'As one looks back upon the Apostolic Age, the prevalent impression is that of the spiritual atmosphere of a religious revival; and such in fact was the atmosphere of the Apostolic Church.'

Church. In view of the dissatisfying inconclusiveness of studies of the organized life of the early Church, it is not surprising that scholars ceased to present elaborate descriptions of that organization, and instead concentrated their energies on various isolated elements such as the Apostolate. The attempt to find one organizational principle to comprehend the life of the Primitive Church in Protestant scholarship seemed to be inconclusive, if not abortive, apart, of course, from Anglo-Catholicism, which had insisted on such a principle in the divinely ordained prerogative of the Apostles.

II

T. W. Manson in his recent lectures, *The Church's Ministry* (1948), recalls how Dr. William Temple, at the Faith and Order Conference at Edinburgh in 1937, pleaded for concentration on 'the business of framing an adequate doctrine of the Church' because this, he thought, would lead to a solution of problems connected with the Ministry and Sacraments.[23] Strangely enough it was in fact a similar direction that New Testament scholarship took after it became apparent that agreement on the nature of the organized life of the Church was unobtainable:[24] scholars generally tended to turn from questions of organization to the idea or doctrine of the Church in the New Testament. The nature of the Church rather than the form of its life assumed primary importance.

The inconclusiveness of previous studies was not the only factor in this change. The collapse of the atomistic individualism that characterized so much of nineteenth-century life and thought; the advent of a new social awareness; the new position in which the Church found itself over against the State in so many European countries (the 'scandal' of the Church has become apparent to us modern Europeans, and the intransigeance and 'mystery' of its claims a more stubborn fact than they could have been in the velvety days before the rise of Marxism, Nazism and their like)—these factors contributed to the change that we have noticed. In addition, the oecumenical

---

[23] *Op. cit.*, p. 10.

[24] It is part of the exceeding greatness of Hort's *The Christian Ecclesia* that even in the eighties it did not succumb to organizational minutiae to the neglect of the 'idea' of the Church. See his *Recapitulation, op. cit.*, pp. 225 ff.

movement has not left scholarship untouched;[25] and, finally, as we saw at the beginning, the theological renaissance of our time, which is rooted in those factors which I have already noted, has inevitably and particularly quickened interest in the theological meaning of the Church.[26]

However we assign the causes for it, the fact is evident that the relevant New Testament scholarship has been more preoccupied in our time with the nature of the Church than with its organization; and this preoccupation has been fruitful in results. With admirable clarity Linton has pointed out those ways in which scholarship has made possible a new understanding of the Church. Four disciplines within the New Testament field in particular have contributed richly: they are:—

1 *The Lexicographical.* The examination of the term *ecclêsia*, for example, has greatly enriched our theological understanding of the Church as the *qehàl Yahweh*. I shall also have occasion to refer later to studies of the term *apostolos*.

2 *The Theological.* In earlier days the eschatological interest of Jesus was deemed to preclude any possibility that He envisaged a Church. But a better understanding of the eschatology of Judaism has led to the interpretation of the Church as the eschatological community of Jewish expectation. So far from appearing as an impossibility for the mind of Jesus, the Church now appears almost as a necessity for that mind; the appearance of the Messiah involved the appearance of the Messianic community of the End.[27] Similarly the work of Dalman, Otto, Dodd and others on the meaning of the phrase *The Kingdom of God* has made any merely Ritschlian understanding of it impossible: and with the Kingdom goes the Church.

3 *The Sociological.* The attempt to understand the Church as merely one among many societies of a 'similar' kind that flourished in the first century has failed. The sociological approach to the Church, which sought to explain it purely in terms of human relationships,

[25] See the prefaces to R. N. Flew, *op. cit.*, and G. Johnston, *The Doctrine of the Church in the New Testament*, pp. 133 ff.; also p. 5 above.

[26] On all the above, see Linton, *op. cit.*, pp. 132 ff.

[27] So too Streeter's assumption, *op. cit.*, pp. 69 ff., that the anticipation of the near approach of the End in the Early Church made it largely indifferent to questions of organization, is by no means as obvious as it once was.

has consequently given place to a new kind of sociological approach, which strictly speaking is not sociological at all, in which the peculiarity of the Church as a divine-human society is recognized, a peculiarity which demands peculiar categories for its explanation. As Johnson has expressed it, it is the *differences* between Christianity and its rivals in the first century, and not its similarity to them, that are now recognized to be significant.[28]

4 *The Historical.* Coincident with all the above there has emerged a new conservatism in the treatment of those passages in which the founding of the Church is directly ascribed to Jesus. In particular, Matthew 16:17-19, is not now so certainly treated as unauthentic: e.g., Flew's reaction against its rejection is well known.[29] But not only so: the whole dogma of critical orthodoxy, as it has been called, that Jesus founded no Church has been seriously questioned, and shaken, if not dismissed.

Lexicographical, theological, sociological and historical studies then have led to a new awareness of the nature of the Church. The new awareness has been exemplified with distinction in two English books—that of R. N. Flew, *Jesus and His Church* (1938), and G. Johnston, *The Doctrine of the Church in the New Testament* (1943); I do not think that it is an exaggeration to say that these, and similar studies, have revealed considerable unanimity as to the theological interpretation of the Church. Flew's book has especially established the essential unity of the teaching of the various New Testament documents as to the nature of the Church. The Church is God's creation: it has come into existence through human response to the saving work of God in Christ, the Messiah of Jewish expectation: as such it is the eschatological Israel of God, and is marked by the eschatological gift of the Spirit and is thus enabled to be the missionary agent in bringing the promises of God to all those afar off. I know of no better summary of the New Testament doctrine of the Church than that given by Johnston:[30] 'The existence of the Church was a result of divine activity and of human obedience to the word of God. Its members became partners in a great fellowship, baptized

---

[28] *Op. cit.*, p. 33. Cf. Karl Holl, *Ges. Aufsätze*, ii, p. 9.

[29] *Op. cit.*, pp. 123 ff. In addition, work by Jeremias and others points in the same way.

[30] *Op. cit.*, p. 132.

into a single society where, by union to the Lord, they could enjoy a certainty of final salvation, were able to worship God in reality, in praise and prayer and the Eucharist. Through Jesus Christ incarnate, crucified and risen, Jew and Gentile alike shared an experience of forgiving grace. Invisible bonds of the Spirit joined the widely separated congregations to one another. This spiritual Israel was a new community, one in faith and loyalty to the expected Messiah and Lord, a divine family, itself a word of God to the nations as it witnessed to Jesus Christ.' The discovery of the unity of the New Testament doctrine of the Church is a significant part of that synthetic movement in New Testament studies with which we all are familiar.

III

From the above it will have appeared that New Testament studies in the last seventy-five years have revealed a curious dichotomy. On the one hand, there has emerged a marked unity as to the essential nature of the Church as the eschatological people of God in Christ. On the other hand, there has emerged an equally marked disagreement as to the way or ways in which that people was organized, if, indeed, in its earliest stages we could speak of its being strictly 'organized' at all. The nature of the Body of Christ has become clear; but there is division as to the form or forms that that Body has assumed. In other words we have, broadly speaking, attained a unity of conception as to the significance of the Church, but have achieved no corresponding unanimity as to the right way or ways, as the case may be, in which it should be organized.

It is at this point that we have to recall Jenkins' words that we must recover a conviction that Church order is divinely ordained. In the light of our discussion this means, I presume, that the unity of our conception as to the significance of the Church demands also a unity of conception as to the way in which it should be organized. Let me illustrate by reference to Judaism. The ground of Judaism is the *Torah*, and, through the travail of centuries, Judaism has evolved an outward organization which effectively bears witness to the centrality of the *Torah*, the Synagogue, an institution which expresses the genius of Judaism, and everywhere gives to it, even in its most 'liberal' forms, a marked unity. I take it that we are concerned to discover whether the New Testament points us to a Christian counterpart of what the Synagogue is for Judaism, to a divinely ordained norm which expresses the nature of the Gospel, as the Synagogue expresses the nature of Judaism. Jenkins and others would have us assume that there is such a norm—reformable, indeed, according to the Word of God, but nevertheless well defined.

With the assumption that Jenkins makes, Roman Catholics would agree; and they would meet it with the assertion that the prerogative of the Apostles and the primacy of Peter are the clue to the divinely ordained form of the Church. Similarly within Anglo-Catholicism, e.g., in the manifesto *The Apostolic Ministry*, it is maintained that there is one divinely ordained form of the Church—a form depending on what is called *The Essential Ministry*, the Apostolic ministry, which is the 'divinely ordained ministerial instrument for securing for the Church of God its continuous and organic unity, not as a club of like-minded worshippers or aspirants to holiness, but as a God-given city of salvation'. This ministry is 'the earthly pivot round which the whole organic life of the Church' is to revolve.[31] It need hardly be said that both Roman Catholics and Anglo-Catholics claim the support of the New Testament for their contentions.

This is not the place to give a detailed criticism, even if we could, of *The Apostolic Ministry*. Its thesis that the unity of the Church depends on an episcopate which can claim an unbroken succession from the first Apostles, who were deemed to be not merely the ambassadors of Christ but in some sense His representatives in person, is open to criticism, as we shall see later, on theological grounds. But to criticize it on these grounds at this stage of our argument would, I think, be to prejudge the issue. Therefore I now merely point out two valid criticisms of the theory from the New Testament point of view. These are:—

1. There is the awkward fact that the term Apostle, derived from the Aramaic *shâliach*, can hardly bear the weight that is put upon it. Many a theory in the New Testament has come to grief on the rock of Greek grammar: T. W. Manson has conclusively shown that the

[31] *The Apostolic Ministry* (ed. K. E. Kirk) London, 1947, p. 8.

thesis of *The Apostolic Ministry* is wrecked on the rock of lexico-
graphy. There is enough in a name sometimes to carry a vast
structure: but there is often not enough in a name to do this. This
is the case with the term *shâliach*. We can here only refer to pp. 31 ff.
in Manson's *The Church's Ministry* for details.

2. In the second place, the facts of history bring this theory to
grief. The claim to an unbroken succession for the episcopate from
the first Apostles cannot strictly be proved or disproved. But certain
facts in the New Testament make it impossible to accept it. Canon
Lacey, it will be remembered, was content to speak of Paul as a
dangerous exception to the rule that the one sign of an Apostle is
express appointment by other Apostles.[32] But a view of the Church
and Ministry which makes of the ministry of Paul a dangerous
exception, and, therefore, surreptitiously questions the validity of the
Pauline mission, is self-condemned. In an illuminating review of *The
Apostolic Ministry* Dr. Telfer [33] has expressed this with telling force:
it is surely of the utmost significance that the New Testament
depicts the greatest experiment perhaps in all the history of the
Church—the Mission to the Gentiles—as taking place without the
authority of the Twelve.

I have above cursorily referred to two facts, out of many others,
which at least justify us in questioning the thesis of *The Apostolic
Ministry*, as it touches on the New Testament. But this thesis has
been advanced in a far more subtle and challenging way in a book
which, to their own disadvantage, it seems to me, the authors of *The
Apostolic Ministry* ignore. In his book *The Gospel and the Catholic
Church* (1936), A. M. Ramsey has argued cogently that the episcopal
is the form of Church order which itself expresses the Gospel.
According to Ramsey, the New Testament itself reveals that the
outward order of the Church is no indifferent matter, but is related
to the inner meaning of the Church and to the Gospel itself: he holds
that for the New Testament, as for us, the Apostolic Succession is
important on account of its evangelical meaning.[34]

It would be impertinent to dismiss Ramsey's deeply moving book

[32] Cited by C. H. Dodd in *Essays Congregational and Catholic* (1931), p. 8.
[33] *J.T.S.* xlviii (1947), p. 226.
[34] *Op. cit.*, p. vi.

in a few sentences, but, at the risk of great presumption, I shall point out why it seems to fail in its claim. There are three reasons:—

1. Although Ramsey insists that his appeal is not to history but to theology, nevertheless, when he has to deal with the Papacy, which naturally forms a rock of offence for his theory, he shifts from an appeal to theology, very conveniently, to an appeal to history:[35] this inconsistency in his approach is disturbing. The appeal to history is as devastating to Ramsey's view of the episcopate as it is to the Papacy. Thus when Ramsey writes such a sentence as: 'There is no Christian community mentioned in the New Testament which has not behind it some authority responsible to a larger whole . . .'[36] we must rejoin that we simply cannot know what every community of Christians in the first century was like or how they were founded or to whom they felt or did not feel, responsibility.

2. The emphasis that Ramsey, like the authors of *The Apostolic Ministry*, places on the Apostolate, as such, is questionable when judged by the New Testament, as we have already seen. But there is a further point. He writes of the function of Apostles as that of witnessing to the historical facts of Christ:[37] the Apostle *qua* Apostle, the later Bishop *qua* Bishop, is 'sent to bear witness to the historical events'. 'The Apostle, and the Bishop after him, is the link with the historic events. . . .' It is Ramsey's conviction that there is an office in the structure of the Church which of itself *witnesses* to the historical events on which the Gospel rests. But is it merely stupid to ask what we mean by *witnessing*? Can an office *witness*? It has often been the case that a bishop has witnessed to the historical events, but not merely by being a bishop. To witness to events is to commit oneself personally to them: and those people who are witnesses to the Gospel facts, surely, are not those who necessarily hold an office designed for that purpose, and are therefore officially appointed witnesses, as it were, but those who have most responded to the facts, be they bishops or others. It seems to me that Ramsey's argument that the structure of the Church and particularly the episcopate witness to the Gospel is *logically* convincing, apart from the inconsistency we

[35] *Op. cit.*, p. 65; but see also p. 233.
[36] *Op. cit.*, p. 46.
[37] *Op. cit.*, pp. 60 f.

mentioned above, until one asks what exactly he means when he speaks of an office *witnessing* to the Gospel. To ask this question is to realize that his whole method of dealing with the Gospel and the Church, profoundly religious as in one sense it is, nevertheless involves their mechanization—a mechanization which he establishes with an altogether admirable mathematical precision.[38] This leads me to my third point.

3. On page 83 we read: 'But certain actions in [Christ's] work of grace are confined to the Bishops . . .' The logic of Ramsey's position here works itself out: the grace of Christ is humanly conditioned: it is caged in an office. To this we shall return later: we are content here merely to state the point.

In the light of the above, we cannot accept the view of those Christians who claim that the form of the Church, which rests on the so-called Essential Ministry, is uniquely sanctioned by the New Testament. But we now go on to recognize that no other form of Church government or order regarded as sacrosanct by our Puritan forefathers can claim the unique sanction of the New Testament. We must state, quite brutally, that neither Congregationalists nor any other Free Churchmen can claim to be the sole heirs of the New Testament in their Church life. The critical discipline which enables us to meet the pretensions of Rome and of Anglo-Catholicism at the same time undermines the often smug complacency of Free Churchmen. The arguments, for example, which were used to justify Congregationalist policy in the Puritan era can no longer carry conviction. This has been forcibly brought home to us by those scholars who have insisted that there is no one form of Church life presented to us in the New Testament, and that, on the contrary, the New Testament presents us with many forms of Church life. The dichotomy in New Testament studies, to which we referred above, between the unity of our conception of the nature of the Church and our disagreements as to its form or forms is no mere accident, but a necessity, because the Churches of the New Testament are like a coat of many colours, they vary both in foundation and in organization.

---

[38] Our criticism holds despite Ramsey's careful insistence that no office is to be thought of in isolation from the Body: the Body itself has been mechanized. See p. 82.

The chief protagonist of this view, of course, has been Streeter. In *The Primitive Church* (1929) he maintained the thesis of a primitive diversity in Christian institutions tending towards uniformity: in this diversity 'the Episcopalian, the Presbyterian, the Independent can each discover the prototype of the system to which he himself adheres'.[39] Thus in Jerusalem there was a Church organized more or less as a synagogue with a normal body of presbyters (elders), but where James, the brother of the Lord, had such a unique position that Streeter feels justified in calling him a kind of bishop. Moreover, the necessity for supplying relief for the poor led to the appointment of seven almoners, who seem to have been regarded by the author of Acts as deacons.[40] 'But', writes Streeter, 'the situation at Jerusalem was unique. We cannot safely deduce that in the Gentile Churches the primitive form of government even roughly corresponded to a threefold hierarchy of Bishop, Presbyters and Deacons.'[41] Thus the Church at Antioch was not modelled on that of Jerusalem.[42] There the chief officers were prophets and teachers. So too in the Pauline Churches the evidence is thus summarized by Streeter: '(There) is a movement away from the state of things implied in 1 Corinthians— where pre-eminence in the Church depends on the *personal* possession of some spiritual gift (of which "government" is one of the least esteemed) [and where at first the "elders" were of minor importance and prophets and teachers were the chief, as in all Gentile Churches] —and towards a state of things where importance is attached to the holding of *an office* invested with recognized authority' [i.e., where the elders were given greater importance].[43] In addition to all the above Streeter claims that the Johannine Epistles prove that not later than A.D. 100 mon-episcopacy was in being in some churches in Asia.[44]

This position has received the benediction of C. H. Dodd who does not see how Streeter's main conclusions can be shaken:[45] the studies of Flew and Johnston both seem to assume Streeter's conclusions, and T. W. Manson accepts it. Writing of the end of the New Testament period the last scholar asserts: 'It is evident that at

[39] *Op. cit.*, p. ix.
[40] *Ibid.*, pp. 72 ff.
[41] *Ibid.*, p. 74.
[42] *Ibid.*, pp. 74 f.
[43] *Op. cit.*, pp. 82 f.
[44] *Ibid.*, pp. 83 ff.
[45] *Op. cit.*, p. 3.

this stage in the history of the Church there is still a good deal of fluidity.'[46] 'The total picture of congregational life in its worship and in its organization (even) down to about the middle of the second century is inevitably fragmentary and incomplete . . . one thing that immediately emerges is that at this stage it is idle to look for any hard and fast system, for rigid uniformity of worship or organization.'[47] To judge from the unanimity of the scholars that I have already named, it would appear that the diversity of form in the life of the Church in the New Testament should become a dogma of critical orthodoxy; but it will immediately be noticed that these scholars belong, all except one,[48] who is a Scottish Presbyterian, to the Free Churches, and, quite naturally, their views may be suspected of reflecting, however unconsciously, their denominational loyalties; and it becomes incumbent upon us, therefore, to enquire how Streeter's views have been received in other than Free Church and Scottish Presbyterian circles. One thing is immediately apparent, that those views have not been treated with anything like the same deliberate seriousness outside Free Church circles as within them. Thus Bishop Headlam [49] was content to dismiss Streeter's work in this field in a footnote: writing on the Biblical basis for the origins of the Christian ministry he deals with Streeter summarily by saying that 'although original, stimulating, and ingenious' Streeter's 'theory (which is elaborated for a purpose) really does not help us'. The authors of *The Apostolic Ministry* are even contemptuous of Streeter, and dismiss his thesis without discussion.[50] So too it is significant, but more understandable because of his strictly theological methodology, that Ramsey only once refers to Streeter in *The Gospel and the Catholic Church*—and then only to criticize his view of Ignatius.[51] In view of such almost contemptuous dismissal of Streeter's views in much Anglican writing we must protest that contempt is not argument, and is even worse than scientific guessing such as Streeter unfortunately undoubtedly indulged in. We must submit that that scholar's views deserve far more serious consideration than has hitherto been accorded to them in Anglican circles. Nevertheless,

[46] *Op. cit.*, p. 60.   [47] *Op. cit.*, p. 65.
[48] Streeter himself, however, was, of course, an Anglican.
[49] *The Ministry and the Sacraments* (ed. R. Dunkerley) (1937), p. 336 n. 1.
[50] pp. vi, 253 n. 2, 290 f.   [51] p. 78.

we hasten to add that they have not, in fact, been without considerable influence even in those circles. This is clear from *The Report of the Commission on Christian Doctrine appointed by the Archbishops of Canterbury and York in 1922* (published 1938),[52] where we read: 'It has been a common practice to search the New Testament for precedents and principles of Church Order, with the understanding that if these were found they would at once be decisive. . . . There is not sufficient agreement among scholars to give hope of unity through such an appeal; and there are those who hold that more than one form or Order can be illustrated from the New Testament. Appeal to the New Testament therefore fails to produce agreement.' Many Anglicans, it would appear from such words in the Report, would submit to Streeter's conclusions or at least allow them sufficient force to modify their views, and induce them to defend Episcopacy on other grounds than New Testament History; and it was claimed by the great Cambridge scholar Creed,[53] that in *The Primitive Church* 'the historical reconstruction is based throughout upon a thorough survey of almost all the relevant texts. Where evidence is clear, the main stages of the history are firmly yet cautiously marked out.'

But what of continental scholarship? Here again it is surprising, as far as I am aware, how little Streeter's conclusions have been deliberately dwelt upon. Thus Linton refers to Streeter once only, and that in a footnote,[54] and ignores him even in a section dealing with different conceptions of the Church in various groups in primitive Christianity.[55] Nevertheless, it is probably correct to say that the outcome of Streeter's main contention of an original diversity would appear to be acceptable to many continental scholars, although his detailed expression of that diversity does not seem to have been much considered. That there were grave differences among early Christians as to the form of the Church is emphasized by Karl Holl,[56] who finds a deep cleavage, which he probably over-emphasizes, between the Church at Jerusalem and the Pauline Churches. The same position is largely maintained by Lietzmann. Moreover, he makes it

[52] p. 117.   [53] *J.T.S.*, Vol. XXI (1930), p. 196.
[54] *Op. cit.*, p. 104 n. 1.   [55] *Op. cit.*, pp. 183 f.
[56] *Der Kirchenbegriff des Paulus in seinem Verhältnis zu dem Der Urgemeinde* (1921).

perfectly clear that any dogmatism as to the form of the primitive Churches, such as is necessarily implied in the theory of the authors of *The Apostolic Ministry*, is misplaced. 'We have not the slightest information', he writes, 'about the size of the [Christian Missionary] Churches or the nature of their constitution.'[57] And again: 'There is no doubt that these numerous separate churches brought to expression a host of differences in outer appearance and inner life, and that these differences derived not only from the personalities and the customs of their founders, but also from the geographical and ethnographical, the social and religious conditions of their members.'[58] In another connection Lietzmann writes: 'It is extremely difficult, and at bottom impossible, to describe the development of the earliest constitution of the Church, because our sources only rarely give an answer to the many questions which we propose to them. In the early period, these appeared as outer matters, and unworthy of description; when they began to be of theological importance, the observer's outlook was influenced by theory.'[59] And this, it seems to me, is the only fully justifiable attitude to take.

In view of the dissentient voices we have mentioned above, it may be an overstatement to call Streeter's theory a dogma of critical orthodoxy. But, in my judgment, it is sufficiently convincing at least to establish that there was considerable variety in the forms of Church life in primitive Christianity. The one criticism we are tempted to make of Streeter, apart from his scientific guesses so-called, is that, despite his recognition of the multiplicity of forms, he has probably, in view of the missionary nature of the Churches concerned, too much systematized the various differences, and that the situation was even more fluid than his classification suggests.

IV

The outcome of our survey of the relevant New Testament scholarship during the last seventy-five years is to show that the New Testament itself confronts us with two alternatives;

---

[57] *The Beginnings of the Christian Church* (1937), Eng. Trans., p. 71.
[58] *Ibid.*, p. 174.
[59] *The Founding of the Church Universal* (1938), Eng. Trans., p. 75.

either we find, by the suspension of our critical judgment, that the Church assumes one form based on an essential ministry or determined by some other principle, as the case may be, or we accept the fact that the primitive Christian movement assumed a diversity of forms. And, since the former alternative is closed to us, we must accept the second and admit that Church life in the New Testament is a coat of many colours. To use Quick's [60] metaphor, the relation of the Church to its external order in the New Testament is analogous not to the relation of a man to his own body, which is joined indissolubly to him under all earthly circumstances, but to that of a man to his clothes, which he can change at will. The Church in the New Testament can assume many forms, and is not limited to any one particular form which is peculiarly the expression of its very being.

The importance of this conclusion can hardly be exaggerated. It seems to me that at this point we must part company not only with Roman Catholicism and Anglo-Catholicism, but also with any attempt to squeeze the Body of Christ into conformity with any single, fixed, and necessary mould or form, even though we may concede that that single form may be reformable. Readers of Roman Catholic writers must recognize the cruciality of this issue. Congar's words in *Divided Christendom* are unmistakably clear. Referring to this issue as one of major importance he writes: 'We must emphasize the significance in authentic Christianity of the external form of the Church's unity, etc. . . . To break the unity of the institutional Church was (for Paul, and the early Fathers, as well as for those of the fourth and fifth centuries) to break the unity of the mystical body. . . .'[61] In the face of such statements we must insist that the foundation document of our Church life, as of our faith, reveals that the Primitive Church never knew that *institutional* unity which Roman Catholicism and Anglo-Catholicism claim to be a necessity of the true life of the Church. Over against the artificial uniformity which Romanist and Anglo-Catholic scholars have imposed on primitive Christianity, we can only with difficulty resist the temptation to suggest, as more in accord with the facts, that the New Testament presents us with just that fissiparous fertility which Bishop

---

[60] *The Doctrines of the Creed*, pp. 330 f.
[61] *Op. cit.*, pp. 74 f.

Kirk of Oxford so much detests in non-episcopal Christendom; but nevertheless the temptation is to be resisted for reasons we shall see when we ask the next question.

If we accept the diversity of form which the New Testament presents, and, therefore, must reject, on the basis of the New Testament at least, Jenkins' view that there is revealed to us a divinely ordained order of Church government, are we then to conclude from the New Testament that Church Order is irrelevant to the Gospel? This has been the tacit assumption of many since the publication of Streeter's great study. Streeter himself would seem to imply that necessity or expediency is the determinative factor in the history of the development of the forms of Christian life.[62] T. W. Manson comes very near to the same position. 'We talk glibly', he writes, 'about "our unhappy divisions"; but, in truth, so long as we are under one supreme Head, our divisions must remain essentially unreal.'[63] Manson's point of departure [64] is the effectiveness of the various forms which the Church has assumed, and, apart from the one all dominating principle that the Church is the Body of *Christ*, it is a pragmatic not a theological test that he applies to all these various forms, i.e., Church order in the New Testament is secondary, derivative, dependent and functional, not dogmatic in its significance.

But although Streeter's contention of a primitive diversity seems incontestable, we must also insist that the New Testament does not leave us without much guidance as to the outward form of the Church, and in the following pages I shall seek to point out certain marks of the Church's life in the New Testament which, whilst not supplying us with a normative pattern, nevertheless, do provide us with certain criteria with which to judge any form which the Church may assume. These criteria are here set down not necessarily in order of their importance, but as they seem to have emerged from our studies.

1. Let us begin with the assertion that the primitive Christian communities were subject to order. Few would now agree with Sohm that the Church of the New Testament was a purely spiritual

---

[62] *Op. cit.*, pp. 261 ff.   [63] *Op. cit.*, p. 89.

[64] *Op. cit.*, p. 5. For a criticism of Manson by M. Bruce, see *Friends of Reunion Bulletin*, No. 31, November, 1948.

society, which had no need of any specific outward order. Flew's criticism of Sohm is apt. 'If the Church is a visible society of men, it cannot dispense with some kind of form, with some rules, however loosely framed, some generally received order of life which controls action in cases of perplexity. If "law" be interpreted in this sense, there is already a divinely sanctioned law in the Christian community from the beginning.'[65] The primitive Churches, however diverse in form, were not formless: the early Christians were neither enthusiastic cranks nor merely a horde.[66] In this connection it is important to recall that the Christian movement did not begin with a *tabula rasa*, because the early Christians were, most emphatically, not innocent neophytes in religion, as it were, but members of the true Israel, an Israel that was New but also Old, and they consequently, quite consciously, drew upon a long tradition of worship and discipline in the religious life. It must never be forgotten that behind the Church lies Judaism, and, although the extent to which the worship and life of primitive Christians are indebted to the Synagogue, both by way of attraction and of conflict, is now a matter of acute debate,[67] that the Synagogue supplied the Primitive Church with much of its form can hardly be doubted.

Thus Christian worship from the beginning owed its proanaphoral form at least to the Synagogue. The pattern of its worship —praise (1 Cor. 14:26; Eph. 5:19; Col. 3:16)—the reading of Scripture (1 Tim. 4:13; 1 Thess. 5:27; Col. 4:16)—prayers (Acts 2:42; 1 Tim. 2:1-2)—the sermon (1 Cor. 14:26; Acts 20:7—the Amen (1 Cor. 14:16)—a confession of faith, not necessarily the formal recitation of a creed—all these elements were moulded for the Church by the Synagogue. So too in such things as the separation of male and female worshippers, the veiling of women and the attitude of standing in prayer we see the influence of the Synagogue.[68] Again the observance of Sunday is to be connected with the observance of the Jewish Sabbath. By a kind of assimilation it is probable

---

[65] *Op. cit.*, p. 186. [66] Hort., *op. cit.*, p. 52.

[67] See O. S. Rankin, *The Journal of Jewish Studies*, Vol. 1, No. 1 (First Quarter, 1948). The discovery of the Qumrân Community adds great force to what we write above, see pp. 70 ff., 108 ff., above.

[68] See respectively 1 Cor. 11:6 ff.; Mark 11:25 (but cf. Acts 21:5, 9:40, 20:36); Phil. 1:27; Eph. 6:14; 1 Tim. 2:8; 1 Tim. 2:9 ff.

that at a very early date the Sunday gathering or service attained among Christians the kind of importance that the Sabbath Synagogue service had for Jewry, although its doctrinal significance was found in the commemoration of the Resurrection of the Lord.[69] There were other forms which the Church was not slow to take over from the Synagogue, e.g., the laying on of hands,[70] Baptism; and the Passover was not without its influence on the Eucharist whether the Last Supper was strictly a Passover meal or not.[71] Yet again the disciplinary methods employed by the early Christian communities appear to have been those perfected within Judaism. Dr. Dodd's careful comparison of Church discipline in Matthew and Paul reveals a common pattern obviously borrowed from the Synagogue.[72]

Our purpose in enumerating these points at which the Church drew upon an already existing tradition of worship and discipline is to enforce our contention that however much enthusiasm was a mark of the Primitive Church—and to deny that enthusiasm is to be perverse—nevertheless, it was a disciplined enthusiasm; Church life in the New Testament was from the first ordered. But here we must voice a caution. Not only was Church life ordered, it was also creative and spontaneous. By this I do not merely mean that the Church richly developed its own peculiarly Christian elements of worship, like the Eucharist, but that it manipulated traditional forms freely, and experimented not only with traditional forms, but often, and quite freely, in defiance of them. Thus, although rooted in the synagogal tradition, the Church allowed women to pray and prophesy:[73] even Paul a Rabbi can countenance such a radical departure from tradition as still frightens the Lambeth Conference:[74] not only so, but the 'holy kiss' is practised among people only lately in the Synagogue.[75] Such facts point to the spontaneity of Christian worship. Ordered it was but not stereotyped: it reveals that live interchange of tradition and freedom which is the genius of great

[69] The Sunday is the first day of the week, Acts 20:7; 1 Cor. 16:2; the day on which Christ was raised from the dead, Matt. 28:1; Mark 16:2; Luke 24:1; John 20:1.
[70] Acts 6:6, 8:17, 13:3, 19:6; 1 Tim. 4:14; 2 Tim. 1:6.
[71] See commentaries ad loc.
[72] Expository Times, Vol. LVIII, No. 11 (1947), pp. 294 ff. See also p. 103 above.
[73] 1 Cor. 11:4 f.
[74] Lambeth Conference, 1948, Part I, p. 52.
[75] Rom. 16:16; 1 Cor. 16:20.

music, art, and poetry, as of living religion. But the full significance of this fact—the fact which accounts for that disconcerting element in the worship of the Primitive Church to which Manson[76] refers—can best be seen when we turn to the next point.

2. I have insisted on the ordered life of the Primitive Church. Dix's picture of early Christian worship in his great book *The Shape of the Liturgy* (Date of Preface, 1943) is ridiculously dignified, but perhaps it is no more erroneous than that too exaggerated emphasis on the mild anarchy of early Christianity which Protestants have not seldom rejoiced in and which is merely a fiction of the imagination. But having said that, let me insist again that there is no single ordered pattern to be discerned in all this liturgical and disciplinary activity of the Early Church. To illustrate, let us look at the order of Church Service which our Puritan forefathers derived from the New Testament.[77] Every particular element in their order is derivable from some portion of the New Testament, but not from any one form which was universally followed. The worship of the Primitive Church did not conform to a single type.[78] Even in such a pivotal act of worship as the celebration of the Eucharist we find in the extant sources alone at least four different accounts of its institution. Dr. Vincent Taylor has examined the place of the Eucharist in the primitive communities and has convincingly argued, it would seem, that the Eucharist 'did not everywhere and always become a *central* feature in the life and worship of the primitive communities'.[79] Or let us consider entry into membership of the Early Church. Johannes Weiss had to distinguish three stages in the development of Christian thought on this question, and the same variety appears in T. W. Manson's treatment of the same question in a recent number of the *J.T.S.*[80] What we are concerned to emphasize is that there is no

[76] *Op. cit.*, pp. 56 f.

[77] See Horton Davies, *The Worship of the English Puritans*, London, 1948, pp. 51 ff.

[78] Cf. Lietzmann, *The Beginnings of the Christian Church*, pp. 193 ff.

[79] *The Atonement in New Testament Teaching*, pp. 236 f.; cf. Dix. *op. cit.*, pp. 6 f. We have italicized the word *central* in the quotation from Taylor because it is difficult to think that there would be communities where there was not some kind of celebration of the Eucharist. This is not maintained by Taylor. The Eucharist and Baptism would be handed on to communities by the first missionaries (see Manson, *op. cit.*, pp. 58 f.) wherever they might be.

[80] *Vol. XLVIII*, No. 189–90, pp. 25 ff. (Jan.–April 1947).

stereotyped order of worship and life presented to us in the New Testament, and that it is futile to imagine that we can discern a fixed norm for the details of our worship and Church life therein. The New Testament presents what would seem to be certain unvarying constants in the life of the primitive Church—the Eucharist, Baptism, the Reading of Scripture, Prayer, Praise, Exposition, etc.—but in what proportion their due exercise consisted is not revealed to us. In other words, part of the pattern of Church life in the New Testament is its variety, is the absence of a fixed norm to which all must conform. The variety which Streeter discerned in the various structures and emphases in Theology in the Primitive Church necessarily recurs in its worship and life generally. Variety is part of the spice of that Church's life. But here again we must be cautious.

3. The variety of Church orders and life in primitive Christianity did not destroy the awareness of the essential unity of Christians. 'One thing is clear,' writes C. H. Dodd, 'that the governing idea in the New Testament is that of the one Church—a unique society constituted by an act of God in history.'[81] The Scandinavian scholar Stig Hanson has devoted a volume[82] to this unity of the Church in the New Testament. The Church, he has reminded us, is the eschatological community of God, and a mark of that eschatological community is that it is destined to inaugurate the eschatological unity which is to undo the divisive forces of the world. The present world is divided by the opposition between God and idols, Israel and the Gentiles, God and Satan, but all these forms of opposition are overcome in Christ, and, because Christians are one with Him, in the Church: the Church is to restore the broken unity of the universe. No one can read the New Testament without immediately being aware that it thrills with the sense of barriers long-standing being broken down. Diverse in its external expression the Spirit is nevertheless creative of unity, a unity, we emphasize, which is not dependent on a unity of outward form nor destroyed by varieties of outward form, but which transcends all merely organizational

[81] *Essays Congregational and Catholic*, p. 15.
[82] *The Unity of the Church in the New Testament, Colossians and Ephesians*, Uppsala, 1946.

differences. Moreover, allied with this radical unity of Christians in the New Testament is the universalism of their appeal. It is not necessary at this time of day to state that in the Second Adam all are one. Nationalism, class, sex—the divisive factors of history—these 'in Christ' and in His Church in the New Testament are transcended. The unity of the Primitive Church is a unity not only in diversity of form but in universalism of life. It will not be necessary to illustrate both these aspects—Unity and Universalism—in the life of the Primitive Church: full justice has been done to them by scholars in our own day.[83]

This then is the third mark of the New Testament Church: unity in the faith and universalism in appeal are not broken by diversity in organization. The Church is a unity in diversity. The full significance of this must be emphasized. In words we have already partly quoted, Congar declares: 'St. Paul and the early Fathers, as well as those of the fourth and fifth centuries, had no notion whatever of a mystical Body which was not corporeally visible or was not a definite and individual reality, identical with and indissociable from the apostolic Church. To break the unity of the institutional Church was, for them, to break the unity of the mystical Body—or rather, since the heavenly unity of the Body cannot be broken—to be separated from it. *For the unity of the one was the very form, on the human plane, of the other.*'[84] Congar cannot emphasize sufficiently the significance in authentic Christianity of the external form of the Church's unity: 'It is of the essence of the Church,' he writes, 'on earth to have an unchangeable human form of its unity.'[85] Congar's false distinction between the Mystical Body of Christ and the actual Body cannot here detain us, but we point out his condemnation of the oecumenical movement on the ground that it does not embody the true unity of the Church, because that true unity demands a single institutional form. He contrasts *catholicity* which is 'the taking of the many into an already existing oneness, and which postulates a unity definitely institutional and ecclesiastical in the strict sense of the word'—he contrasts this *catholicity* with mere *oecumenism* which is merely 'the introduction of a certain unitedness into an already existing diversity

---

[83] See especially Johnston, *op. cit.*, index under '*Church*'.
[84] *Op. cit.*, pp. 74 f. Our italics.   [85] *Op. cit.*, p. 100.

—oneness in multiplicity. . . .'[86] But we must insist that such oecumenism as Congar condemns is what we find in the New Testament. The Council of Acts 15 is oecumenical: it brings together two Churches differing in their structures, but nevertheless aware of their mutual dependence. And this, if I understand it, is the paradox and danger of Jenkins's position in *The Gift of Ministry* as in *The Nature of Catholicity*, that while he has effectively helped us to free the nature of Catholicity from the institutionalism of Rome, he also invites us to submit ourselves to another yoke of bondage—to a new kind of form of the Church which we are to discover—reformable indeed, as we stated above, but nevertheless fixed. Lest, however, we should be tempted unjustly to reject Jenkins's plea, let us go on to the fourth mark of the Church in the New Testament which we notice.

4. Our emphasis on the unity and universalism, and yet on the diversity of Church life and order in the New Testament, must not hide the fact that there is a fourth characteristic which is important— that Church order in the New Testament is an evolving order. Here again our debt to Streeter is immeasurable. With great clarity he has marshalled the evidence for the view that 'within the period covered by the writings of the New Testament itself, there is traceable an evolution in Church organization parallel to the evolution in theology'. He finds in the primitive Church 'an original diversity, a rapid evolution in response to urgent local needs, to be followed later by standardization up to an efficient uniform model'.[87] The evidence for this we have touched upon in arguing for the diversity of New Testament forms of Church life above; we saw that Church order culminated in a kind of mon-episcopal system in the Johannine epistles.

Now Streeter,[88] in introducing his thesis that the organization of the primitive Church leads on to a marked uniformity, refers to the famous *Essay on Development* (1846) in which J. H. Newman explains the development of the institutions of the Church, as of its doctrine, as the reaction of the living organism to a changing environment; and it seems to me, that the study of the form or forms of the Church's life in the New Testament inevitably leaves us

[86] *Op. cit.*, p. 101.   [87] *Op. cit.*, p. 72.
[88] *Op. cit.*, p. 70.

with a question. The question is whether that development of primitive Christianity into that unity which we call the Catholicism of the Patristic period is a legitimate development, or a necessary development, or a perversion; e.g., Sohm, you will recall, claimed that that development meant not only a change in the Church's constitution but in her faith. It is not strictly the province of a student of the New Testament to answer this question, but he must point out that it must be posed. He can also endeavour to prepare the way for its answer by stating wherein, in his judgment, lies the heart of the matter in the New Testament conception of the Church in relation to its form or forms, and thus what the ultimate criterion is for any or all forms that the Church's life may assume. This brings us to the fifth point.

5. The central fact about the Church in the New Testament is that it is a society called into being by the direct act of God in Christ. Without Christ there is no Church. The Church is, therefore, completely dependent upon Christ: it came into being at His call.[89] It follows that while the Church is dependent upon Christ, Christ is not, in the same way, dependent upon the Church. Christ, so to speak, can exist without the Church, but the Church cannot truly exist without Christ: in other words it is Christ who is constitutive of the Church. The action of Christ is free: He calleth whom He willeth unto Himself. The Church cannot limit His freedom, or dictate the terms on which He acts. Any Church order, therefore, which presumes to impose terms upon the sovereign freedom of Christ, which limits His activity to certain prescribed channels, episcopal or other, is a denial of His sovereignty: it ignores that distinction between Christ and His Church which, despite the New Testament insistence upon the solidarity of Christians with Christ, is preserved for us in the equal insistence on Christ as the Head of the Body.[90] Recent theology has recalled us to the Kierkegaardian principle that there is a qualitative difference between Creator and creature: so, too, the New Testament often recalls us to the qualitative difference between Christ, the Creator of the Church,

---

[89] This is expressed by T. W. Manson, op. cit., p. 21, in unforgettable words.
[90] Flew, op. cit., p. 160, writes: 'The Lordship of Christ is the constitutive fact for the church.'

and the Church, His creature. This is the real issue that Paul faced in Galatians.

The relevance of all this to our problem is obvious. We have previously criticized *The Apostolic Ministry* on lexicographical and historical grounds: we now point out the theological gravamen of our charge against the position it maintains, and the approach we offer to the question posed by the *Essay on Development*. We can best express our case by referring again to Ramsey's criticism of the Papacy. After arguing that the historic episcopate is a *necessary* expression of the Gospel, he goes on to discuss the Papacy in the following words:—

> 'The question at once arises whether the Papacy is an equally legitimate development, growing out of a primacy given by our Lord to S. Peter and symbolizing the unity of the Church. . . . A Papacy, which expresses the general mind of the Church in doctrine, and which focuses the organic unity of all the Bishops and of the whole Church, might well claim to be a legitimate development in and through the Gospel. But a Papacy, *which claims to be a source of truth over and above the general mind of the Church, and which wields an authority such as depresses the due working of the other functions of the one Body* fails to fulfil the main tests (of a true development).'[91]

Notice the words in italics:—this is a justifiable complaint that Ramsey makes against the Papacy. But we may ask whether when he himself writes that 'certain actions in (Christ's) work of grace are confined to the Bishops'[92] he does not ascribe the same power 'to be a source of truth over and above the general mind of the Church' and to depress 'the due working of the other functions of the one Body' to the Episcopate; and does not Anglo-Catholicism, like Roman Catholicism, by making a particular episcopal structure of the Church a necessity to Christ, make that episcopal structure stand where it ought not, in a position to dictate to the Lord of the Church? But the Spirit bloweth where it listeth. It has, in fact, flowed through the channels of Episcopacy, it has also flowed outside those channels. Those channels may have helped His coming at times, but they have never been the necessary condition of that coming. The development of Episcopacy in Patristic Catholicism, may have been a necessary development in the sense that it was expedient, and we may

---

[91] *Op. cit.*, pp. 64 f. [92] *Op. cit.*, p. 83.

agree with Jenkins, in the same way, that it may possibly be that in our day and generation an outward form of unity would be expedient. But this is quite another thing from admitting that any one particular form of the Church is to be regarded as of divine appointment. The ultimate New Testament criterion of any Church order, therefore, is that it does not usurp the Crown Rights of the Redeemer within His Church.

And this has certain corollaries which bring me back to that distinction which Congar, in true Roman fashion, drew between the Mystical Body of Christ and the Visible Body. He draws certain contrasts between them: we illustrate these briefly (but relevantly).

The Mystical Body is an organism. The only hierarchy (within it) is that of holiness and virtue in accordance with a greater or less degree of living faith and union with Christ. The actual value of each member is a personal and interior thing inherent in himself: he is worth what he *is*. Here we are in the personal and moral order of the relation of each to his destiny and to the mystery of God in Christ, which is the concrete form of that destiny.[93]

The Visible Body is an organization. A strictly social hierarchy, graded not according to personal worth but to functions, powers and actual competence. The worth of each member is independent of his personal quality: he is worth not what he is personally but what he represents in relation to the common good. . . .

It will be seen that the distinction mentioned enables Roman Catholicism to postulate an empirical form of the Church which in all points of organization can and does conform to what we may call 'the world', as the above quotation makes clear. In fact, it would seem that, for Congar, it is the exigencies of existence in the world not the nature of the Gospel that is to determine the form of the Visible Church. Thus, for example, Roman Catholicism can conceive of the Church Visible treating persons not as persons, but independently of their personal value: apparently to be a cog in the ecclesiastical machine, a condition which Bishop Kirk of Oxford

---

[93] *Op. cit.*, pp. 76 ff. In fairness to Congar we must also refer especially to p. 76, n. 2.

feared may well be the lot of Anglican Bishops of the future, can be a common *and accepted* occurrence in the Roman Catholic Church. There are two standards of judgment—one for the Invisible Church and one for the Visible.

Now it is one of the great services of T. W. Manson's book that it insists again on the falsity of any such distinction as Roman Catholics, and others, make between the Visible and the Invisible Church.[94] He has not only recalled us to the fact that that of Christ is the only *essential* ministry in the Church, the significance of which we saw above, but also to the fact that the empirical Church is *The* Body of Christ, and that its place is here and now in the world of space and time.[95] This means that there are no two standards by which we are to judge the form of the Church—one for the Invisible and the other for the Visible Body. The visible form of the Church is itself always subject to the Lord of the Church, and whatever form the Church assumes must be judged, not by the exigencies of the powers of this world, but by Christ. And at this point I am not quite clear as to the position taken by T. W. Manson to which we referred above. He seems to scatter his benedictions on the different Church orders as long as they fulfil the function of bringing men into the Kingdom.[96] But, it seems to me that his own emphasis on the central concept of the Church as the Body of Christ, taken with the due seriousness which he desiderates, supplies us with a criterion of all Church orders, and enables us to condemn certain forms, or aspects of forms, even though they may be effective. It is possible for the Gospel to be effective in spite of, not because of, the form of a particular Church, and that because, as Dr. Manson points out, Christ acts with sovereign freedom. But this does not mean that the Gospel itself does not supply us with a criterion for judging and even condemning a particular order. Thus, to particularize, the kind of hierarchical system implied in Roman Catholicism, on the one hand, and the kind of califate that we saw in the Salvation Army under the Booths on the other, or again the kind of selfish isolationism prevalent in many Independent Churches—these things are a denial of the Christ we have learned. These radical criticisms of Church

---

[94] *Op. cit.*, pp. 87 f.; cf. G. Johnston, *op. cit.*, p. 125.
[95] *Op. cit.*, p. 88.   [96] *Op. cit.*, p. 88.

order, I feel, are implicit in Dr. Manson's assumptions, but he has not always made them sufficiently explicit.[97]

We are now perhaps in a position to draw the threads of our argument together. The New Testament would not seem to present us with a single fixed pattern of Church order which we are to regard as normative: but it does provide us with certain criteria which can guide us. The Primitive Church appears in the New Testament as an ordered or disciplined community, despite its diversity of organization it is profoundly aware of its essential unity, and, moreover, it is constantly evolving by adapting itself to ever-changing conditions that it may properly fulfil the two main tasks committed to it. In answer to the question how far that varied evolving pattern is normative for us I can only refer again to T. W. Manson's words on pp. 85 f. of his lectures, and quote words from Hort with which Manson substantially agrees: 'The Apostolic Age is full of embodiments of purposes and principles of the most instructive kind: but the responsibility of choosing the means was left for ever to the Ecclesia itself, and to each Ecclesia, guided by ancient precedent on the one hand and adaptation to present and future needs on the other. The lesson book of the Ecclesia, and of every Ecclesia, is not a law but a history.'[98] These words of the great Anglo-Catholic scholar are a fitting conclusion to our discussion[99].

[97] Dr. Manson does work out the implications of his position with much detail, however, in the last lecture. See, e.g., pp. 93 ff.

[98] *The Christian Ecclesia*, pp. 232 f.

[99] A learned review of this chapter, on its appearance, was published by T. H. Parker, in *The Church Times*, London. To this I am greatly indebted: it is warmly recommended to all who would understand and appreciate some of the positions rejected in the above.

X

LIGHT ON THE MINISTRY
FROM THE NEW TESTAMENT

I

Since 'The Ministry' in the New Testament, as indeed at all times and places, only has meaning in the light of the Church, it is in this light that we shall seek to understand it. The Church is the eschatological community of God, the community of the End. This is the new and enriching understanding of it which modern scholarship has brought to us.[1] The Ecclesia of the New Testament is essentially an eschatological community enjoying the eschatological gift of the Spirit;[2] it brings to fruition the purpose of God, revealed in the Old Testament, to create a people for himself. It is no sporadic phenomenon, but the outcome of a long historic process stretching back to the call of Abraham or to the Exodus from Egypt or, if we prefer, before the creation of the world. That this is true to the New Testament is abundantly proved by those portions of it where such an understanding of history is explicitly revealed. We need only refer to Gal. 3:6, 17, 29; Rom. 9–11; Heb. 1:1; and to the prologue of the Fourth Gospel, where also the concept of the Church which we have suggested probably comes to the fore.[3] And this concept, it is clear, implies a philosophy of history: it can preserve us from thinking of the Church as a mushroom growth of the first century and remind us that it is as old as creation. But it can also do something more important: it can reveal to us the real purpose of the Church.

[1] The literature on all this is vast: see especially Linton, *Das Problem der Urkirche in der Neueren Forschung*, 1932.
[2] Acts 2:5 ff., 9:31, 15:28; Gal. 3:3–5; 1 Thess. 1:5; Eph. 4:4; 1 Cor. 3:16.
[3] J. Menoud, *L'Église et les Ministères*, 1949, p. 7, speaks of the consensus which has now been reached as to the nature of the Church in the New Testament.

What do we mean when we claim that the Church is the eschato-logical People of God, that it is the People of the End? This question can only be answered in the light of Jewish eschatological ex-pectations. Following Hanson, we may express the essence of these somewhat as follows:[4] Judaism came to regard the world as the creation of the One God, which was intended to reflect the oneness of its Maker, to be a unity. In the beginning, this oneness was a reality; the cosmos as a totality, man included, 'obeyed' God. But sin entered upon the scene, and with it disunity of all kinds: this disunity expressed itself as enmity between man and man, in the family between Cain and Abel, within the nation itself between rich and poor, then between Jew and Gentile, and particularly and funda-mentally, of course, between man and God. But despite man's fall Judaism continued to believe that God was still God, and that, there-fore, ultimately His will would be done.

How would this take place? It would take place in the future; but there were different ways in which this future was conceived. Some thought that a Messianic figure, a Son of David, powerful like the first David, would arrive and inaugurate his kingdom on this earth. Others despaired of this earth entirely and looked for a supernatural figure, the Son of Man, who should inaugurate a new heaven and a new earth. Probably we are not to think of any one well defined and generally accepted Messianic expectation, but of a rich variety of expectations much intermingled. However conceived, the End would be like the beginning; just as at the creation God's will gained untrammelled obedience from the created order and from man himself, so at the End there would be a corresponding obedience. The result of this obedience would be the inauguration of unity, i.e., the re-creation of the broken unity between man and man, and between man and God. And this is the purpose of the community of the Messiah or of the community of the Son of Man—to inaugurate this unity, the eschatological unity of which the initial unity of creation is the prototype.

The most impressive expression of this is found in the Epistle to the Ephesians, where Paul, or at least one of his followers, sets forth the

[4] Stig Hanson, *The Unity of the Church in the New Testament, Colossians and Ephesians*, Uppsala, 1946.

purpose of the Church. C. H. Dodd has summarized this as follows:

[In Ephesians the Church is regarded] as the society which embodies in history
the eternal purpose of God revealed in Christ. This purpose is the ultimate unity
of all being in Him. While in the universe at large there are still unreconciled
powers affronting the sovereignty of God, the ultimate issue is certain. God has
determined to 'sum up all things in Christ'. That might be pure speculation,
but for the fact that history and experience witness to the reconciling power
of Christ in the creation of that supernatural society in which warring sections
of the human race are perfectly reconciled into a whole of harmoniously
functioning parts—the Church. That Jews and Gentiles should have found their
place in the unity of the Church seems to the writer the most signal manifestation
of reconciling grace. The enmity of Jew and Gentile was one of the fiercest in
the ancient world: and the unity of Jewish and Gentile Christians in the one
church *a mystery and a miracle*. He saw that the reconciliation was not accom-
plished by any kind of compromise between the diverse parties, but by a
divine act creating out of both one new humanity. This new humanity is
mediated by Christ. He sums up in Himself the whole meaning of God, and
communicates Himself to men so that humanity may come to realize and express
that meaning. The Church is 'in Christ'; it is His body, and its members have
'put on' the new humanity which is Christ in them (2:11-22). . . . In the great
universe, too, there is movement toward unity and completeness: Christ's
work will not be done till the whole universe is one in Him, to the Glory of
God. The living and growing unity of the Church is, so to speak, a sacrament
of the ultimate unity of all things.[5]

But not only in Ephesians does this become clear. The Pauline
doctrine of Christ as the Second Adam is pertinent here. Paul
accepted the traditional Rabbinic doctrine of the unity of mankind
in Adam. That doctrine implied that the very constitution of the
physical body of Adam and the method of its formation was
symbolic of the real oneness of mankind. In the one body of Adam,
east and west, north and south were brought together, male and
female. Paul, when he thought of the new humanity being incorporated 'in Christ', conceived of it as the 'body' of the Second Adam,
where there was neither Jew nor Greek, male nor female, bond nor
free. The difference between the body of the First Adam and that of
the Second Adam was for Paul that whereas the former was animated
by the principle of natural life, was *nephesh*, the latter was animated

---

[5] *The Abingdon Commentary*, Nashville, 1929, pp. 1222 f.; cf. 2 Cor. 5:19.

by the Spirit; and the purpose of God in Christ is 'in dispensation of the fullness of times' to 'gather together in one all things in Christ' (Eph. 1:10), i.e., the reconstitution of the essential oneness of mankind in Christ as a 'spiritual' community, as it was one in Adam in a physical sense.[6] Finally, we refer to the Farewell Discourses in the Fourth Gospel where the meaning of the Christian Ecclesia comes to full expression again. Christ prays not only for the Twelve but for Christians yet unborn. 'Neither pray I for these alone, but for them also which shall believe on me through their word; that they all may be one; as thou, Father, art in me and I in thee, that they also may be one in us: that the world may believe that thou hast sent me' (John 17:20–21).

So far, we have stated two things about the Church; first, that it is the eschatological People of God and, secondly, that its aim is the re-creation of the unity which mankind has lost. We now have to enquire how the Church is to accomplish this. And that brings us to our present concern: it is through the life of the Church, or, to be more accurate, through the life of Christ in the Church. But what does this mean?

Let us retrace our steps a little. We saw that the Church is the eschatological, Messianic community gathered by Jesus, the Messiah. But this community is not a community standing over against him, as it were; it is a community which is integrally bound up with him. It is so closely knit to Christ that, in Pauline language, it can be said to be 'in Christ'. To use the famous Pauline metaphor again, the Church is the *Body* of Christ, it is the extension of His Being; quite literally Christians are to form the eyes, the feet, the ears, the mind of Christ. (The notions of corporate personality, derived from a Semitic background, which lie behind such a conception of an extension of the Being of Christ in His followers, are indispensable to the understanding of the New Testament doctrine of the Church, although we can only refer to them here in passing.) In other words, since the Church is the Body of Christ, it is called upon to perform His work: the Church is the continuation of the life of Jesus, the Messiah.[7]

---

[6] See for the evidence W. D. Davies, *Paul and Rabbinic Judaism*[2], 1955, pp. 53 ff.

[7] See especially T. W. Manson, *The Church's Ministry*, London, 1948, *ad loc.*

But what was the nature of that life? It can be summed up in one word—ministry (*diakonia*). 'The Son of Man came not to be ministered unto, but to minister, and to give his life a ransom for many' (Mark 10:45). This was the secret of the Messiahship of Jesus, that it was the Messiahship of a Suffering Minister. T. W. Manson in his book *The Church's Ministry* has given the reasons for choosing this word 'ministry' as that which best describes the public career of Jesus. They are three: (1) It reflects the fact that in Jesus we have the actualization of the purest and most satisfactory formulation of the remnant ideal in the Old Testament, the picture of the *Servant* of the Lord in Deutero-Isaiah;[8] (2) it accurately describes the kind of activities which make up the Gospel record of the life of Jesus; and (3) it provides the standard for the life of His followers. Thus this self-giving ministry of Christ becomes the norm for the life of the Church, its pattern: the life of the Church is to be the continuation of that ministry, and, in so far as this is actually the case, the Church heals as He healed, and restores as He restored, the brokenness of men. It is then by its *diakonia*, in which and through which the Living Christ continues His work, that the Church is continuously re-creating the unity that the world has lost.

II

But we are particularly concerned not with the ministry of the Church as a whole, the ministry of what we may call Christian *agape*, which is the lot of *every* Christian, but with the ministry of 'ministers' as such, i.e., the ministry of people who have been set apart, in whatever way, for specific tasks in the Church. How does 'the ministry' in this strict sense fit into the ministry of the Body as a whole? Clearly, to take seriously what we have sought to reveal about the nature and purpose of the Church, and about its continuation of the ministry of Jesus as a means of fulfilling that purpose, has important consequences for the understanding of the specific character of 'the ministry'. Let us gather up the chief of these consequences as follows.

First, all ministry in the Church, as the New Testament under-

[8] Mark 10:45, which possibly echoes Isaiah 53.

stands it, is the activity of the Living Christ Himself; it is the gift of His grace to His people. It is no accident that every significant term that has historically come to be used of 'ministers' in the Church is applied in the New Testament to Christ Himself. Thus Jesus is called a deacon, a servant (Rom. 15:8; Luke 22:27; Mark 10:45; Phil. 2:7); He is an apostle and High Priest (Heb. 3:1); He is bishop and shepherd (Heb. 13:20; 1 Pet. 2:25, 5:4). This fact emphasizes the truth on which we have insisted that all ministry is His ministry. He is always present in the ministry of His own. So in Luke 10:16 we read: 'He that heareth you, heareth me; and he that despiseth you despiseth me, and he that despiseth me despiseth him that sent me.' Thus again for Paul the preaching of God's word, for instance, is in truth God's own word, through which God Himself works in the Body, as in 1 Thess. 2:13: 'For this cause also thank we God without ceasing, because, when ye received the word of God which ye heard of us, ye received it not as the word of men, but as it is in truth, the word of God, which effectually worketh also in you that believe.'[9]

But, secondly, if all ministry is the ministry of Christ Himself, then it also follows from this that there is no ministry in the Church which is merely the result of human merit. Every ministry in the New Testament is the activity of the Living Christ, so that there is no truly Christian ministry which is sustained out of our own resources as it were. There is no merit on the basis of which we become the 'ministers' of Christ: the New Testament refused to contemplate any such 'ministry'; none ever deserves to be a minister, or, as we more often express it, *ought* to be a minister in virtue of any moral or other qualities he may possess. On this basis 'the ministry' is an impossible calling; it is not a human possibility, as indeed every minister knows. The truly typical call into 'the ministry', of whatever kind, is that of Peter depicted for us in Luke 5:1–11. Peter is called to become a fisher of men, but the outcome of his first encounter with Christ is the exclamation, 'Depart from me, for I am a sinful man, O Lord.' It is of the grace of Christ's call that he enters 'the

[9] Cf. Gal. 1:9–10; Acts 4:29. I am much indebted in all this to the penetrating study by E. Schweizer, *Das Leben des Herrn in der Gemeinde und ihren Diensten*, 1946; cf. T. W. Manson, *op. cit., ad loc.*

ministry', not of his own merit; it is of the grace of Christ also that he remains in it when he would sometimes like to leave it. Recall the words of Luke 22:3, 23:31 f., 'and the Lord said, Simon, Simon, behold, Satan hath desired to have you, that he may sift you as wheat: *But I have prayed for thee, that thy faith fail not*: and when thou art converted, strengthen thy brethren. . . .' In Paul the awareness, not only of inadequacy, but of utter unworthiness to be a minister of Christ is sometimes overwhelming.[10] That every virtue and every victory in ministry, whatever it may be, 'is His alone' is writ large on page after page of the New Testament.

Again, thirdly, there is a further consequence of the conception of the Church which we have found in the New Testament. Since the Church is the Body of *Christ*, and since it is the Church as such that continues His ministry, there can be no one other 'ministry' which is essential in the sense that it is this one ministry that constitutes the Body.[11] The only *essential* 'ministry' in the Body is the ministry of the Living Christ Himself.[12] And to take seriously the thought that the Body is the Body of Christ Himself makes otiose any essential ministry other than His own. In His body every member, however lowly, has his ministry; there are no idle members. But on the other hand there are no members which can lord it over the Body. There are no higher and lower ministries in the Church of the New Testament; it knows no distinction of cleric and lay; there is no priesthood in the New Israel such as there is in the Old Israel because the New Israel in its *totality* is a priesthood.[13]

And it is at this point that we must reject the claims of Anglo- and Roman Catholicism, not only on the historical and lexicographical

[10] 1 Cor. 2:1 ff.; 1 Cor. 15:8 ff.; 1 Tim. 1:1 ff. So much is Paul aware that he is an apostle merely because of the grace of Christ that the term *grace* becomes for him a synonym for the *apostolate,* as in Rom. 1:5. (Here the connecting *kai* is meant to identify the two terms.) He defines his apostolate as 'the grace that is given to me of God'; cf. 1 Cor. 3:10; Gal. 2:9; Eph. 3:2, 7; 1 Cor. 15:10; cf. also 2 Cor. 4:7; 1 Tim. 1:12 f.

[11] See *The Apostolic Ministry,* ed. K. E. Kirk, London and New York, 1947.

[12] Cf. T. W. Manson, *op. cit.*

[13] 1 Pet. 2:5; Heb. 7:24 f. (here Christ is the eternal priest, but has no successors); Rev. 1:6; 5:10; 20:6. See Lightfoot, *The Epistle to the Philippians,* 1903, pp. 181–269; Schweizer, *op. cit., ad loc.*; Menoud, *op. cit.,* pp. 18 ff.: 'De même que c'est l'Église et non le fidèle qui est le corps du Christ, c'est l'Église et non le fidèle qui est un sacerdoce' (p. 21).

grounds which have often been pointed out,[14] but on theological grounds derived from the New Testament. The Church is completely dependent upon Christ: it came into being at His call: it is His body—the Body of His creation. It follows that while the Church is dependent upon Christ, Christ is not in the same way dependent upon the Church. Christ, so to speak, can exist without the Church, but the Church cannot truly exist without Christ: in other words, it is Christ who is constitutive of the Church. The action of Christ is free: He calleth whom He willeth unto Himself. The Church cannot limit His freedom or dictate the terms on which He acts. Any Church order, therefore, which presumes to impose terms upon the sovereign freedom of Christ, which limits His activity to certain prescribed channels, Episcopal or other, is a denial of His sovereignty. To make the Papacy or the Episcopacy a necessity to Christ is to make both the Papacy and the Episcopacy stand where they ought not, in a position to dictate to the Lord of the Church.

The Spirit bloweth where it listeth. It has, in fact, flowed through the channels of Episcopacy, it has also flowed outside these channels. These channels may at times have helped His coming, but they have never been the necessary condition of that coming. The development of Episcopacy in Patristic Catholicism may have been a necessary development in the sense that it was expedient; in the same way it may possibly be that in our day an outward form of unity would be expedient. But the ultimate New Testament criterion of any 'ministry', as of any Church order, is that it does not usurp the crown rights of the Redeemer within the Church: the real danger of both Roman and Anglo-Catholicism is that they imprison the Spirit of Christ in an order.

In the light of all that this asserts negatively about the ministry, that is, in defining that in which the ministry does not consist, we may well ask in what, then, does the ministry consist? What is its justification or its *raison d'être*?

In seeking to answer this question we now refer to another danger which always dogs the Church. This danger is the direct antithesis of that constituted by Roman and High Anglican claims; but it is no less real. It is the danger of believing that because the Church is

[14] See Chapter IX.

the Body of Christ and that He is working in and through it, so that all is of His grace, then we need no form or order for the Body at all, or at least we can treat its form or order cavalierly. It is the danger into which Sohm fell when he asserted that the organized structure of the Church in itself involved a departure from the pristine purity of the spiritual fellowship of the saints.[15]

But what are the facts as the New Testament presents them? Let us emphasize, as strongly as possible, one central thing. The fact that all is of grace does not mean that Christians are absolved from responsibility in the Body. The same kind of paradox presents itself in New Testament ethics. The New Testament, which asserts that all is of grace, is also full of imperatives—exhortations—pleas—warnings. Phil. 2:12 f. reads, 'Wherefore, my beloved, as ye have always obeyed, not as in my presence only, but now much more in my absence, work out your own salvation with fear and trembling. For it is God which worketh in you both to will and to do of his good pleasure.' God's grace does not do away with the necessity of works. The Church is Christ's and His Spirit bloweth where it listeth, but it must blow through *Christians*: He cannot act mechanically. Without denying His own nature, He cannot treat men as marionettes or puppets: He demands their active co-operation. Thus the Spirit demands confession, the active response of the soul to Christ, and in Matt. 16:18 the Church is said to be built on one who thus confesses. This kind of confessing response lies behind every ministry in the Church. But the Spirit in the Church demands not only confession but action, the awareness of the claims of human need and practical response to meet them.

This means that Christians cannot be a group of people enjoying ecstatic irresponsibility or basking in the warmth of an irrelevant emotionalism: they must accept the challenge of the demands made upon them by Christ in facing the order and the quality of their own life as they confront the world. This is the meaning of the appointment of the Seven in Acts 6:1 ff. Hort [16] has unforgettably expressed the meaning of that appointment. It was

not only a notable recognition of the Hellenistic element in the Ecclesia at

[15] *Outlines of Church History*, E.T., M. Sinclair, 1895, pp. 32 ff.
[16] *The Christian Ecclesia*, 1897, p. 52, our italics.

Jerusalem, a prelude to greater events to come, but also a sign that the Ecclesia was to be an Ecclesia indeed, not a mere horde of men ruled absolutely by the Apostles, but a true body politic, *in which different functions were assigned to different members, and a share of responsibility rested upon the members at large, each and all*; while every work for the Ecclesia high and low was of the nature of a ministration, a true rendering of a servant's service.

It is the same acceptance of responsibility that lies behind all the specialized 'ministries' of the Church. It is not that the Church submitted to an order of ministry imposed upon it from above, which it was compelled to obey, but that Christ, acting in the Church, created 'ministries' to fulfil His purposes. That is, 'the ministry' is determined not by status conferred but by function fulfilled.[17] Thus while the New Testament recognizes no distinction between cleric and lay, nevertheless, despite the fact that ministry is the function of the whole Church, it does recognize a distinction between 'ministers' set apart for specific functions and the rest of the faithful (Phil. 1:1; Acts 15:22).

III

But what are those functions for which the Church must particularly set certain ministers apart? They can be broadly distinguished under two heads.

First, there is the proclamation of what the New Testament calls the *Kerygma*, the preaching. The Gospel in the New Testament is the good news of the glory of God (1 Tim. 1:11; 2 Cor. 4:6). But this glory is revealed in an Event—in the coming, the life, death, and resurrection of Jesus Christ. It is this Event in its totality, by which the world is redeemed, that first called the Church into being; and on its further proclamation does the continuance and expansion of the Church depend. 'Il ne suffit pas pour sauver le monde,' writes Spic, 'que le Christ soit mort et resuscité. Il faut en outre que ces faits soient divulgés et qu'on y croie.'[18] The Church can only live by witnessing to the Event which gave it birth.

Now that was the essential function of the Apostolate, the most important and, indeed, unique ministry of the New Testament. The

[17] See T. W. Manson: The New Testament Basis of the Doctrine of the Church, in *The Journal of Ecclesiastical History*, Vol. I, No. 1

[18] Spicq, *Saint Paul, Les Epîtres Pastorales*, 1947, p. 226.

Apostles were, first and foremost, witnesses of the Resurrection (1 Cor. 9:1), and some also, in order still more to ground their witness to the event, of the earthly life of Jesus (Acts 1:21–22). They were bearers of the tradition, stewards of the *Kerygma* (1 Cor. 4:1). Thus even Paul, despite his strong assertion of his direct commission to be an Apostle from the Risen Christ (Gal. 1:1), is also anxious to be rooted in that tradition which the other Apostles safeguarded, lest he should be labouring in vain. Although the Apostolate, as such, could have no successors, it remained the quite fundamental task of the Church to carry on the 'apostolic' witness to the Word made flesh. Henceforth it could do this only by being true to the tradition received from the eyewitnesses, the Apostolate; and thus from the earliest days it had not only to set men apart (by the laying on of hands or otherwise) to be guardians of this tradition which they had directly received, but also had to recognize the need to maintain them materially.[19] The case of Timothy is here instructive. He is called upon not to succeed in any office, i.e., not to be in the Apostolic Succession in the Roman sense, but to continue in the things which he had learned.[20] In short, he is to be the minister of the Word of God which he has received from the Apostolate.[21]

But it is clear that there would come a time when those responsible for witnessing to the Event would have no direct relation to the eyewitnesses of that Event at all. And Cullmann [22] has again recently reminded us that in time the witness to the Event came to be deposited and safeguarded in the Canon of Scripture. In the fixation of the Canon, about the middle of the second century, the concern of the Church was just this: to be true to the apostolic witness; and when we consider the vagaries of extra-canonical tradition, we cannot doubt that it succeeded in being so. But the consequence is that henceforth the ministry of the Word becomes a ministry which wrestles with the witness of the Canon to Christ and, having wrestled with it, proclaims it. In this sense, as in others, 'the ministry' is today, as always, to stand in that apostolic succession which witnesses to Christ: thus only will it be true to its specific task, and thus renew

[19] 1 Cor. 9:1 ff.; cf. Menoud, *op. cit.*, p. 38.
[20] 2 Tim. 3:14; cf. Titus 1:9.
[21] Cf. Schweizer, *op. cit.*, pp. 75 ff.
[22] *Christ and Time, ad loc.*

in the experience of men that crisis which was constituted by the impact of Him who was the Word made flesh. The ministry is, therefore, not essentially concerned with the speculative flights of reason nor primarily with the intuitions of the light within, but with a particular history—that of Jesus, the Christ. It is called in the most literal sense to be a steward of what was in Him revealed; and it is the supreme virtue of stewards that they should be faithful to that which they have received.

We must at this point refer to the Sacraments, because both Baptism and Eucharist, like the Apostolate, are concerned with *Kerygma*, i.e., their aim is to set forth that event which is the ground of the Church. Baptism takes us back both to the baptism of Jesus at the hands of John in Jordan and to the 'baptism' which He underwent on Calvary. Flemington is right in defining it as '*the Kerygma in action*, the means whereby the saving Act of Christ's death and resurrection is made available for successive believers within the Christian fellowship'.[23] Similarly the Eucharist proclaims the Lord's death (1 Cor. 11:26), i.e., it is again the *Kerygma* in action. Thus Baptism and the Eucharist are intended to fulfil the same function as does the Canon: they are both designed to witness to the Event. The Sacraments take us back through symbolic acts directly to the Person of Christ; the Canon mediately through the apostolic witness.

But since the Sacraments are kerygmatic, can we discern their relation to the human custodians of the *Kerygma*, the 'apostolic' ministry? In 1 Cor. 1:17 Paul asserts that his primary task is not to baptize but to preach the gospel: apparently he assumes that the administration of the Sacrament could be delegated to other ministers, who were not so much concerned with the founding of new churches as with the upbuilding of churches already founded. His reason for asserting the primacy of preaching is not that he regards Baptism as unimportant, but that the local situation at Corinth demands that he should avoid giving occasion for any misunderstanding of its meaning, such as that there could be baptism into his own or any other name, and not solely into the name of Jesus.[24]

[23] *The New Testament Doctrine of Baptism*, London, 1948, p. 123.
[24] See Flemington, *op. cit.*, pp. 53-4.

Indeed another part of the same Epistle, 1 Cor. 10, makes clear how profound was Paul's appreciation of Baptism.

We have no direct guidance from the Pauline corpus, or from the rest of the New Testament, as to whose duty it was to baptize or to celebrate the Eucharist; and we do not know that Paul himself (1 Cor. 1:14 f.), Peter and the Eleven (Acts 2:38 f.), Philip the Evangelist (Acts 8:12 f.), and Ananias (Acts 9:18) did perform baptisms.[25] It seems fair to infer that usually, if present in the gathering, an Apostle would naturally perform the act of Baptism and celebrate the Eucharist, and probably, in the absence of such, prophets or teachers would be responsible. It is true that we have no specific directions on this matter till we come to the second century,[26] nor can we be sure that Baptism and the Eucharist were in every church regarded as central or important in the life of the Church,[27] nevertheless that the Sacraments were always the concern of 'the ministry' we cannot doubt; and this because, although it is possible with Sohm to overemphasize the part played by the Eucharist in the development of the organized ministry of the Church, it is not possible to overlook the seriousness with which the New Testament treats the sacramental presentation of the *Kerygma*. Very often, we may be sure, the ministry of the Word coincided with the ministry of the Sacraments. The ease with which Paul and the Fourth Gospel use the Sacraments for didactic or edificatory purposes merely serves to reinforce their significance for the *Kerygma* of the Church.[28]

This didactic use of the Sacraments leads us to the second function which the Church had to maintain. The preached Word is constitutive of a community and occurs within a community, in the Church. The Church saw the need not only of proclaiming its preaching, but of expounding its 'teaching'. The distinction between these two functions has been defined by C. H. Dodd as follows, although it should not be too hard pressed:

[25] It is possible that Acts 20:7, 11 point to the celebration of the Eucharist by Paul.

[26] See Menoud, *op. cit.*, p. 42, n. 2.

[27] Vincent Taylor, *The Atonement in New Testament Teaching*, pp. 236 f.

[28] See Cullmann, *Le culte dans l'Église primitive*, 1945, pp. 25 ff.; Rom. 6:3, 4; John 3:5 f.

The New Testament writers draw a clear distinction between preaching and teaching. This distinction is preserved alike in Gospels, Acts, Epistles and Apocalypse, and must be considered characteristic of early Christian usage in general. Teaching (*didaskein*) is in a large majority of cases ethical instruction. Occasionally it seems to include what we should call apologetic, that is, the reasoned commendation of Christianity to persons interested but not yet convinced. Sometimes, especially in the Johannine writings, it includes the exposition of theological doctrine.[29]

How wide the teaching was can be judged from the ethical sections of the Pauline epistles. Church and state, sex, social conventions, class distinctions, 'nationalism'—they all are treated by Paul. And the aim of the teaching can be gleaned from certain terms used of the Church. It is a building into which the individual is to be built up (Eph. 2:19 ff.): or again it is, by implication, a school where the individual Christian is to be taught the culture of Christ (Rom. 16:17; Eph. 4:20). Always it is the effect on the Body of Christ, not its brilliance or originality, that is the criterion of the 'teaching' (1 Cor. 14:2 ff.).

These two functions are those which the Church of the New Testament has to safeguard. It is this that 'the ministry' in the New Testament is designed to do. There came into being, called of Christ in the Church, first 'apostles', who because it is on their witness that the Church depends, can be called along with Christ the foundation of the Church (Eph. 2:20; Matt. 16:18). Paul would next apparently place the 'prophets', whose task it was under the inspiration of the Spirit to expound a message in terms understandable to all rather than in unintelligible tongues (these prophets soon disappeared from the life of the Church).[30] But it was the teachers who appear to have been nearest to the Apostolate;[31] it was their task not only to interpret the Christian message in the light of the Old Testament, but also to expound the meaning of the Faith; it is significant that in the Pauline epistles the teaching ministry is the only one, apart from the Apostolate, which is allowed to live by the gospel (Gal 6:6). The other ministries in the New Testament are too numerous to mention here, but we may safely assert that they all subserved,

---

[29] *The Apostolic Preaching and its Developments*, 1937, pp. 1 f.
[30] See 1 Cor. 12:8-10, 28-30; Eph. 4:11.
[31] 1 Cor. 4:17; 2 Thess. 2:15; cf. Col. 2:7; Eph. 4:21.

broadly speaking, the two functions to which we have referred. These are everywhere and always the peculiar concerns of 'the ministry'.

Let us now, finally, gather together what we have written. The Church, which 'the ministry' serves, is the eschatological community, the people of God, the Body of Christ, which continues His ministry and is designed to serve in the re-creation of the unity which mankind has lost. And in this people of God we found two functions that had constantly to be fulfilled, if that unity was to be regained: namely, the proclamation of the Event, which created and still creates the people of God, both in Word and Sacrament, and the upbuilding of this same people by *didache*. It is in terms of these two functions that the peculiar responsibility of 'the minister' within the ministry of the Body is to be understood.

INDEXES

I. OLD TESTAMENT REFERENCES

II. REFERENCES TO THE APOCRYPHA AND PSEUDEPIGRAPHA OF THE OLD TESTAMENT

III. NEW TESTAMENT REFERENCES

I Thess.		Philemon	
1:9	187	16	153
2:13	236		
2:14	184 n.15, 187	Heb.	
5:27	72 n.25, 219	1:1	231
II Thess.		3:1	236
2:3f.	191	4:10	74 n.33
2:6f.	180	7:24f.	237 n.13
2:8–10	191	13:20	236
2:15	244 n.31		
I Tim.		I Peter	
1:1f.	237 n.10	1:11	60
1:11	240	2:5	237 n.13
1:12f.	237 n.10	2:22	129 n.31
2:1f.	219	2:25	236
4:13	72, 219	5:4	236
4:14	220 n.70		
II Tim.		II Peter	
1:6	220 n.70	2:1	185 n.16
3:14	241 n.20	Rev.	
4:16–18	192	1:6	237 n.13
		4:7	85, 86
Titus		5:10	237 n.13
1:9	241 n.20	20:6	237 n.13

IV. QUOTATIONS FROM THE DEAD SEA SCROLLS

(See pp. 119f. n.5 for a list of the edition used in the text.)

The Manual of Discipline		*The Manual of Discipline*	
1:5	127	3:7	101
1:9	121	3:13	127
1:11	127, 170 n.64	3:13ff.	155, 158, 159, 172, 173
1:11f.	122 n.12	3:13–4:26	103, 154, 163
1:12	126	3:19ff.	173
1:13	121	3:24	123 n.17
1:14	158	4	138 n.66
1:22f.	123 n.17	4:2	128
2:2	121	4:3	169
2:3	101, 128 n.30, 131	4:5	127
2:22	123, n.17	4:9–11	161
2:26	127, 150	4:18ff.	129, 165, 176 n.86
3:1	126, 127, 150	4:20	150, 152, 168, 169 n.62
3:2	125, 150	4:20f.	168
3:3	125 n.21, 150	4:22ff.	176 n.86
3:4f.	150	4:25	176 n.86
3:6	127	5	122 n.12, 138 n.66
3:6ff.	150, 152	5:2	122 n.12

V. QUOTATIONS FROM RABBINICAL LITERATURE

VI. REFERENCES TO HELLENISTIC AUTHORS AND TO EXTRA-CANONICAL CHRISTIAN WRITINGS

VII. AUTHORS

VIII. SUBJECTS